YIELD

amplify
an imprint of Amplify Publishing Group

www.amplifypublishinggroup.com

Yield: How Google Bought, Built, and Bullied Its Way to Advertising Dominance

For more information, please contact:
Amplify Publishing, an imprint of Amplify Publishing Group
620 Herndon Parkway, Suite 220
Herndon, VA 20170
info@amplifypublishing.com

Library of Congress Control Number: 2025904849

CPSIA Code: PRFRE0425A

ISBN-13: 979-8-89138-617-4

Printed in Canada

YIELD

How Google Bought, Built, and Bullied Its Way to Advertising Dominance

ARI PAPARO

amplify

an imprint of Amplify Publishing Group

CONTENTS

A NOTE ABOUT SOURCING

This book was written based on two primary sources: in-depth interviews with over sixty executives and witnesses to the events described, and the thousands of pages of evidence made public as part of the Department of Justice's antitrust suit against Google's ad tech group in the Eastern District of Virginia. These sources are cited in the endnotes. In many cases, anonymity was granted to interviewees because the parties remain witnesses to unresolved court cases or remain under NDAs with their former employers.

The author has also been a personal witness to many of the events that are described here, if not an active participant. The narrative leans on his experience and often describes some of the more technical aspects of how the industry works without citation because it is based on his general knowledge as a practitioner. In the handful of cases where a factual claim or quote is directly from the author, it is described in the endnotes as such.

GLOSSARY

The advertising world uses lots of terminology and acronyms. In this book I try to make it clear what things are and how they work, rather than relying on jargon.

Ad exchange: A system that allows publishers to auction off their ad inventory to the highest bidder.

Ad network: An intermediary that matches demand from ad buyers with inventory from sellers in a variety of ways.

Ad tag: A short snippet of HTML and JavaScript that, when rendered by a browser, calls an ad server or other advertising technology company to retrieve an ad.

Advertiser ad server: A system that allows an advertiser or agency to manage their ad buys across many publishers and receive unified reporting on those results.

Agency trading desk: A division within a larger agency that focuses on programmatic buying of ads and acts as a "center of excellence" for the rest of the group.

Demand side platform (DSP): A system for allowing ad buyers to target and execute advertising buys on ad exchanges.

First-price auction: An auction where the highest bidder pays exactly what they bid.

Floor price: The minimum value a publisher is willing to accept for a given ad impression sold through an ad exchange.

Header bidding: A method of collecting bids from ad exchanges or other parties within the browser and inserting the winning bid into the ad server.

Header wrapper: Software that helps publishers manage header bidding.

Impression: A single ad shown to a single user on a webpage, phone, or other device.

Mediation: A term used in mobile apps for calling multiple ad servers in sequence to maximize revenue. Essentially, mediation is the mobile in-app version of the waterfall (see next page).

Private marketplace (PMP): An arrangement where a buyer and seller agree on ad inventory to be transacted; this is similar to how direct deals work, but the transaction takes place programmatically through an ad exchange and typically a DSP.

Programmatic: A catch-all describing buying and selling ads using ad exchanges and related technologies.

Publisher ad server: A system that allows a publisher to determine which ads show in which slots on their webpage, mobile app, or other media. The determination of the correct ad may be influenced by price, priority, or other business rules.

Real-time bidding (RTB): A system whereby ad exchanges auction ad inventory through real-time connections with DSPs or other buyers.

Second-price auction: An auction where the highest bidder pays one cent more than either the next highest bidder or the floor price if there are no other bidders.

Supply side platform (SSP): A largely abandoned term, this is sometimes used interchangeably with ad exchange or with the combination of yield managers and ad exchanges.

Waterfall a.k.a. daisy chain: An inefficient technique whereby a publisher calls for an ad from a third party, then if no ad is available, calls another party and so on until they get a paid ad.

Yield manager: Companies that helped publishers make more money from their ad network partners. These companies are now mostly considered ad exchanges.

DoubleClick and Google Product Names

Google has a habit of renaming its products in confusing ways, so we use the most common generic names in the book. Sometimes it is necessary to use contemporaneous names or acronyms.

AdX: The commonly used nickname for the ad exchange originally built by DoubleClick, then migrated to Google. The exchange has had numerous official names, like DoubleClick Marketplace, but everyone calls it AdX.

AdMob: An ad exchange that specializes in mobile app-based ads.

Accelerated Mobile Pages (AMP): A Google initiative to create open standards that would speed up mobile web pages.

DART for Advertisers (DFA): DoubleClick's advertiser ad server, renamed Google Campaign Manager.

DART for Publishers a.k.a. DoubleClick for Publishers (DFP): DoubleClick's publisher ad server, renamed Google Ad Manager (GAM).

Display and Video 360 (DV360) f.k.a. DoubleClick Bid Manager (DBM): Google's demand-side platform for larger advertisers to buy ads programmatically.

Google Ad Manager (GAM): The publisher ad server offered by Google that replaced DFP. Originally this only included the ad server, but in the late 2010s, they started using this name to refer to both the ad server and the ad exchange as a bundle.

Google Ads f.k.a. AdWords: The system where advertisers place their ad buys across Google Search, the display ad network, and YouTube.

Google Analytics: A free analytics tool used to track activities on websites and apps.

Google Campaign Manager (GCM): Google's revamped version of DFA, DoubleClick's advertiser ad server.

Google Display Network (GDN) f.k.a. Google Content Network: The display and video ad network built on top of Google Ads. At some point Google stopped using this term and started referring to this as just part of Google Ads. In this book we simply call this the "Google ad network."

Open Bidding f.k.a. Exchange Bidding f.k.a. Exchange Bidding Dynamic Allocation (EBDA): Google's answer to header bidding, allowing other ad exchanges to bid directly into the publisher ad server.

TIMELINE OF EVENTS

November 1, 2004	DoubleClick explores strategic options
April 2005	First ad exchange on Right Media
April 26, 2005	DoubleClick acquired by Hellman & Friedman
March 20, 2006	DoubleClick acquires competitor Falk
October 9, 2006	Google to acquire YouTube
October 17, 2006	Yahoo invests in Right Media
March 2007	Viacom sues YouTube
April 4, 2007	*Times* profile of the DoubleClick exchange
April 14, 2007	Google to acquire DoubleClick
April 29, 2007	Yahoo to acquire Right Media
May 18, 2007	Microsoft to acquire aQuantive
July 25, 2007	AOL acquires Tacoda
July 26, 2007	Microsoft acquires AdECN
August 9, 2007	WPP to acquire 24/7 Real Media
August 9, 2007	AOL to acquire AdTech
September 2007	AppNexus founded as cloud provider

September 2007	MediaMath founded
September 18, 2007	PubMatic debuts at TechCrunch 40
March 11, 2008	Google-DoubleClick closes
March 13, 2008	Google announces free ad server
March 12, 2009	Google accepts third-party cookies
September 17, 2009	Google launches AdX 2.0
February 10, 2010	AdMeld Partner Summit introduces RTB
June 3, 2010	Google acquires Invite Media
June 9, 2011	Google to acquire AdMeld
December 2, 2011	AdMeld approved by DOJ
December 6, 2011	AOL-Yahoo-Microsoft sales alliance
March 22, 2012	AdMeld to be integrated into AdX
July 2012	Marissa Mayer becomes Yahoo's CEO
January 2013	Dynamic Revenue Share in AdX
August 7, 2013	AOL acquires Adap.tv
November 2013	Project Bernanke
March 6, 2014	Comcast acquires FreeWheel
Spring 2014	Global Bernanke
Spring 2014	Sell-side Dynamic Revenue Share
January 15, 2015	Facebook starts the "pivot to video"
May 12, 2015	Verizon acquires AOL

May 12, 2015	Facebook Instant Articles
June 18, 2015	First mention of "header bidding"
June 29, 2015	Microsoft outsources ad sales
August 6, 2015	First GitHub commit for prebid.js
October 7, 2015	Google AMP
January 2016	"Wrapper Wars" in New York
April 13, 2016	Open Bidding (EBDA) in beta
July 25, 2016	Verizon acquires Yahoo
December 2, 2016	Amazon TAM
March 31, 2017	Last Look removed for Open Bidding
June 8, 2017	Open Bidding open beta
July 2017	Poirot in DV360
October 1, 2017	Apple's ITP removes cookies from Safari
August 2018	AT&T acquires AppNexus
September 2018	Poirot 2.0
December 14, 2018	Facebook-Google alliance(Jedi Blue)
March 6, 2019	Google announces first-price auction
April 18, 2019	Raucous meeting at Google with publishers
May 2019	Unified Pricing Rules
September 9, 2019	50 states announce broad investigation of Google
January 2020	Google to remove cookies in "two years"
April 11, 2020	Facebook exits open web, focuses on app
December 16, 2020	State antitrust case led by Texas announced

January 2021	UK gains oversight over Privacy Sandbox
June 2021	Google €220 million fine in France
June 2021	EU opens antitrust investigation
September 1, 2021	PE buys Verizon Media, renames it Yahoo
September 2021	Apple's ATT prevents in-app tracking
December 21, 2021	Microsoft acquires Xandr (formerly AppNexus)
January 24, 2023	DOJ antitrust suit against Google
February 2023	Neal Mohan becomes YouTube CEO
June 13, 2023	EU issues Statement of Objections
July 25, 2023	YouTube revenue exceeds that of "Network"
April 2024	Judge Mehta finds Google has search monopoly
July 22, 2024	Google reverses approach on cookies in Chrome
September 9, 2024	DOJ trial in the Eastern District of Virginia
December 2024	Canada files case against Google
April 2025	Judge Brinkema rules Google to be a monopoly in the ad-tech market

HOW ADVERTISING TECHNOLOGY WORKS AT GOOGLE (DIAGRAMS)

The way advertisements end up on web pages is surprisingly complex and has evolved significantly over the past decade. The following diagrams are simplified but give some perspective on how Google and others have tried to advantage themselves in the flow of data and information as these decisions are made.

Pre-2007: The "Waterfall"

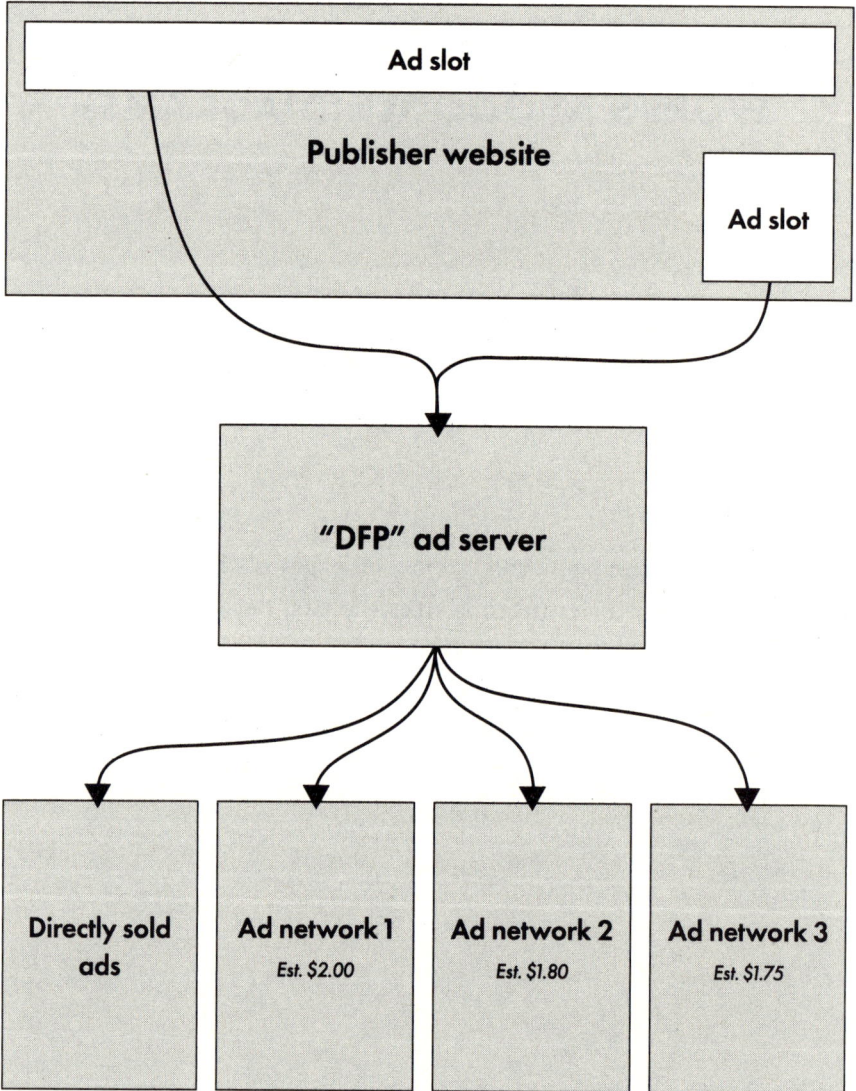

Ad slot

Publisher website

Ad slot

"DFP" ad server

| Directly sold ads | Ad network 1 *Est. $2.00* | Ad network 2 *Est. $1.80* | Ad network 3 *Est. $1.75* |

Serve direct ads first, then try ad networks

Ad networks called sequentially in a "waterfall" based on estimated prices

2007-2014: AdX Dynamic Allocation (First Look)

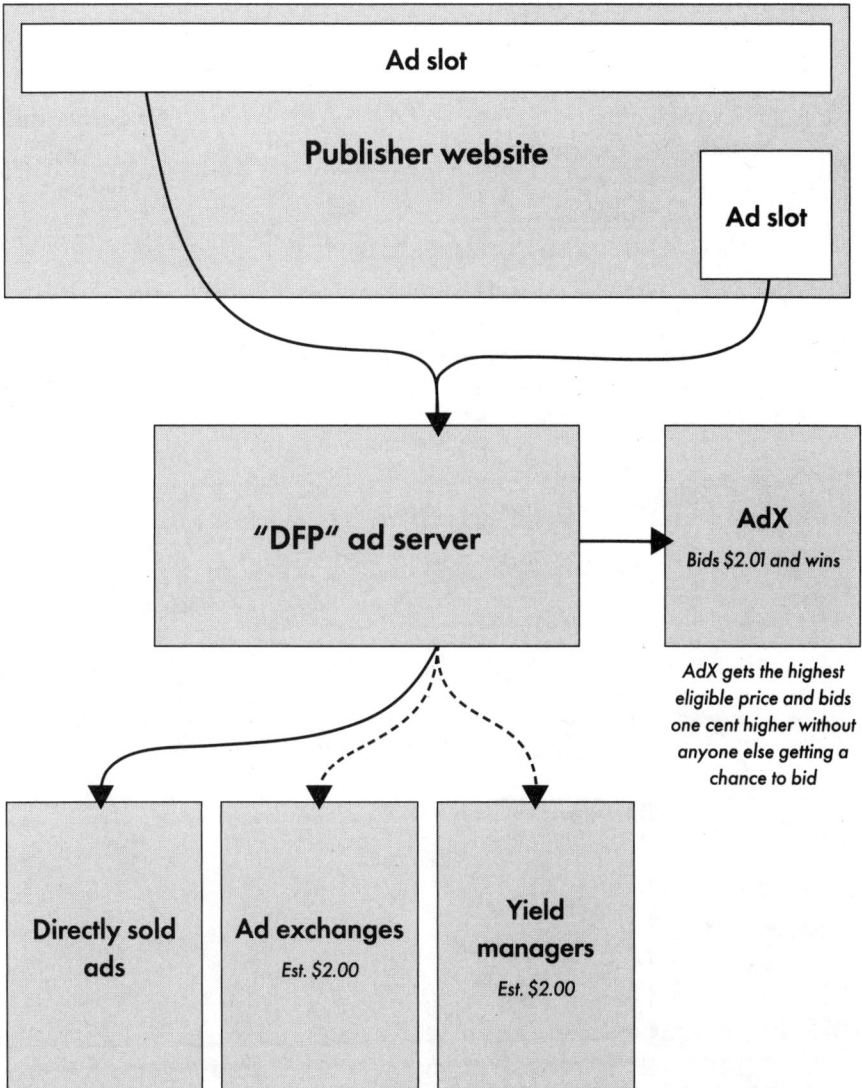

Ad slot

Publisher website

Ad slot

"DFP" ad server

AdX

Bids $2.01 and wins

AdX gets the highest eligible price and bids one cent higher without anyone else getting a chance to bid

Directly sold ads

Ad exchanges
Est. $2.00

Yield managers
Est. $2.00

2014-2019: Header Bidding with AdX "Last Look"

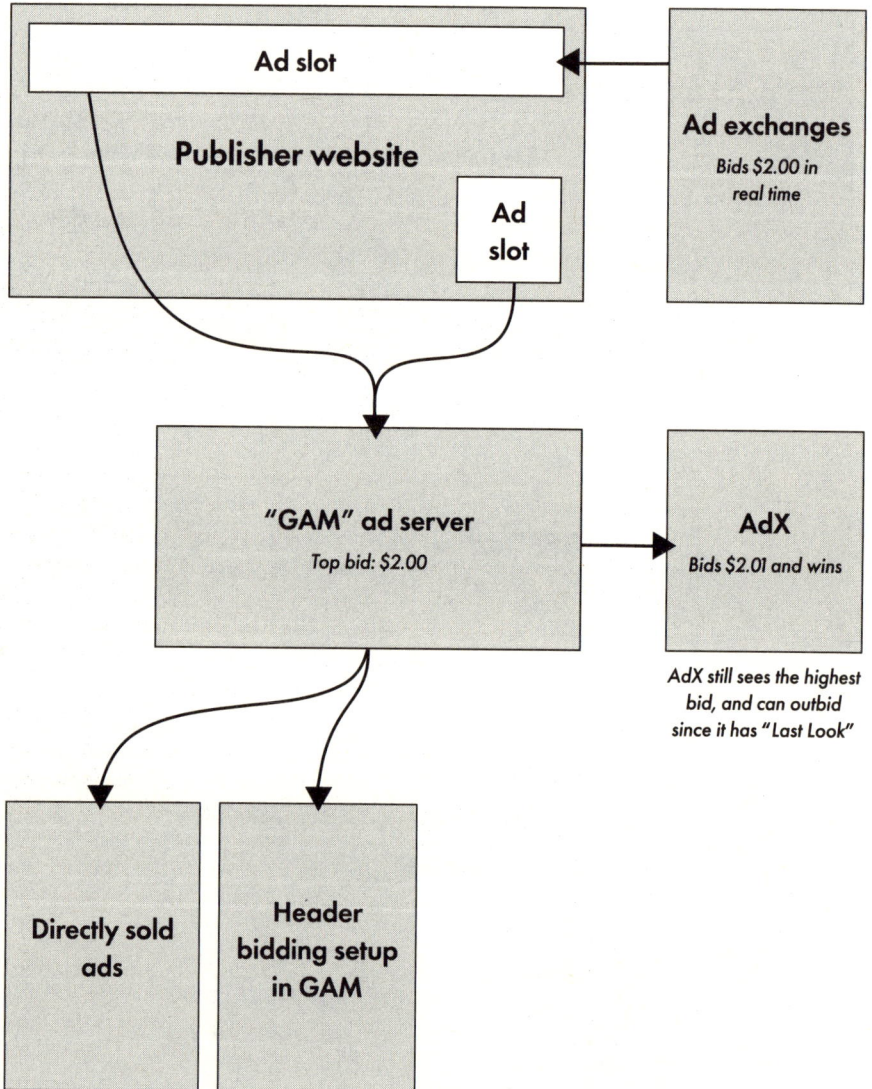

2019-Present: Header Bidding and Open Bidding

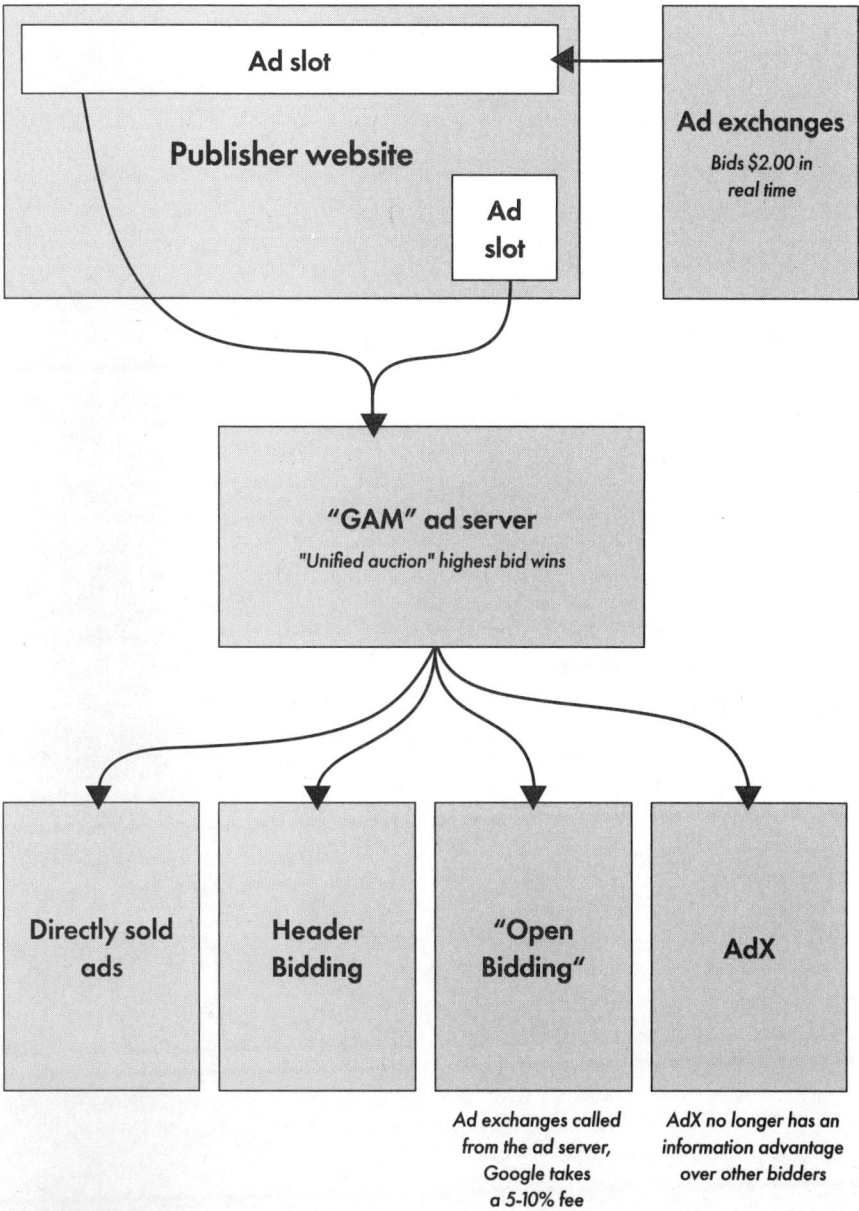

INTRODUCTION

S teph Layser couldn't believe what she was hearing. Along with about thirty other publishing executives, she was at Google's imposing New York headquarters listening to product managers announce changes to how Google's advertising products would work.

Steph represented News Corp, the owner of media properties Fox News, the *New York Post*, and the *Wall Street Journal*, among others. News Corp was one of Google's largest publisher customers, and they had been using—and paying handsomely for—Google's advertising software for decades. Like the other attendees, Steph was an expert in yield management and operations, the dirty business of managing the ads on publisher websites to squeeze every penny out of the content and hopefully pay the journalism bills.

The first half of the presentation was quite upbeat. Google was switching the way it ran auctions for advertising to the more desirable "first-price" method—a change many publishers welcomed and felt was past due. Then Google dropped a bombshell. A new feature was being

1

rolled out that would restrict the ability of publishers to set different pricing levels for different sources of ads.

It didn't take more than a moment for the assembled audience to understand the impact of this change. Publishers regularly set higher prices when Google was selling their ads, as compared to other partners. They also might set lower prices for another seller to help build a stronger relationship, meet business commitments, or reduce their dependence on Google. These were all common techniques that were proven to generate incremental revenue. This product change was touted as an enhancement, but clearly it was designed to end these practices and give Google an advantage in the marketplace.

The room erupted, and decorum was lost. Steph and others hurled angry and accusatory questions at the speaker. At one point the speaker joked he could use a drink, despite the meeting taking place well before lunch. Sarah Sluis from the trade site *AdExchanger* put it best, dryly reporting, "It did not go well."

While the relationship between publishers and Google had at times been fraught, never had anyone seen a move with such naked self-interest. Announcing this as a new "feature" for publishers struck attendees as gaslighting. Even employees inside Google agreed. For months leading up to the fateful meeting, in internal emails employees worried this change would look bad and that publishers would be upset. The warnings went unheeded. After all, what could publishers do about it when they were stuck using Google's technology?

The complaints from publishers were mostly ignored. The new pricing rules were rolled out with some minor modifications, and effectively there was nothing to do but accept it. The trust between publishers and Google, already fraught, was gone forever.

For years leading up to this moment, publishers were in a low-grade conflict with Google while also largely dependent on it for vital ad revenue and search traffic. Google had made it nearly impossible for publishers to switch off their advertising software. Google's ad exchange, which sold ads on their behalf, was integrated in a way that intentionally prevented other exchanges from competing on a fair basis. More sophisticated publishers had even seen evidence there was something amiss with the auction mechanics that determined which ads would serve on their sites—it sometimes seemed like fingers were being pressed on the scales. Now, for the first time, the malfeasance was nakedly apparent.

Within two years of this dustup, state, federal, European, and civil antitrust lawsuits had been filed against Google's advertising business. Discovery in those suits found behavior that went well beyond the pricing rules and uncovered secret projects, with code names such as Bernanke and Poirot, intended to manipulate the market and increase Google's dominance, as well as a secret pact with archrival Facebook, which gave off the appearance of collusion. The whole industry had been stunned by Google's ten-year run from bit player to absolute dominant force within display advertising. When the methods by which they got there were uncovered, it gave credence to the most paranoid fantasies of competitors and customers alike.

The fate of Google's ad business, and with it the ad-supported digital publishing model, is now being decided by judges and juries in Brussels, Virginia, and Texas. The first domino to fall came from the federal courts, when Judge Leonie Brinkema of the Eastern District of Virginia ruled Google to be an abusive monopoly in advertising. The ultimate remedies, and remaining cases around the world, may determine the future of media and journalism.

Google is best known for its consumer products: Search, Gmail, Maps, and Android. But advertising has always paid the bills, and the company is the largest seller of ads in the history of the world. Most of Google's advertising is tied to search—many of those blue links on the search results page are paid for by advertisers and generate literally billions of dollars for the company every single day.

Less well known is Google's dominance in display and video ads—the squares and rectangles dotting your favorite websites and apps. Google went from a minor player in display advertising to a position so dominant they could change the rules on a whim, rendering multibillion-dollar media companies like News Corp and Gannett helpless to control their own destiny.

The traditional media business, and the journalism it supports, is a shadow of itself. Newspaper employment has declined 80% since 1995, and similar declines have been seen in other media. This decline is structural and driven by consumers getting their news and information in different ways. Media companies are adjusting to the new environment with new approaches, such as paywalls and email subscriptions. In the end, though, a large portion of the journalism, content, and entertainment we all enjoy is paid for by ads.

The ads shown on websites like nytimes.com are bought and sold through a surprisingly complex thread of companies using technology more akin to what you would expect to see on Wall Street. Within a couple of hundred milliseconds, dozens of buyers might transmit their bids for ads on a single page, with machine learning and AI driving the processes to select those offers with the best performance. Outside of those directly involved, few may be aware of the complexity of the advertising ecosystem. But the way it has evolved—and been manipulated—has had a direct, ongoing effect on the economics of publishing and journalism.

Like the other markets where Google competes, the advertising business has been radically disrupted by technological innovation. Within the span of twenty years, ads went from being bought and sold by humans, over the stereotypical "three martini lunches," to globally traded commodities bought and sold like stocks. As this transition unfolded, control over the inventory sold by publishers, and the demand from advertisers, shifted to the technology innovators. Through a series of acquisitions, exclusive relationships, and market manipulations, Google took the helm of this enormous market and never looked back.

This is the story of how technology separated publishers from control over their advertising revenue and the decades-long attempt to claw it back. It follows Google's rivals trying to chip away at the company's dominance, publishers hacking code to generate more revenue, and ultimately regulators and policymakers hauling the company into court.

PART I

THE RACE TO THE STARTING LINE

CHAPTER 1

WELCOME TO SILICON ALLEY

The right ad to the right person at the right time.

—Unknown

Brian O'Kelley didn't think he was changing the world. He was just trying to make his customers a little more money. Brian was the CTO of Right Media, a little-known technology company based in the Flatiron neighborhood of Manhattan. Right serviced a bunch of customers that also were hardly household names. Companies such as Matomy Media out of Tel Aviv were ad networks, essentially middlemen, who would buy ad space from publishers looking to make money and sell the space to marketers looking to reach the right customers on the web. These were not glamorous Madison Avenue creative houses like Ogilvy or Y&R. They were nameless, faceless optimizers looking to squeeze pennies out of every transaction.

Brian's insight was that digital advertising was essentially a *valuation* problem. If you could value every ad properly, you could figure out the best one to show at any time, on any website. Previously everyone in advertising thought this was a *matching* problem, where the goal was to "show the right ad to the right person at the right time." From Brian's point of view, the right ad was the one willing to pay the most, making publishers the most money and giving the advertiser the most value. This was in sharp contrast to the idea of traditional media planning where a twenty-something at an ad agency recommended what to buy via PowerPoint.

From this insight was born the first advertising exchange. Once you could value every ad, you could also trade them. Like the Nasdaq, an ad exchange could match ad buyers and sellers in near real time, based on price, providing better results for everyone. The first ad exchange transaction took place within Right Media in April 2005 and would revolutionize the entire industry. As a side effect, it would disrupt the traditional relationships between publishers and agencies, and instead put the largest technology companies, like Google, Yahoo, and Microsoft, in the driver's seat.

This ad exchange breakthrough would start within the decidedly unsexy world of banner ads but over the next decade would become the way most ads on websites, billboards, iPhones, and TVs would be bought and sold. It represented a fundamental change to the advertising business because it separated the buying and selling of ads into distinct activities that could be performed by different companies. From the first Ivory Soap ads in newspapers to the video ads on the Yahoo homepage, every single spot was bought and sold by two parties who connected directly. Even in the case of ad networks that worked across many publishers, there would be contracts with each publisher and each advertiser and they would only match the two within a closed system.

With an ad exchange, a publisher could offer its ad slot for sale and any buyer anywhere in the world could theoretically win an auction to show their ad. In financial terms, the market went from one entirely based on *futures* contracts to a *spot market*. This innovation would be especially important to companies like Google, Yahoo, and AOL, who all controlled a lot of "supply" to sell and advertiser "demand" looking to spend—making the market more efficient would almost certainly add to their profits.

The idea for an ad exchange was not entirely new; people in advertising had been talking about liquidity and marketplaces for quite some time. It was during the dot-com era of the 1990s at industry pioneer DoubleClick that the seed of the idea was first planted and, later, where it would turn into a global phenomenon under Google's ownership.

"Welcome to Silicon Alley" read DoubleClick's billboard opposite the iconic Flatiron Building on the corner of Twenty-Second Street and Broadway. After a successful IPO in 1997, the company had real swagger, and the sign was a symbol to the world that the company was the big player in this emerging New York tech scene. There were lavish parties for advertisers and agencies, including an infamous Oompa Loompa themed bash that involved hiring little people as waiters. The headquarters took up a full block on West Thirty-Second Street and included a basketball court. This was a company that was making a mark.

Founded by the "two Kevins"—Ryan and O'Connor—DoubleClick was an innovator in the early days of internet advertising, selling and placing banner ads across a network of thousands of websites ranging from the *Wall Street Journal* to small blogs run by solo entrepreneurs. The company did not own any websites or create any content itself; it sold ads on other websites through its ad network. Ad networks had developed quickly when the web first became popular with consumers because it was easier for advertisers to place an order with a single company rather than try to buy ads from tens or hundreds of different publishers. Many publishers had put up websites in the 1990s out of a sort of FOMO, without much of a real business plan. When advertisers became interested in the online audiences, they had little idea of how to sell or service the business, so outsourcing made a lot of sense.

As publishers saw traffic to their websites grow, they wanted to sell those ads themselves, in the same way they sold print, radio, or TV spots.

While sales might come relatively easy, managing the ads themselves was surprisingly complex. It was not only that a publisher might need to have an engineer or other technical person incorporate the ads into the webpage; often advertisers would also have detailed specifications for when and how their ads should show—for example, only in the United States or only during daytime hours. As sales grew, this problem quickly became unmanageable, and thus a new type of software product was created, called an "ad server."

Ad servers are complex and powerful tools that help publishers manage which of their ads show up on which pages of their sites and, eventually, on which mobile and TV apps. Ad servers need to consider many factors to determine which ad to show at a given time. The advertiser might specify the flight dates, the time of day, the geography, the portions of the site, and many other factors. Larger publishers will often employ large teams of people to run their ad operations, or "ad ops." These people work like air traffic controllers, helping the sales force land new deals while also maneuvering existing orders to make sure they meet the advertisers' orders for delivery, budget, and pricing.

A key part of the job in ad ops is maximizing the "yield" of the publisher's inventory. In the airline business, yield means making the most money on every seat on the plane—an empty seat is a wasted opportunity. The same is true for ad slots on a website—if the user visits the page and nothing shows, you have effectively lost money. The ad ops teams balance delivering the ads that were booked directly by the sales team with selling the ads through indirect sales channels like ad networks. While DoubleClick was the largest ad network, they were not the only one, and the ad ops teams would use the ad server to try to eke out extra pennies from whoever was willing to pay for the "remnant" slots. This unsold inventory was largely an afterthought since the prices were so much lower than direct but over time became the battleground that would turn the entire business on its head.

Wenda Harris Millard was DoubleClick's sales leader. She came from *Family Circle*, where she was the publisher of the country's number-one women's magazine. She remembers hearing about the opportunity at the then-unknown DoubleClick and thinking, "I don't want to work with geeks." In a three-hour meeting, she got over her fear of geeks and was charmed by Kevin O'Connor, remarking, "I wasn't sure if he was a genius or a lunatic." She joined the company as employee twelve and helped grow it to over three thousand employees and a half billion in revenue. The DoubleClick ad network was her baby, and she saw it grow from being a rounding error of revenue for publishers to being a real business they took quite seriously.[1]

The actual mix of publisher websites on the network had lots of variation and included odd sites like IBM's patent lookup service, in addition to brand-name publishers. The company saw the opportunity with some of the "long tail" content but worried about tarnishing the reputation of the primary business with a whole bunch of webpages no one had heard of, with content produced by amateurs or at least by non-journalists. To protect the company's primary brand, DoubleClick, they created a new network for these sites, called Sonar.

Wenda recruited Michael Walrath for Sonar, later calling him "brilliant." Just a couple years out of college, Michael quickly became the star salesman on the Sonar team. The Sonar business was unsexy enough that it was banished from the company's expensive headquarters and sent to an old office that suffered from shoddy air-conditioning. The direct response advertisers Sonar sold to were willing to work with long tail websites because they cared much less about the quality of the content or the way their brands appeared on the page. All they wanted was performance—meaning clicks, conversions, and downloads. The types of brands that ran on primetime TV were being handled by the salespeople back at the mother ship with the big expense accounts, while Michael and crew sold to a motley assortment of smart kids who knew how to make money on the nascent web.

Michael instinctively knew that this type of long tail inventory could generate performance with the right offers. Instead of trying to sell campaigns to individual advertisers or agencies, he focused on selling space to other ad networks. In the same way DoubleClick's own ad network represented many advertisers across websites, when Sonar sold a single ad placement to another network, it might represent tens or hundreds of advertisers, and they could choose which ad to show on the fly to get the best results.

The only problem was delivery. His customers wanted more opportunities to show their ads, but they were strictly limited in the price they would pay since their goal was to maintain a margin. The best ad slots would go to the premium advertisers, while Sonar and its customers were picking up scraps. He wasn't content to just let this go. He wanted to really understand how the vaunted DoubleClick technology worked and how it decided which ads to show on which pages. He reached out to a friendly product manager, Matt Philips, to get a tutorial on ad serving.

The Sonar network and the rest of DoubleClick all ran on the company's DFP ad server. Matt gave Michael a link to put into his browser that was only available for employees to see the inner workings of the ad server for any given campaign. All Michael had to do was change the "ID" field within the link to look at any campaign in the system. What Matt told him to look for was a special metric called the Satisfaction Index. This metric showed whether the campaign was properly delivering according to the advertiser's deal parameters. An index of 100 meant it was in good shape. Over 100 meant it was delivering too fast and needed to slow down. Under 100 meant the ad needed to catch up and would serve more.

Since most DoubleClick customers were big, traditional media companies who had sales forces to sell expensive ad campaigns directly to agencies, the ad server was primarily built around an assumption that the best ad to serve was the one that matched the desired *delivery* goals of the advertiser. Effectively that's what the Satisfaction Index measured, the likelihood the ad would deliver on time and on budget. There was little consideration of whether an ad performed better for the advertiser.

Michael's Sonar customers cared enormously about whether the ads "worked" or not, so there was a big mismatch between what they were trying to accomplish and what the technology was designed to do. While Michael could bring in these valuable ad network buyers, willing to spend as much as possible to get performance, the ad server would just slot them in with all the other buyers and hope for the best. Since the average price they would pay was lower than brand advertisers, they would always be starved for impressions and set as lower priority in the server. He devised a hack.

He called Jonah Goodhart, who, with his brother Noah, operated a scrappy ad network called Colonize. These guys were consummate dot-com entrepreneurs who could figure out how to make money by arbitraging the cost of banner ads against the performance requirements of their advertisers. Unbeknownst to Michael, Jonah was still an undergrad at Cornell University and operating this side gig from his dorm, while also being one of DoubleClick's largest customers. The proposal Michael pitched was to write an order for a million dollars—much more than Jonah would normally commit to—but to set the order to run for just one week. Michael assured him it would never actually run that much budget and he would only pay for what was actually delivered. Jonah was skeptical but trusted Michael and decided to give it a shot.

When Jonah's oversize order was entered into the ad server, the Satisfaction Index went crazy because it was so far away from hitting the totally unrealistic delivery goals. The *unsatisfactory* index would then force the ad server to show the ad as often as possible, within the targeting parameters, which is exactly what Jonah and team wanted. At the end of the week, Jonah might have been billed only a quarter million dollars against the huge paper commitment, but his ads showed much more often and to higher-priority audiences than ever before.

Once the hack proved to work, Michael went bananas, selling oversize orders to all his ad network clients while getting kudos from upper management for the eye-popping bookings he rang up every day. He ended up personally representing 40% of all Sonar revenue. No one seemed to care that this hack was taking away delivery from potentially more valuable customers and, probably, the overall company was losing money. Michael had created a trading strategy that paid him rich commissions at the expense of the fancy brand advertising being sold at headquarters. The insights from this hack would lead to the development of a totally new kind of advertising technology.

David Rosenblatt was the first product manager for DoubleClick's ad server. When he joined in 1997, there were only eight ad serving customers and the vast majority of the company's revenue came from selling ads rather than selling software. It was David's first job since getting his MBA from Stanford, and little did anyone suspect he would eventually rise to become the company's CEO.

David is not particularly loud or physically intimidating but had a way of cutting through any problem, or any meeting, to get to the point. He frequently interrupted a speaker giving a long PowerPoint presentation with a pointed question about the implication that the presenter had not even considered. He had a habit of asking presenters to ignore all their slides and instead just say the two or three things that had to be done to be successful. This style proved valuable in the world of advertising and amid the dot-com era, where so much nonsense could cover up the important facts and truths.

The entrepreneurial spirit of DoubleClick was also a big part of David's success. He grew the ad server business by working arm in arm with his sales lead and ignoring the noise from the larger and more successful ad network side. He and the company's CTO, Dwight Merriman, sold Dell Computers an advertiser-facing ad server product before it even existed, then spent the plane ride home from Dallas figuring out how to build it.

When the dot-com bubble burst in 2001, roughly 70% of Double-Click's customers went out of business,[2] often without even a forwarding address. Media spending has always been highly cyclical, so the recession that followed was devastating to everyone selling ads. Since so much of the ad spending on the early web was "round-tripping" between venture capital funded start-ups and their venture-capital-funded publishers (estimated at over 70%!), the effect of the bust on digital ads was exceptionally severe.[3] The DoubleClick ad network revenue plummeted, and in 2002 that division was sold off for less than $15 million.[4] More than half the company's remaining revenue came from software sales that David had either built, managed, or acquired. Having grown most of the important products, David was made the company's president and was put in charge of day-to-day operations.[5]

In the years that followed, the company diversified, adding tangentially related products such as email management and marketing automation workflow. The ad servers were cash cows, but it was hard to see them as a source of growth or worthy of investment given the moribund state of digital media. The online advertising business hit a peak of $8.2 billion in revenue at the height of the boom in 2000, but even with ever-growing consumer internet usage, three years later spending was still almost a billion shy of this peak.[6] The advertising world watched with awe the new phenomenal growth of search ads being built by Google on the West Coast, but within traditional publishing there was not a clear path forward for monetizing content.

By 2004 DoubleClick was a sleepy, slow-growing software company with a shrinking market capitalization and the aura of a firm that had seen its best days in the rearview mirror. Almost all the big media companies relied on DoubleClick's ad server for their digital business operations. The advertiser-facing ad server was also growing quite quickly into a second major software business. It was not the most glamorous technology, but they were very sticky products that were hard to replace and met real business needs. Little did anyone suspect at the time that this humble software platform would become the linchpin of control over the entire web advertising market.

Cofounder Kevin Ryan was in charge as CEO but maybe looking forward to new adventures (he would later found or cofound Gilt Group, MongoDB, *Business Insider*, and dozens of other companies).

In November of that year, the board concluded that there needed to be changes that would be difficult to accomplish as a public company. It put itself up for sale, hiring investment bankers Lazard Frères to manage the process.[7] About five private equity funds kicked the tires, but curiously, given DoubleClick's central place in the advertising world, there were no strategic, nonfinancial bidders. Google took a meeting but did not ultimately bid. Yahoo, AOL, and Microsoft were not interested. Only one final bid was made, by San Francisco-based private equity firm Hellman & Friedman[8] along with JMI Management. The transaction closed in 2005 for a price of $1.1 billion. The actual cost to these firms would turn out to be much less, since the amount being paid for equity was only $342 million, with the remainder in debt. Net of the cash on the books of DoubleClick, it was even substantially lower, maybe as low as $250 million.[9] This was a company that was generating over $300 million in annual revenue and $37 million in net income, so this was quite the bargain.[10]

For the leading light of New York's technology scene, this was an inglorious exit. Not only had the company's IPO priced their stock at roughly double the exit price,[11] but the market capitalization had at one time reached over $15 billion.

For David, it was time to get to work. Kevin Ryan and a bunch of other executives departed when the deal closed, and David was made CEO. He reshuffled the management deck to get the company ready to restart growth. He brought in a longtime IBM executive, Marianne

Caponnetto, to lead sales and marketing. In technology, HR, and finance, he promoted existing senior managers who had been at the company to executive roles. The most important role to fill, though, was product management. If the company was to grow, it would be through innovation and product development. There were a number of talented VP-level managers in the product team, but David felt that none were clearly ready to lead the team into this new era. He looked outside the company, to someone who had been in the trenches during the earlier stages of the company.

———————

Neal Mohan joined DoubleClick in 1999 through the acquisition of a competitive ad serving company, NetGravity.[12] Neal had a management role in client services and became a valued contributor, focused on business operations—essentially an offshoot of accounting and analytics. During the bust period, he became a self-described "hatchet man,"[13] coordinating and executing the many rounds of layoffs that became a sort of background noise for those in the tech sector in 2002 and 2003.

Neal left to get his MBA from Stanford, and alum Rosenblatt was happy to write his recommendation. Two years later, when the deal to take DoubleClick private was set to close, it lined up with the same moment Neal was graduating from business school. David reached out. Neal already had an offer to join Google in its OSO group, which was essentially a very large sales and service organization reporting up to Sheryl Sandberg that catered to small and midsize customers. Google was an incredibly prestigious company to work for, and the job matched the kind of work Neal had done prior to getting his MBA. Also, he lived in Palo Alto, so it was local. Neal was so close to accepting that Google had already printed his office nameplate.

But David had a hunch. Even though Neal had no experience in product management or strategy, was located on the wrong coast, and had not worked for DoubleClick for years, he felt that he would bring some level of cohesion to the product function at the company. He pitched the idea and ultimately persuaded Neal to give up the perfect Google offer to take a flier on the new DoubleClick. This was a hunch that would pay off for both of them.

David, Neal, and the rest of the management team got working fast to right the ship and restart the company's growth. They sold or shuttered unattractive parts of the business, invested in the dominant ad serving software products that had been let languish for years,[14,15] and acquired some strategic assets like a video ad platform.[16] Within a year the company would be a quite attractive software company, with 50% annual growth and 30% profit margins.[17] The real strategic value, though, would come from control over the platform itself.

CHAPTER 2

A STUPID FEATURE

The ad exchange started as a "stupid feature"... to bid on
overflow inventory from other networks and vice versa.[1]
—Brian O'Kelley

When DoubleClick sold off its media business after the dot-com crash, star salesman Michael Walrath found himself unhappy and looking for something new. Because of the bad economic environment, the prices that publishers could get for digital ads had fallen off a cliff, and that glut of affordable inventory gave room for a proliferation of ad networks. These networks were essentially in the business of buying cheap ad inventory from publishers, then marking it up and driving (or even guaranteeing) performance for advertisers. It was a great time for Michael to start a company focused on the network business.

Michael quit, and with some invested capital from his sibling clients Jonah and Noah, as well as Matt Philips as his product lead, started Right Media. The first iteration was simply a media consulting company, where he would help his clients get more inventory and performance by being smarter about understanding how the technology worked. In other words, he would hack the systems for them. His vision was a lot larger. He recalled thinking that "the way ads were being sold mechanically and economically made no sense; if you just served the highest value ad, you would make more money for everybody."[2] Going back to his days at DoubleClick, Michael and his boss at the time, Bill Wise, would often brainstorm about what they called the Ad Nasdaq, a trading environment that would democratize advertising and let anyone buy or sell ads without all the complexity and hassles inherent in running a complex operation.[3]

Right Media quickly evolved from consulting to also transacting as simply another ad network. AOL was their largest client, buying ads at low cost in order to get sign-ups for their dial-up and broadband services. Michael realized they were not going to scale this business as a makeshift ad network and they needed to build their own technology. He did not want to repeat the mistakes he saw (and exploited) at DoubleClick. Rather, he wanted to build a new type of ad server, one that optimized to revenue rather than delivery. He needed someone to help him build the technology.

Michael had gotten to know Joe Zawadski, an early digital advertising pioneer who had started a company called Poindexter. Joe came to New York with a degree from Harvard and spent a couple of years as an investment banker before striking out on his own in the new and uncertain Silicon Alley tech scene. Poindexter was described as an "optimization" company, which meant it would both help publishers decide which ads would show on their site (what would later be called "yield management") and help advertisers pick which creative to show when they bought digital ads. This technology was inherently limited since it could not affect the price paid for the media or the choice of what to buy. All it could do was optimize what had already been bought. Michael and Joe agreed on a deal to build the new Right Media ad server as a new joint venture in which Poindexter would provide the technology and Michael would sell the ads.[4] Progress on the technology was slow and behind schedule when Poindexter's board killed the deal. The ad server Michael wanted would still come to fruition almost by accident. Right Media was subleasing an office—really a closet—from Poindexter, and that was how he found his CTO.

Brian O'Kelley can be an intimidating figure. The six-foot-five former college basketball player makes no apologies about his competitive streak. Combined with his habit of dressing in torn T-shirts and flip-flops, he gives off the contradictory air of both not giving a shit and being willing to do anything to win. After graduating from Princeton with a computer science degree in distributed systems, Brian moved to New York at just the wrong time, the difficult economic years after the dot-com bust. At the time, if you were a technologist in New York, you were likely to end up in either advertising or finance.

Brian ended up at Poindexter, hired to make its software scale. With the Right Media ad server project not happening (or happening slowly), he saw this as an opportunity. He asked Michael and Matt out for lunch. They picked a place across town to add to the stealth. Brian made a proposal to switch sides. Instead of working as a contractor for Poindexter, he would work for Michael and Right Media directly. A deal was made, and as a side effect, they would need to find new office space.

Brian, Matt, and their team were tasked with building out what was probably the first ad server designed specifically for performance. They delivered an initial version in about six weeks. The real breakthrough came when calculating the expected value of each impression and doing it in near real time. This might seem easy at first glance, since the ads have prices associated with their orders. For a performance ad network like Right, though, the value might vary depending on the type of performance. Consider two advertisers, one that is brand focused and wants to pay a fixed rate, $5 per thousand impressions, and another that wants clicks and is willing to pay $1 for every visit to their website. To determine which of those two ads would be better to serve, you need a common metric. In this case the ad server had to calculate the *expected value* of the click-driven ad and compare it to the fixed $5 bid for the brand advertiser. In this simplistic example, if the ad server expected more than five clicks for every thousand impressions, then the click ad should serve at a higher priority.

These calculations had to be done extremely quickly and on hundreds—or thousands—of ads eligible to show in each ad slot. The inputs to the calculation might include the time of day, the website or placement, the user's location, and the browser. To make it more complex, not every ad gets clicked as often, so the calculation needed to take into consideration the performance of that particular creative and advertiser. It also had to make educated guesses about these values in cases where there was little historical data, like when an ad just started running for the first time.

At first there was only one customer for this new kind of ad server, Right Media itself. Michael and his team continued to hawk AOL sub-scriptions and rack up margins. This would only be the first step.

Brian was not content to just sit behind the scenes coding. He started attending industry events, working on the business side, and generally learning the ad network business. At long-forgotten conferences, like the Ad:Tech events, various middlemen and, frankly, bottom-feeders would come from around the world, compare notes, and do deals in the under-belly of advertising. The ad networks attending the show were often building their own technology, at great expense, since the leading ad servers were not built for this kind of optimization. For an ad network that was focused on generating margin with performance ads, an ad server like DoubleClick's was just the wrong tool for the job.

It was at one of these events that Brian met Bob Regular.* Bob ran an ad network called Kitara, and it operated on an ad server his team in Tel Aviv built from scratch. The server was struggling with some of the basics, like properly tracking ad clicks, and overall was not generating the results

---

* That is really his name.

he was hoping for. After Bob learned about what they had built at Right Media, he wanted to try it for himself. Brian jumped at the opportunity and engaged deeply with Bob and his team, understanding their requirements and making multiple trips to Israel to work with the team. After a couple of months, Kitara turned off its own technology and switched to Right's ad server. He would not be the last.

During a trip to visit Regular and the team in Israel, Brian realized that there was a mismatch in advertising demand that perhaps he could fix. The Right Media ad network often had quite a bit of available ad inventory in Europe but had very few advertisers who wanted to buy ads in the region. Some of the Israeli ad networks had demand in Europe, as they did more business with agencies in London and Paris. Swapping inventory between two different ad networks using manual methods, like cutting and pasting between them, would be complex and error-prone. Brian's ad server was already able to use its expected value calculations to estimate how much a given ad impression was worth to a given advertiser. Why not, he reasoned, just show the ad with the highest value, even if it came from a different customer?[5] At the time, he thought of this as just a "stupid feature" to flow demand between customers in Europe.[6] The importance became obvious once they saw the results.

Building this cross-customer exchange was not as easy as it sounded at first. After a couple of weeks of work, they were ready to try. In April 2005 Brian "flipped the switch," and the first two ad networks, Right's and Kitara, were connected. With just these two nodes of the network connected, revenue almost magically went up by 15% overnight. No new advertisers were signed up, and no new publishers were providing inventory. Just by matching demand and supply slightly more efficiently, everyone was better off. It was akin to Goldman Sachs and J. P. Morgan suddenly being given access to each other's orders after trading stocks only among their own customers. All the prices, matching, and liquidity instantly improved. Michael's original vision was coming true, though in a roundabout way.

There was no press release or marketing event to herald the new offering. Once it was clear this technology made more money, word of mouth within the tight-knit community of ad networks took hold and there was a stampede to Right Media, both for the ad server and this new "ad exchange" that magically increased yield.

———————

The ad exchange attracted attention and prompted Yahoo to invest $40 million for a minority position in Right Media.[7] The news of the investment was kept out of the press, but for people in the advertising world, it came as a shock. The company few had heard of, with second-tier middlemen clients, was suddenly partnering with Yahoo, the most powerful digital media company of the time.

With the investment and the exchange growing like wildfire, Right Media was adding people and customers at a breakneck pace. Internally the company was in chaos. More than one set of executives was sleeping together, and after-work happy hours and drinks were a constant. The product side was straining as well. The volume of transactions on Right Media scaled from about 2 billion per month in 2005 to over 100 billion per month in 2007.[8]

Once Right Media's system started having some level of liquidity between buyers and sellers, it opened a number of new opportunities to grow. In 2005 the company launched DMX, a product that allowed publishers to sign up on their own to be part of the network and to put tags on their websites to make passive money.[9] This directly competed with Google AdSense, but since it focused on display ads instead of text likely netted higher prices for the publishers. They also created a console for ad buyers to place bids and orders against the inventory in their exchange, possibly the first instance of a "demand" platform.

While it may have seemed like connecting customers in an exchange was now a solved problem, it turned out to generate an ever longer list of new ones. Each customer on the exchange needed to sign a contract with every other trading partner and handle all the billings and reconciliations themselves. Fraud became a problem, as generating fake websites, or fake traffic to those sites, could almost instantly turn into profits.

These operational problems paled compared to the internal drama. Brian, with a taste of what he could get done when given a chance, essentially started running his own company within Right. He tightly ruled over his engineering team and shunted to the side business hires and others who would distract from his vision. He and Michael stopped talking.

There were stories of Brian seeing one of his engineers in a conference room with a salesperson and barging in to break up the meeting. If the business side wanted to talk to engineering, it would go through him.

A possibly apocryphal story goes that an important client came into the Right office and had probing questions about how the algorithms worked exactly. Brian was summoned to the meeting and was a bit piqued to have his technology put under the microscope, especially by non-technologists. He plopped his bare feet on the table, pulled out his laptop, and with a few keystrokes disabled the algorithm on that clients' campaigns—causing them to immediately start spending budget wildly and without any controls. He suggested they could tell the algorithm worked by seeing what happened when it was turned off.

The last straw may have been when Brian burst into a board meeting to which he was not invited. There was discussion of selling the company, with a price of $250 million targeted. Brian was furious. He thought they were on the road to building the next great multibillion-dollar technology company. For Michael and the board to consider exiting was like selling his child. Brian would ultimately be correct about the price being too low, but maybe not in the way he was hoping.

CHAPTER 3

SUPPLY AND DEMAND

None of us knew what we were buying.[1]

—Gokul Rajaram

Gokul was getting frustrated. He was a director of product management at Google, arguably the most dynamic and innovative company in Silicon Valley. He had teams of the most talented product and engineering minds in the world. He had access to more advertisers than had ever existed on any ad platform in history. Yet he could not get the really big advertisers to buy display ads from Google, and working with premium publishers was an operational nightmare. They had all the ingredients to bridge their success in search ads to win in the adjacent market of display advertising, but it was simply not working.

In 2005 Google's revenue exceeded $6 billion and the company was growing at an astronomical 92% annual rate. The search giant was poised to become an era-defining company with products in areas as disparate as mapping, health, and search. Expanding from search ads—a virtual license to print money—to the seemingly much less complex area of display advertising seemed easy.

Google AdWords* launched in 2001 and had grown to be the largest single source of unique advertising demand in the world. It became dominant simply by being the only way to buy ads on Google Search, the company's flagship product. There were literally *millions* of advertisers on AdWords. With its heritage in search ads, virtually all the demand it controlled at the time was in the form of text snippets, not images or videos, but that seemed like a solvable problem.

Google also already controlled a significant volume of publisher ad space through AdSense. Launched in 2003, AdSense was a hugely successful program that allowed publishers to make money off text ads from Google's search advertisers. The program was the brainchild of founder Sergey Brin and was first built by Susan Wojcicki. Susan was the longtime head of ad products for the company and the owner of the actual garage in which Google had been first built. The program was so impactful that Susan was given a "founder's award" of millions in stock bonuses.[2] As the first product manager for AdSense, Gokul had expanded the program to allow publishers of any size to sign up and immediately start making money, a huge innovation at a time when the typical ad network sales process involved phone calls, complex contracts, and faxes. His work earned him the honorific "the Godfather of AdSense."

The next step would be to bring display advertising into the mix, getting Google AdWords buyers to adopt imagery, and expanding AdSense to more premium sites. Gokul and team launched the Google Content Network in 2004. GCN, as it was known, essentially allowed image ads to run on AdSense publishers. This was a deeply unspectacular launch since, among other problems, the advertisers buying Google Search did not have any image ads to run. The first iteration of the product simply made images out of the search text ads—problem solved!

---

* AdWords is the product for buying ads. Later the name was changed to "Google Ads."

AdWords eventually supported letting advertisers upload image ads on their own, but this just raised other issues. The click-through rate on text-based search ads was extremely high since the ads were finely tuned to the search terms. A consumer searching for "ukulele" might respond really well to an ad selling that exact item. But image ads on websites—even if they were for ukulele lovers—were never going to perform at that level, causing buyers to get confused and frustrated at the relatively lower performance.

Larger advertisers, and the big agencies that represented them, understood this dynamic. After all, they were buying billions of dollars of display ads and rarely would evaluate their investment entirely by click-through rates. When Gokul spoke to these advertisers, though, they had a very different problem. While they understood the value of the giant AdSense footprint, they wanted to evaluate ad performance using cookies, and Google most definitely did not like cookies.

Cookies at the time were the lingua franca of display advertising. Small text files stored on the user's web browser, they do not in and of themselves mean anything. As a user takes actions and "surfs the web," however, the cookies can be associated with those activities. For example, if the user sees an ad and then five days later visits a website for that same advertiser, those two data points can be associated via the cookie, and assumptions can be made about the value of the ad in driving the site visit. This exact type of "attribution" is what advertisers were asking Gokul for. More specifically, advertisers were asking for a *policy change*; they wanted to run ads on the Google Content Network but only if they could track those ads using the ad serving technology from DoubleClick or its rival Atlas and get proper attribution. These companies would be *third parties* to the transaction, with Google and the advertiser as the first and second parties. Google cofounder Larry Page simply would not allow these to run through his platform, fearing that they might collect or exploit data about their users or do something else nefarious. "I lost count of the number of times I went to Larry asking for third-party pixels," Gokul would recall ruefully.[3]

On the publisher side, there were also problems. The text ads in AdSense were primarily being placed on webpages based on the context of what the pages were about, rather than any information about the user viewing the ads or other signals that might indicate their preferences. As a result, AdSense monetized best on niche sites, blogs, and long-tail content where large, mainstream advertisers might not be as well suited. This, as well as the fact those publishers had fewer monetization options, meant AdSense catered primarily to very small publishers. The big publishers might use AdSense as a last resort if there were no other options for monetizing an ad slot, but their primary ad network partners were those focused on display ads and premium brands.

As Gokul talked to more premium publishers, it became obvious that the AdSense tags would always be placed somewhere deep in the bowels of DoubleClick's ad server and Google's access to the inventory would be intermediated by opaque and unpredictable processes. If there are two things Google product managers hate, it is being disintermediated and being subject to inefficient processes.

One option for Gokul to solve his problems was to acquire a company in the advertising space. Google had taken a look at DoubleClick during the Hellman & Friedman sales process but likely concluded the company was too much of a mess to bother. DoubleClick's main rival, aQuantive, owned the Atlas ad server for buyers but did not have a publisher product. This meant an acquisition might solve the cookie dilemma but not the inventory access problem. "We didn't know what we were buying," Gokul said about these early investigations.[4]

Gokul and team decided to build instead of buy. They embarked on a major investment program to close the gaps in its display strategy by building ad servers to compete with DoubleClick. On the buy side was GFA, or Google for Advertisers, which was intended to be a free tool for larger advertisers to manage all their display spend across Google and other supply sources. This would compete head-to-head with Double-Click's industry-leading DFA, or DART for Advertisers, product but would likely undercut it on fees and offer other advantages, such as integration with the popular Google Analytics tool. Even though this new tool would use cookies for tracking, these would be *first party* and owned by Google so would pass muster with Larry and other executives.

On the sell side, Google was building GFP, a free alternative to Double-Click's DFP publisher ad server. The strategy was to give away the ad server and in exchange get more inventory to feed into AdSense and monetize.

In typical Google form, there were a bunch of other products under development to disrupt other aspects of what was perceived to be the inefficient and fragmented display advertising world. Google Ad Planner was a media research and planning tool that would compete with ComScore and Nielsen by including data on a long tail of millions of websites, instead of just the top 500.[5] Survey tools were being developed to better understand the impact of ads on brand awareness and affinity. Design tools of various kinds were intended to make the process of creating ads easier.

The investment level in all these initiatives was very high, and nothing was yet showing real, concrete results. Compared to the launch of AdSense—an instant blockbuster—these display products were harder to build and required an uphill climb to get adoption from customers, even when subsidized or free. For the advertiser product, in particular, the large agency customers were hugely demanding and would not entertain switching systems without considerable effort. On the publisher side, there was a clear opportunity to service smaller website owners who might not need a complex ad server, but disrupting DoubleClick's position with premium publishers seemed nearly impossible.

Despite this struggle, there were two things Google had in abundance: ambition and cash. Maybe Gokul could solve his problems at the right price.

CHAPTER 4

PROJECT WOLF

DoubleClick to Set Up Exchange
for Buying and Selling Digital Ads
—New York Times

In an episode that sounds like it was cribbed from a spy novel, a former Clicker* who worked in the ads group at Google made a surreptitious phone call to their former colleagues at DoubleClick. The message: "They're coming after you."[1] This news was then confirmed by employees at YouTube. The video sharing site had just been acquired by Google, but the ads on the site were still run by DoubleClick's ad server. The YouTube team was being pressured to move over to a new system being developed internally to replace DoubleClick.[2] It was clear that Google was building an ad server.

Google already had AdSense, an ad network that monetized unsold publisher inventory. It was quite an easy supposition that they might give away an ad server for free and in exchange ask publishers for their ad inventory to sell. DoubleClick had sold its ad network business years

---

* Clicker = DoubleClick employee

earlier and did not have any comparable offer. It is hard to compete with a free product. They felt like sitting ducks.

DoubleClick's enterprise-level ad serving could probably withstand that competition for some time, given the complexity and high demands of major publishers. Smaller publishers, and those that had fewer direct ad sales, though, would likely find an offer for free ad serving attractive. It did not go unnoticed that the general theme of an established company getting cannibalized by "worse" competition from the bottom of the market was right out of popular business books like *The Innovator's Dilemma* by Clayton Christensen[3]—it usually ends poorly for the incumbents. David would later say that at this moment he felt like he was clinking champagne glasses on the bridge of the *Titanic*.[4] Everything seemed great for the company—it had never felt better—but the most powerful and innovative company in the world was pointing a well-funded iceberg directly in its path.

Realizing the company needed to focus on the threat of Google, newly minted head of product management Neal Mohan assembled a team of the top product and engineering brains in the company to form a new task force, called Project Centillion. A centillion is a very large number—a one followed by three hundred zeros. The name was chosen because a "googol" is also a very large number, but not quite as large—a one followed by a mere hundred zeros. Centillion was essentially a brainstorming environment where every product, technology, business, or regulatory idea to stop Google was considered.

The PowerPoint deck that summarized the Centillion recommendations was subtitled "Strategically Neutralizing the Google Threat" and identified five strategies. Four of these were new product offerings, along with one "nonmarket" strategy that recommended lobbying, press outreach, and various other hardball tactics.[5] The basic conclusion was that while Google had a big advantage in monetization based on its millions of search advertisers, it was going to take years for them to break through to large publishers and agencies. DoubleClick, on the other hand, had deep relationships with traditional publishers, and to survive it needed to help bring these companies actual revenue, not just software. How this would be accomplished, exactly, was still being debated. The other insight was more cultural. "Google was easily distractable and fickle," a former employee would recall. "If DoubleClick puffed out its chest and looked hard to beat it, they would eventually give in."[6]

Economically, transacting media was going to be much more attractive than selling software. While DoubleClick was the dominant ad server, it was not immune to competitive pressure. Falk, a German start-up with a youthful CEO of the same name and an aggressive expansion strategy, would continually undercut publisher ad server pricing until DoubleClick just gave up and bought the company.[7] Other competitors like 24/7 Real Media and AdTech would offer one-cent-per-thousand rates for ad serving because unlike DoubleClick, they still operated media ad networks and could cross-subsidize their technology fees. With all this competition, average ad serving rates had plummeted to as low as one to three cents per thousand ads. It was certainly possible that ad serving might become free, even without Google's new entry. If a new product from DoubleClick could reasonably charge 15% to 20% of the media it transacted, that represented an order of magnitude more revenue per impression and a huge opportunity.

Many on the DoubleClick management team knew Michael Walrath from his days at Sonar and had been tracking Right Media, despite the fact that it had been working mostly under the radar and avoiding press mentions. There was clearly something going on there, as word spread of a new product they had created called an "ad exchange" and a large investment they had subsequently received from industry juggernaut Yahoo. Joe Zawadski had left Poindexter and was doing consulting on the changing currents in digital advertising. He got the assignment from Neal to help figure out some of this stuff for DoubleClick and would help educate the product team on what was going on and where it was likely to head.*[8]

While Right Media's customers were unglamorous middlemen scraping for spare pennies, DoubleClick's included all the largest and most attractive digital media companies: Hearst, Meredith, Condé Nast, the *Washington Post*, the *Wall Street Journal*—the list goes on. While these publishers all deployed large and professional sales teams to sell their ads, a sizable portion of their revenue was generated indirectly by ad networks. Customers spent huge amounts of time and effort in deeply inefficient processes to optimize this indirect revenue through the ad server. By building an ad exchange on top of the ad server, DoubleClick could optimize all those indirect impressions for the publishers and take a nice fee on every transaction. Inside the company this was sometimes called the "100% publisher strategy," meaning it was aimed at all the publisher's monetization needs, not just the ads they sold directly.

On the advertiser side, there was something in the air as well. Start-ups like Tacoda and Poindexter were using data to get better results for advertiser customers. DoubleClick had a huge presence on the buy side but was not innovating and was more focused on workflow. It was not yet clear how any of this would shake out, but Neal and the product team had the general realization that DoubleClick was in a prime position to innovate in matching ad buyers, sellers, and data. To be successful, this effort could not be run by an ad hoc committee like Centillion. Neal and David needed to build a team.

Michael Rubenstein had come a long way from a small Canadian email marketing start-up to become the leader of the biggest and most

---

* Joe used the money from consulting with DoubleClick to start his new company, MediaMath.

important deals at DoubleClick.[9] Imagine the stereotype of an aggressive salesperson—loud, extroverted, and stopping at nothing to close the deal; Michael was the polar opposite. He is polite, with youthful good looks and a distinctively Canadian friendliness, and you might wonder how he amassed his track record of closing huge deals and partnerships. Later in his career, he modestly noted that one of his real talents is "dealing with difficult people."[10]

While DoubleClick had most major independent publishers using its ad server, historically the very largest technology companies, like Yahoo, chose to build their own. Rubenstein had just cracked that nut and convinced AOL—at the time perhaps the second-largest digital publisher—to switch to the DoubleClick technology. In addition to the sheer size of the deal, the reputational win for the company was huge and clearly showed the rest of the market that DoubleClick was the gold standard for large publishers.

The team that implemented AOL had spent untold days and weeks on the project, building custom software, flying back and forth to the company's Dulles, Virginia, headquarters, and basically killing themselves to make it all work. After the dust had settled, many on the team started to look for new challenges.

Rubenstein was at a turning point in his career. Having just completed an MBA at Columbia over nights and weekends, and with DoubleClick going private, he thought maybe it was time for something new. He spoke to David Rosenblatt about his career prospects as he explored what might be next. Rubenstein would start informally working on some of this Centillion stuff, trying to figure out the business side of what the heck this was all about. Rubenstein, for all his talents, was a businessperson, not a product guy. He needed product and engineering talent to help flesh out what the offering would be, along with what might be possible to build on the complex and old DoubleClick infrastructure. As far as he was concerned, there was one man for the job, the same product manager who had helped implement AOL and had worked side by side with

Michael for the previous two years: Scott Spencer. There were only two problems. First, Scott had already quit. Second, many in the company told Michael it was a terrible idea.

———

Scott Spencer was one of the longest tenured product leaders at DoubleClick. An MIT graduate with a deeply technical mind, he took on new product problems like a Greek philosopher looking to probe the depth of the universe. Unfortunately, this approach did not always make a lot of friends. "A bit abrasive" was a description. Or as one person put it in a backhanded compliment, "I actually like Scott."[11]

In his long tenure at the company, Scott had learned how every aspect of DoubleClick's complex "stack" worked and at a level of detail that could not possibly be matched. Scott had served as the product manager for pretty much all the major ad serving products and knew how they fit together. Any type of ad exchange would have to tie deeply into the ad serving technology since it would have to know when certain ad impressions were eligible to be sold to other parties. With a still vague conception of what the product would be, there was no one better suited to build this product.

Nevertheless, some members of the senior team tried to dissuade Rubenstein from bringing Scott on board, arguing that he was too technical and not commercially oriented enough to work with customers and understand their needs. The trust between Scott and Michael from their work on the AOL project was too important to let rough edges get in the way. Scott would stay at the company and join the new team.

In true nerd fashion, Scott came up with the name Project Wolf, not to capture the animal spirit but because "wolf" was "flow" backward. The product would "flow" ads between buyers and sellers. They still were not sure what the product would do exactly. The concept of an "exchange" was nascent, and it was not entirely clear who would be buying and selling ads within the product and how it would work.

With Scott on board, the team needed some engineering firepower as well. Like Rubenstein and Scott, there were a bunch of longtime employees who found themselves underutilized post-AOL and were deeply bored with the ordinary work of running the company. Dritan (Drit) Suljoti, a hacker of a sort, had joined the company in a technical support role when only nineteen years old (a fact that surprised coworkers when they realized they had been serving alcohol to an underaged person at the ubiquitous company happy hours). Even though he had a business degree, Drit liked to play around with web development and JavaScript, skills that allowed him to excel at helping DoubleClick customers with tricky problems like incorporating video and special effects into their ads. Drit rose through the ranks and joined the engineering team, eventually serving as one of the founding members of the R & D function within the company. This small team served a little bit like new product hackers, taking weird ideas and seeing if they were possible with the technology of the time.

The R & D team had just completed a strange technical project for a customer that for some reason had to implement two different ad servers at once. The problem with having two ad servers is that you must choose which one might be the right one to serve an ad on a given webpage and at a given time. The solution the R & D team came up with was for one of the ad servers to "bid" into the other one with the price of the best ad it could find, then the decision could be made based on price.[12] This strange solution (which they later patented) turned out to be an almost direct analog of what would be needed to make an exchange work within the ad server.

Scott and Rubenstein realized that to build a differentiated product, they would need to tie deeply into the publisher ad server. A publisher ad server evaluated every ad available to fill a given slot on a webpage, along with their respective prices and priorities. An exchange offered by a competitor, like Right Media, would have no way of knowing what other ads it was competing with, and the publisher would have to essentially guess the right price and priority to call the exchange and ask for a bid. It would be like selling stocks without a ticker to tell you the market price.

Knowing the pricing of the other ads in the ad server was an enormous advantage. Wolf would be engineered so that it would only flow a new ad from the exchange when the price beat all other eligible ads in the ad server by one cent or more. This feature was sometimes given the misnomer First Look since from the outside world it looked like Double-Click was giving itself priority over other exchanges and ad networks, but that was a misunderstanding. DoubleClick was not bidding first; it was waiting to see what other bids were eligible and at what prices and then bidding last, once it knew the price to win.

The pitch to publishers was they would be taking zero risk by letting Wolf bid since they were never giving up more revenue elsewhere. This was not entirely true. The other ad networks or exchanges were booked in the ad server at their estimated historical value and on a given impression *could* have paid much more than Wolf. The ad server just did not know what the other exchanges were willing to pay in real time the way it did with Wolf. DoubleClick was setting up a two-tier system for demand to compete: one that ran a smart auction against direct demand and one that was stuck guessing the right price and priority.

Scott explained this feature as a way publishers could dynamically allocate their inventory to the exchange, and from that the feature Dynamic Allocation was born. Dynamic Allocation would become the biggest factor in the success of DoubleClick's exchange and its future dominance. It would help make publishers a great deal more money from their unsold inventory, all the while driving competitors mad.

It only took a month to build Ad Square, a prototype of what would become the ad exchange. Publisher reactions were frosty. The feedback showed there was a whole lot more to do. The idea that advertisers would be able to buy ads using technology, instead of the traditional channels, was deeply unsettling to the folks whose job it was to sell those very ads. Every publisher the team spoke to demanded that direct sales channels be protected from this technological menace.

Some of the best engineers at the company were brought on to help turn the prototype closer to reality. The publisher feedback meant that all sorts of controls needed to be built to restrict which kinds of ads the exchange could sell. Dynamic Allocation was great on a whiteboard, but in reality it had to be carefully implemented into the complex and aging ad serving stack to meet publisher business models.

Like the nine circles of hell in Dante's *Inferno*, the publisher ad server had developed with distinct strata, defined in sixteen levels of *priorities*. The priorities may have started as simply higher or lower than one another, but over time they had accumulated distinct meanings and behaviors that publishers understood and depended upon. Level 4 was not just slightly higher than level 5; it also meant the ad was a "sponsorship," which had distinct rules for how fast it would deliver and pace against goals.[13] The solution to the publisher challenge of assuring the exchange would not interrupt direct sales was to restrict Dynamic Allocation to only compete with certain low priorities in the ad server, those 12 and lower, which were designated as Bulk. Bulk priorities were generally only used for ad networks and other indirect sources of ads, and certainly these could be preempted by the exchange if it could beat their prices. No one imagined at the time that the ad exchange might have premium ads to compete with the direct sales in priorities 1 through 11 or generate prices high enough to be worth overriding those direct orders. This assumption would change quite a bit over time.

With the prototyping and feedback in hand, the project was taking shape. It was a big project and was going to require focus and significant funding. Neal and David, along with the Wolf team, took the proposal to the new owners at Hellman & Friedman, asking for additional funding beyond what was in the standard operating plan. Under the heading "What Is Project Wolf?" a slide gave a coherent answer that would largely still be accurate today: "Wolf is an automated way for Buyers of inventory to access publisher inventory, and for Sellers to streamline the sales process and improve overall yield."[14]

In a distinct break from the way DoubleClick had previously been positioned, the board deck put the company side by side with the offerings from media giants Yahoo, AOL, Microsoft, and Google. The proposal would dip DoubleClick's toe back into the media business, and that business was a dance of giants. The proposal was for an incremental 100 employees, or roughly 10% of the company's total headcount, to support this new product.[15] Wolf would move forward, and in the process, DoubleClick would regain some of its swagger.

The product was renamed AdX—the normally stolid Rubenstein uncharacteristically claims this shortened name, in this exact capitalization form, came to him in a dream.[*]

While Scott, Drit, and some of the best engineers at the company built the product, Rubenstein went on a road show to talk to buyers and sellers about AdX. It was not particularly hard to get meetings given DoubleClick's central place in the media ecosystem. Once the ad prioritization problem had been sorted, publishers were excited and got on board with the exchange. After all, they were being offered extra revenue with no risk. In an environment where print, subscriptions, and traditional revenue were all under threat, anything that

---

[*] A decade later, despite many renaming efforts by Google's marketing team, that three-letter name would remain ubiquitous.

might bolster digital revenue was worth trying. Buyers, on the other hand, were a little more complicated. Who exactly would want to buy ads in this exotic new way that had no relation to the current ways of doing business?

The first group of buyers were ad networks. Ad networks were effectively resellers of publisher inventory, like the original media business of DoubleClick from the 1990s. Publishers had lots of choices for ad networks and might dole out inventory in all kinds of inefficient or imprecise ways. Networks had to beg, borrow, and steal to get access to publisher inventory—or more realistically they just had to guarantee higher payments. The exchange offered a way for the ad networks to bid on inventory they wanted instead of getting whatever a publisher might have doled out for them. This could be a boon to their businesses.

The second group was made up of the folks who had been jealously watching the ad networks operate for a decade—the big advertising agencies. It was no secret that ad networks were taking in big margins by connecting buyers and sellers without any pricing transparency. If the buyers got the performance they demanded and the sellers got a good price for their inventory, everyone was happy. It seemed like the agency's job of buying media for their customers and driving performance was quite like what the ad networks were doing, for much less margin. Why should agencies get billed on a "time and materials" basis when ad networks could take a flexible spread?

The Wolf deck presented to the board suggested a 5% fee for transactions through AdX. At some point this would change to a much steeper 20%, which is what it remains today. From Rubenstein's customer meetings, it seemed like no one cared too much about the fee since the way it was billed was essentially baked into the transactions. For publishers, the fee was invisible. The fee calculation was performed by the exchange before the bid was made, so the publishers only saw the bid *net* of any fees. If a buyer bid $1.00, the publisher would see a bid of $0.80 ($1 minus 20%). As long as this net fee still beat the other ads in the ad server, it was worth it. Buyers also did not much care about the fee, as long as they got the performance they wanted.

Acting as a middleman to price-insensitive customers on both sides of the transaction would open many opportunities for profit but also for nontransparent fee structures and shady business practices that would prove difficult to stamp out.

––––––––––

There was a sense in the media world that things were heating up. The digital ad market was back to rapid growth, up 35% in 2006 to almost $17 billion, led by Google's unstoppable search business.[16] The innovation at Right Media and Yahoo's subsequent investment had people talking. While ad networks were still major players, start-ups looking to use data to automate and disrupt the market in smarter, more transparent ways were proliferating.

The smoldering was set ablaze by the April 4, 2007, *New York Times* headline "DoubleClick to Set Up an Exchange for Buying and Selling Digital Ads."[17] The "Business" section feature included a half-page photograph of Rubenstein, Spencer, and Rosenblatt and described AdX as a "Nasdaq-like exchange for the buying and selling of digital advertisements." Rosenblatt's quotes in the piece show the sea change at the company, predicting Double-Click would derive the majority of its revenue from AdX within five years and that the whole value of the company depended on the ability to maximize customer revenue. That was a big break in approach from providing a boring software product with multiyear enterprise contracts.

The article clearly highlighted the innovation coming out of the some-what forgotten stalwart of the New York technology scene. The reporter hinted, likely with some off-the-record input from Rosenblatt and Ruben-stein, "The service may make DoubleClick a more attractive acquisition target." Indeed, it did.

CHAPTER 5

YMAG

We'll do to display what Google did to search.[1]
—David Rosenblatt

It had only been eighteen months since DoubleClick had been taken private, and the company was firing on all cylinders. Rosenblatt had seen this movie before, when the old DoubleClick was worth over $10 billion. He remembered how he and many other employees exercised their stock options to lock in capital gains, only to end up with shares worth less than they owed in taxes. He was still relatively young, with two children at home and a healthy amount of untradeable stock in this rocket ship of a revived company. Perhaps, he thought, it was time to see if there was interest in selling out before the Google iceberg hit.[2]

David approached his board with the idea. They were skeptical and thought the company was primed for an IPO or another good outcome with a little more time. They made him a proposal—go out and talk to one single potential strategic acquirer and gauge market demand, then we can decide if we want to run a real process.

Neal and David traveled to Sunnyvale, California, to meet some friendly faces at Yahoo. Yahoo owned 20% of Right Media, but they were still thinking opportunistically about how to grow their business. The company's premium inventory, like the homepage, Finance, and Sports, were considered "Tier 1" and sold out at premium rates through direct sales deals. There was a huge underbelly of traffic on "Tier 2" areas of the portal, primarily Yahoo Mail, on which the sales force did not focus and where ad slots would often be left unsold. When a consumer is quickly paging through their email, it is generally not a great time to show a premium branded ad for a new car or deodorant. The solution for Tier 2 was likely to be an ad network or exchange that could fill the inventory from indirect sources in an auction, like the one provided by Right Media or maybe the soon-to-launch AdX. Just on that basis, an ad exchange acquisition would be worth a lot to Yahoo.

The corporate development team did a cursory review of the opportunity and quickly came back with an offer of up to $1.5 billion for the company, less than a year after it had been taken private for just $342 million.

David and Neal knew that even though the software businesses of DoubleClick were valuable and generated hundreds of millions in annual revenue, the price for the company was going to be driven by the exchange. Because ad exchanges enabled the separation of buyers and sellers of ads, access to the huge publisher footprint of the DoubleClick ad server could be enormously valuable to companies that had a lot of pent-up ad demand (i.e., lots of advertisers).

There was also the desire to break free of the constraint of only monetizing owned and operated properties (known as O & O) through direct sales. The web was a big place, and new sites were attracting consumer attention every day. Unless you had some way to capture the value of the expanding web, you would inevitably lose market share over time.

In a talk at Google several years later, David laid out clearly the dynamics that drove companies to adopt a network model:

Yahoo towards the end of 2006 reached a basic conclusion that applies to all internet publications, which is . . . your share of the market translates into your share of ad revenues. If you grow share, you get promoted; if you lose, you get fired. And it works like this for TV and print.

Yahoo had applied this model to their own business for years. But the conclusion they reached, which I think is right, is that it is flawed for the internet, because the cost to entry for a new publisher is so low; they'll never be able to grow their audience at the same rate as the internet. You can have some 21-year-old kid come and make a website and get huge share. Look at Facebook. Yahoo's share of audience is significantly diluted. The audience gets diluted. So how do you fix this problem and grow your revenues at the same rate as the internet? It's simple: by selling other peoples' inventory.[3]

Later in the same talk, Rosenblatt laid out the value of owning DoubleClick clearly, saying, "If you don't have access to that inventory, nothing else matters. It turns out that the most efficient way to access that inventory is by owning the primary ad server . . . It allows you as a network the so-called 'first look' at each impression."[4]

Of course, the Yahoo term sheet asked for the deal to not be shopped to others, and, of course, that's exactly what Neal and David proceeded to do. The investors at Hellman & Friedman were excited to potentially exit their investment for a five-times return within less than two years. A process was kicked off, and bankers were interviewed. As part of the bake-off, the investment banks asked them each to value the company. Results all came in within roughly the same range as the Yahoo bid; they all saw the company as essentially comparable to other software companies and valued based on profit multiples, growth assumptions, and the like.

It may be a little hard to imagine today, but in the late 2000s, the advertising business was dominated by what were colloquially known as the "Big Three": Yahoo, AOL, and Microsoft (MSN). These companies captured the lion's share of ad dollars and were considered must-buys by most brands on digital media plans. They had huge sales forces and thousands of advertisers buying banner ads on the sites and on the ad networks they operated. Their fortunes had been on a steady decline, though, since the beginning of the decade. Yahoo's portal was built around utilities like email and news, both of which had been bleeding traffic to more modern and innovative solutions like Gmail and Google News. Microsoft's traffic came overwhelmingly from the Internet Explorer default homepage, and other browsers were steadily eating away at that advantage. AOL, meanwhile, had been disrupted by the move from dial-up to broadband, a consumer change that left them on the wrong side of the unstoppable growth of the internet.

The Big Three were being challenged on all fronts by a technically sophisticated but decidedly awkward newcomer to the display business: Google. Google was dominant in search advertising and was flush with cash from its blockbuster IPO yet was struggling to break into display and video advertising. (The company bought YouTube in 2006 but did not start monetizing it until a couple of years later.)

Tim Armstrong was Google's first employee based in New York City, the capital of the media and advertising businesses. The square-jawed, good-looking head of revenue for the US, he had been working hard to establish Google's bona fides in the media world. Tim had built a relationship with Rosenblatt over the years, so he was the person at Google that David called. DoubleClick was in play.

Tim set up a video conference call with Gokul, Susan, and others who had been leading the display effort at Google. It was easy to justify bidding for the company. An acquisition would solve all of Google's display problems in one go. On the publisher side, it would give privileged access to the largest and most premium pool of ad supply in the world. On the advertiser side, it would transform the cookies in the ad server from the dreaded *third party* to *first party*, thus unlocking advertising display budgets. Finally, it would bring in the expertise of the teams that lived in the display market day in and day out.

Internally, it was called Project Liberty, likely because of the New York location of the target. The rationale for buying DoubleClick was clearly laid out in bulleted form by David Drummond, the company's general counsel: acquire the customers, prevent Microsoft from buying it, and unblock Google's progress on building its own ad server and display ad network.[5] The plan was to buy the company, reduce the head count, make ad serving free, and migrate the customers to Google products in about two years. This was not exactly how it played out.

If they could match the world's largest source of ad demand with the world's largest source of ad supply, they should be able to create an enormous new business. Tim Armstrong imagined the acquisition could improve measurement and targeting of ads across the web, search, and YouTube.[6] In short, it would herald a new era for digital advertisers and publishers.

When Neal put together a model showing how much money an acquirer could hope to capture by buying DoubleClick and its nascent exchange, he called the model YMAG.xls, after the only four companies who could really take advantage of the access to DoubleClick supply: Yahoo, Microsoft, AOL, and Google. The model was tweaked slightly before each presentation to better match the inventory and monetization assets of the target company. In one unfortunate incident, Susan Wojcicki interrupted Neal's presentation to ask why the spreadsheet she was looking at said "Microsoft," to which he coolly but improbably answered, "Typo" and moved on.[7]

Neal's YMAG presentation pitched the buyers that "the winner will be the company with the largest pool of liquidity." In this context liquidity meant the amount of demand and supply matching on the platform. The way to get the most liquidity was to "become the primary ad server to get a 'first look.'" There was also a sense of urgency to act; he asserted, "The race to the finish line is already well underway."[8]

With the insight that the acquisition would unlock huge liquidity for the buyer's existing demand, the model estimated that by buying Double-Click, any of the YMAG companies could generate an additional $2.6 billion in new ad revenue—per year.[9] The bankers thought the whole company was worth $1.5 billion, but Neal was pitching almost double that amount in synergies annually.

The news of DoubleClick's sale process had leaked in the *Wall Street Journal*, with Microsoft identified as the probable buyer.[10] This only served to accelerate the auction, with multiple escalating bids from all four of the YMAG companies.

AOL dropped out, but Google and Microsoft seemed to be bidding without a clear ceiling. "The motivating factor for Microsoft was that Google was interested. They thought, Let's just do it and figure it out later. They didn't really have a strategy," recalled Rosenblatt.[11]

Amusingly, the same rationale was driving the bidding at Google's Mountain View headquarters. Google's David Drummond wrote, "Our interest became more acute after learning that Microsoft had already made a serious offer" and speculated the deal would go for over $2 billion in cash.[12] The internal Liberty deck asked, "How high are we willing to go?"[13]

Google moved fast and acted decisively. They were able to get a signed letter of intent, or LOI, to buy DoubleClick for $3.1 billion. The LOI gave Google exclusivity to negotiate and sign a definitive agreement within about two weeks. The executive team at DoubleClick felt Google was the better home for the company, and at the time there was no company with a more exciting brand.

The Google IPO and their seemingly unstoppable growth had clearly rattled Microsoft. A decade later, the CEO of Microsoft would insightfully testify that "search was the largest software market by far."[14] This sentiment that something profoundly disruptive was happening was undoubtedly a threat to the core of Microsoft's reason for existing as the world's leading software business. Losing the DoubleClick deal to Google would undermine Microsoft's ambition in the media world, which at the time included not only MSN but also Xbox, MSNBC, and—a couple of years later—Bing. It would further cement Google as the dominant provider of advertising software, which was something Microsoft wanted to avoid at all costs.

AOL Time Warner had dropped out of the bidding, but the Mandarin Oriental Hotel in their namesake Time Warner Center on Manhattan's Upper West Side was a convenient, if a bit ritzy, spot for Google and DoubleClick executives to meet for the first time. The agenda was to start the diligence conversations that would get both parties comfortable with a final deal. Google had rented out a whole floor and flown in many top executives to meet the target company for the first time.

The DoubleClick executive team was having a premeeting in the Starbucks on Broadway just opposite the hotel. The company's counsel checked her Blackberry and held it up for David to see. There was an incoming message from Microsoft's corporate development team. They were willing to match the offer for DoubleClick, and the message included an email from

CEO Steve Ballmer in which he opened the door for a much higher offer. Ballmer wrote that if the offer match was not acceptable, DoubleClick should simply mark the paper up to meet its needs and sign it, then Microsoft would review and rapidly countersign to close the deal with minimal negotiation required. Without saying so, Ballmer was communicating "Here's a blank check—tell me what closes the deal." It was like getting a direct message from your exes while on the way to your wedding.

The LOI was signed, though, and was still exclusive, so David and the team went up to the thirty-fifth-floor lobby of the hotel and started to engage in small talk and preparations for the meeting. Something got the better of Rosenblatt, and he sidebarred with Drummond, a key champion of completing the transaction and the ringmaster for diligence. Drummond must have been profoundly shaken by the revelation of the competitive offers—despite the contractual prohibition keeping Double-Click from shopping the company further. While some of the sessions had already completed, he decided on a change in plans. Drummond let the gathered executives know that the remaining meetings were canceled and everyone could head home. It is unclear exactly what his intentions were moving forward, but the news that the bidding war was being restarted had thrown the whole deal for a loop.

A week (or more) went by. Under the LOI, DoubleClick could not engage with the other bidders, so the email from Ballmer went unreturned. Google, for reasons of its own, decided to not engage. There was radio silence and no communication about moving forward. A day before the LOI was set to expire, David and the team got an updated term sheet from Google. The financial terms had not changed, but now the deal included a "hell or high water" clause, meaning that Google was committed to closing the deal without any substantive diligence or other conditions. It was money in the bank. David and Hellman & Friedman took it and ran.

At a price of $3.1 billion, Hellman & Friedman had gotten a return of eight or nine times their money in two years. Executives like David and

Neal got life-changing payouts on their equity. At the time, it was the biggest technology exit in New York history (Bloomberg was arguably more valuable, but it was a private company). The customers, who included almost every major traditional media company and broadcaster, now held the promise that the software they used to run their business would be shepherded by the most advanced and innovative technology company in the world. More than that, the deal would spark a wholesale reshuffling of the digital advertising world's relationships.

The DoubleClick acquisition was announced on April 14, 2007,[15] less than two weeks after the *Times* article touting the new ad exchange. The news would spark a land grab as companies realized they needed to own the technology that would enable them to become liquid ad exchanges and compete in a new transformative era of advertising.

It was 2:00 a.m., and Rob Norman was at a nightclub in Marbella, Spain. He was having a fun night with other executives from GroupM—the largest media buying firm in the world—where he was an executive. His phone rang. It was the boss, advertising legend Sir Martin Sorrell. Rob stepped out of the club to see what the call was about. Sorrell delivered the news that DoubleClick was going to be acquired by Google. What should they do? he asked.

It was not obvious to Rob that this was a major shift, and with a couple of cocktails behind him, perhaps he was not thinking as clearly as would be ideal. He and his team had been negotiating a global ad serving deal with DoubleClick at the time, so that's immediately where his mind went. He told Sorrell that he thought they should go ahead with the deal. Over the course of his multi-decade career, Sorrell had transformed an unknown British public company, Wire and Plastic Products plc, into WPP, the world's largest agency holding company.[16] He was a proven master of strategy and finance and was seeing a couple of steps ahead.

Saving a penny or two on ad serving was not what was concerning the boss. Sorrell was worried how Google's heft and data could tilt the balance of power between media sellers and buyers, potentially out of his favor. "We cannot afford to *not* be in that business," he said, meaning the liquid and data-driven advertising world that was quickly emerging.[17] WPP was going to dive in.

––––––––––

Michael Walrath was keenly aware that the DoubleClick announcement was going to change everything for Right Media and the whole market. He knew who likely bidders were for DoubleClick and wanted to get his company in the best position to sell to one of the losers of that auction. You might call it his personal second-price auction. The company had turned down an acquisition inquiry from Microsoft years earlier, leaving a bit of bad blood in the wake. If Google was buying DoubleClick, that left Yahoo as the most likely buyer for Right Media, especially given their existing stake.

As soon as rumors started circulating, he flew out to meet with the team at Yahoo. He had built a relationship with Yahoo founder Jerry Yang, as well as CEO Terry Semel. Yahoo was already feeling they were likely to be outbid by deeper pockets at Google and Microsoft, but they tried to puff out their chests with Michael to get better negotiating leverage. In a meeting with Jerry and the corporate development team, they made it appear they were considering buying both companies, with Right Media getting the smaller of the two checks. If they already owned DoubleClick, then certainly the value of the remaining 80% of Right would be much less. This strategy may have worked had Semel not dropped into the meeting midway through and frankly stated, "OK, we're not going to win DoubleClick," ruining the posturing and making it clear that Michael was in the driver's seat.[18]

The original investment contract with Yahoo included a clause that gave the portal a limited amount of time to put together a bid if Right ever wanted to put itself up for sale. It was not a right of first refusal but more of a waiting period so Yahoo could get a bite at the proverbial apple before a competitor. The provision was meant to protect Yahoo's investment, but it also had the inverse effect of letting Right force the issue. On the day the DoubleClick acquisition news hit, Walrath sent Yahoo the notice the company was for sale, starting the clock ticking. Michael was summoned back to California, where he had a tense meeting with Jerry and Terry. Jerry was waving around a golf club he liked to twiddle with, and Terry was holding a Louisville Slugger baseball bat. After a lot of back-and-forth, Terry made a show of handing Michael the bat and indicating it was time to make a deal. Thirty minutes later they had the outline of the acquisition—Yahoo would buy the rest of Right Media, the part it did not own, for $680 million.[19]

Brian O'Kelley would not come along for the ride. He was fired soon after the deal was announced. Michael Walrath would later say of Brian, "He was 95% genius and 5% disaster," adding, "He wouldn't have lasted five minutes at Yahoo."[20] Brian made a reported $25 million on his vested shares, but his firing left on the table tens of millions more and put a chip on his shoulder the size of Mount Everest. He got a very small measure of revenge by throwing water on the deal, telling the *New York Times*, "I have to say I giggled . . . there is no way we quadrupled the value of the company in six months."[21] This quote infuriated Jerry Yang and the Yahoo team in Sunnyvale.

Asked whether the firing was deserved, Brian would later admit, "I'm not saying that everyone didn't want to fire me."[22] This would not be the last the advertising world would hear from Brian O'Kelley.

Throughout the DoubleClick process, Microsoft had been giving clear signals that it was willing to pay to play in this market. While it was ultimately rebuffed, Ballmer and company were desperate to not be left behind. Seattle-based aQuantive was a key competitor of DoubleClick, but its ad server was almost entirely used for advertisers and agencies, not publishers. This made the strategic value for capturing publisher inventory much lessened as compared to DoubleClick. aQuantive did operate a performance ad network called DrivePM, so theoretically the ad server and ad network technology could be adapted for the exchange use case. Crucially, though, you would not have the advantage of immediate access to publisher inventory.

Despite these drawbacks, four weeks after the DoubleClick announcement, on May 18, Microsoft announced it would acquire the smaller aQuantive for $6.1 billion.[23] Internally, the Google team would joke that Microsoft got "half the company for twice the price." One Google executive even prank-called Brian McAndrews, aQuantive's CEO, to say, "You're welcome."[24]

While aQuantive had an ad network, it did not have an exchange. To solve that gap, Microsoft two months later bought a little-known thirty-employee company called AdECN for an estimated $50 million to $70 million.[25] AdECN's marketing claimed it was "the only real-time, auction-based, neutral exchange for buying and selling online display advertising,"[26] but despite this positioning, it was virtually unknown in the industry. Microsoft would try to cobble these assets together into a viable alternative to Google and DoubleClick but would struggle to execute.

———————

Two months after the DoubleClick announcement, on July 25, AOL would acquire innovative behavioral targeting company Tacoda for $275 million,[27] and a couple of weeks later, it would buy the second-largest publisher ad server, a Germany-based firm confusingly called AdTech, for an undisclosed price.[28] AOL would combine its ad network Advertising.com with AdTech to offer publishers a viable alternative.

Four months after the DoubleClick announcement, on August 9, Sir Martin and Rob Norman would get into the business they could not afford to not be in by acquiring the number-three publisher ad serving company, 24/7 Real Media, for $649 million.[29] The acquired company would give WPP an ad server and an ad network but most importantly would enable data-driven buying capabilities at the holding company, at just the time those would become vitally important.

In just four months, from April to August 2017, over $10 billion had been spent to acquire advertising technology companies. The common vision was to build liquid marketplaces for ads that would better bring together buyers and sellers—with the winner taking the spoils.

The race to the finish line was more like the race to the starting line.

PART II

"ALL OR NOTHING"

CHAPTER 6

BRING IN THE SNACKS

The markets within the online advertising space continue
to quickly evolve, and predicting their future course
is not a simple task.[1]

—Statement of the Federal Trade Commission concerning Google/DoubleClick

G oogle had been betting on the traditional media business prior to the DoubleClick deal. Lost to history are products like Google Print, Google Radio, and Google TV Ads, all efforts to bring the efficiency of the auction-based search business to unsold inventory in traditional analog media.

Tim Armstrong brought in former entrepreneur Tom Phillips to run the Google Print Ads business. Tom had a strange and interesting background, most notably as the founding publisher of the legendary *Spy* magazine, where, among other targets, the editors spent years mocking then-real estate mogul Donald Trump, coining the description of him as a "short-fingered vulgarian."[2] Tom had previously sold the assets of Deja, an early Usenet discussion board technology, to Google to form what would ultimately become Google News.[3]

Tom realized that the original business plan for Print, to sell remnant ad slots in magazines, did not make sense given the thirty-day lead times for printing glossy monthly content. He pivoted the business to daily newspapers and spent a year convincing 225 publishers like the *New York Times*, *Washington Post*, and *Boston Globe* to try getting some new revenue from this strange experiment.[4] Even with the brand-name publishers and some actual revenue from the program, it was clear to Tom that this was a sort of side project for Google and that the long-term decline of the newspaper business cast doubts about the prospects for Google Print.[5]

Google TV Ads, meanwhile, was an ambitious effort to bring technology into the living room, once again primarily by selling unsold remnant ad slots. Google had a toehold in the industry through a deal with EchoStar, a satellite provider with fourteen million US households under the DISH brand, as well as some other minor cable providers. In addition to its large base of advertisers, Google also brought to bear its technology know-how and promised advertisers more accurate forecasting and reporting through set-top box data, rather than the aging Nielsen ratings. Using this more granular data, Google emphasized that advertisers could reach the same audience as the major cable networks by aggregating smaller audiences from less popular networks into a single buy. This theme of using technology to better meet advertiser needs across a network, instead of direct buys with traditional publishers, would be a recurring one and would deeply impact the future of publishing and broadcasting.[6]

The commercial side for all these media products ran through Tim and was seen by some as a grand experiment. Tim had gained enormous trust and respect with Google's founders, Larry and Sergey, and was given a lot of latitude to pursue projects that were more experimental and commercially oriented. These efforts, in retrospect, were very un-Googley. They relied much more on sales and business development efforts than on technology, and they were operating in markets that many in the Mountain View headquarters viewed (accurately) as being in permanent decline.

With some success under his belt with Print, Tom was asked to expand his purview and manage the commercial side of Google TV Ads, as well as Radio. It was a big promotion, but he was skeptical that the company really had its heart in it.

Just a couple of weeks later, Tom was thrown a curveball. He had heard about the DoubleClick acquisition on the same day as everyone else. Tim grabbed his arm in the company cafeteria and told him, "Stop what you're doing and run this." With his skepticism toward Print and other Google media forays, and his entrepreneurial spirit, he was relieved and excited to take on the challenge. This skepticism proved prescient, as all of these traditional media businesses would end up being shuttered within a couple of years.

Tom wanted to jump right in and start integration work, but he would have to wait almost a year to do anything meaningful due to government review. "I was a camp counselor for a year," he would later recall.[7]

Microsoft was dead set against letting the deal close and executed what *Business Insider* called a "highly organized, highly aggressive lobbying campaign."[8] They hired advertising insider Michael Kassan to try to convince the industry the deal was going to ultimately be bad for them. On the legal front, he was joined by Jonathan Kanter, who many years later would bring the Department of Justice's case against the company. Steve Ballmer also used his influence, calling the CEO of News Corp, for one, to align him against the deal.

By the end of May, the Federal Trade Commission had been assigned to review the deal and had asked the companies a series of detailed questions, known as a "second request." The agency was being actively lobbied by both the competition and a cadre of advocacy groups concerned about the privacy implications of the deal. It would "give one company access to more information about the Internet activities of consumers than any other company in the world," said one complaint.[9] In what would prove an accurate counterpoint, Howard University law professor Andrew Gavil noted, "Strictly speaking, privacy is not an antitrust issue."[10]

―――――――

DoubleClick had an unfortunate history on the privacy front, with a troubled billion-dollar acquisition of catalog data company Abacus Direct during the height of the dot-com era.[11] DoubleClick's data about consumers was always anonymous and based on cookies. It did not own any data or claim any ability to match these anonymous cookies with real-world personal information, like names, email addresses, or phone numbers. Abacus Direct was a data cooperative for the print catalog business, meaning it let its members, who sent out shopping catalogs, mix and match their data with their competitors' data to find new customers. If you have ever gotten a new catalog in the mail that you did not sign up for but seems vaguely aligned with your shopping habits, that is likely thanks to Abacus Direct.

The Abacus acquisition was vehemently opposed by privacy groups. The deal would "fundamentally change the nature of the Web, from one where people's movements in cyberspace are generally anonymous to one where their identity and a large profile moves around with them," said Jason Catlett in a statement from the Electronic Privacy Information Center and Privacy International.[12] Despite lobbying of shareholders and government officials, the deal closed without much difficulty. But that was not the end of the matter.

Soon after the deal closed in 1999, DoubleClick began matching its anonymous cookies with the richer and more personal Abacus database. This would potentially unlock enormous value for advertisers, enabling them to target digital ads to consumers who recently made specific offline purchases or who had a general predisposition to buy certain kinds of products. Even though the privacy concerns had been raised during the acquisition review, it was only after the deal closed and *USA Today* ran a short and relatively innocuous article titled "Cookies: How Sites Know What They Know" that the real trouble started.[13] The article prompted an individual to file a complaint with the California courts, which got the privacy advocates back involved, which then steamrolled into multiple state and federal actions. The FTC and ten state attorneys general quickly opened investigations into the company, and the data matching process was put on hold.[14] "Forget Big Brother," said Michigan Attorney General Jennifer Granholm in a cringeworthy political quote, "truly 'Big Browser' appears to have arrived."[15]

The investigations were settled in 2002 with no admission of wrongdoing but with various controls being set on DoubleClick's privacy policies and use of data. The real impact was that it made the company's brand synonymous with the worst worries about online privacy in the minds of consumers and regulators and put it in the crosshairs moving forward. This episode was so traumatic for the company that it warranted its own Harvard Business School case study.[16]

———

A recurring argument against the DoubleClick-Google deal was around scale and power. Google was just getting too big for comfort, and that scale gave them a data advantage that would be hard to overcome. Sir Martin was outspoken in his concern over the deal and the use of data. "It raises some issues for us. It raises issues as to whether we are happy to let Google have our clients' data and our own data, which Google could use for its own purposes," he told the *New York Post*.[17] A senior executive at Time Warner prophetically offered, "I hope the government starts understanding this power sooner rather than later."[18]

Congress got involved as well. A day of Senate Judiciary Committee hearings brought David Drummond alongside Brad Smith, general counsel of Microsoft, and several privacy advocates to hash out the issues inherent in the proposed acquisition.[19] Senators Herb Kohl of Wisconsin and Orrin

Hatch of Utah opened the hearing with statements of concern about both the market power of the combined company and the privacy issues that could arise. Other witnesses grappled with explaining how it was that Google and DoubleClick were currently in vastly different markets (search and display) yet would become an unstoppable force once combined.

Scott Cleland, a longtime internet policy expert who had served at the Department of State, had the most powerful and easy-to-digest testimony. Speaking to the power of scale, he laid out the case:

> What do people want when they buy advertising? They want an audience, and they will pay for a larger amount if they have a larger audience. So, in this instance, Google's . . . 65 percent of Internet viewer share would be . . . up to about 90 percent, according to my estimates.
>
> Well, they have got 90-percent share of the advertisers, and this is going to give them hundreds of the ones they do not have. So once again, if you are a website, who are you going to turn to? You are going to turn to Google because they are the only game in town that can give you access to all the world's advertisers . . . And Microsoft, Yahoo, and the others? Baby stuff relative to those numbers.[20]

David Drummond responded with a just-the-facts explanation: "I guess I have to express a little bewilderment. I keep hearing that Double-Click is our single largest competitor over and over again . . . We are very different than DoubleClick. We have never sat around the boardroom and talked about our competition with DoubleClick. It is a very different business . . . We do not actually participate in this display ad segment very much. We very much would like to, and that is part of the reason we purchased DoubleClick, because of their tools."[21]

Cleland also raised the alarm bells about the control the combined company might wield on content and information: "What I ask you is:

What checks and balances would exist to Google-DoubleClick's web of market power over the world's information? The combined Google-DoubleClick merger would have little accountability to consumers, to competition, to regulators, or even third-party oversight."[22]

The concern over scale resonated with advertisers but also with advocacy groups. "Whoever dominates the online advertising market has the ability to control the future of diversity and availability of content online," said privacy advocate Jeffrey Chester.[23]

The almost immediate consolidation of the advertising technology market was working against the anti-Google crew. After all, Microsoft owned DoubleClick's chief rival, aQuantive, and through MSN and other properties operated a larger display advertising business than Google. Just a week before Microsoft announced its acquisition, aQuantive's CEO Brian McAndrews boasted in an earnings call that he would take market share as a result of the DoubleClick deal.[24] "Many [ad] agencies, as you know, have outright said Google is an enemy," he added, bolstering his case against DoubleClick.

———

In December 2007, about eight months after the deal was announced, the FTC voted 4 to 1 to close its investigation. In its findings, the agency optimistically stated, "Online advertising fuels the diversity and wealth of free information available on the Internet today."[25] The findings argued that search and display were different markets, that concerns over privacy were out of scope for antitrust and were not limited to this combination of companies, and that the wave of acquisitions had made the market even more competitive than before.

Reading this document in the modern context, one might rightly have sympathy for the commissioners, as they contemplated many of the areas that would later become problematic, even though it would have required great foresight to predict the course of events accurately. Regarding the ad exchange and synergies with Google, the report offers, "The ad inter-mediation market today is highly fragmented and correspondingly com-petitive, and there is no evidence suggesting that DoubleClick is uniquely positioned to significantly enhance* competition in this market."[26] It also discounted "the possibility that Google could leverage DoubleClick's leading position in third-party ad serving to its advantage in the ad inter-mediation market."[27] These statements proved extremely wrong. The combined company would both deeply integrate its ad exchange into the ad server with Dynamic Allocation in a way that would disadvantage rivals and use the demand from Google's search business to make the exchange dominant.

Regarding ad serving, the report discounts supposedly high switching costs for publishers. It then provides a counterfactual scenario that ignores the market power of the DoubleClick ad server and compares it to the nascent Google server: "If Google were to exclusively bundle AdWords with AdSense and DFP . . . they would have already . . . used such a bundle to force customers to adopt the beta version of Google's third-party ad server."[28] In fact, the bundle of AdWords and the publisher ad server would be the tie that multiple customers would later convincingly argue made it literally impossible to switch.

The final paragraph admits "the markets within the online advertis-ing space continue to quickly evolve, and predicting their future course is not a simple task," then closes with a warning: "We want to be clear, however, that we will closely watch these markets and, should Google engage in unlawful tying or other anticompetitive conduct, the Commis-sion intends to act quickly."[29] It did not end up acting quickly.

The only concession from Google was to voluntarily sell the Perfor-mics division of DoubleClick. It was a relatively small business that per-formed search marketing, so the conflict of interest with the search giant was fairly obvious.[30]

---

* The word "enhance" seems wrong here but is in the original FTC document.

Tom's work as "camp counselor" suited him well. He wanted the teams to get to know each other, even though during the governmental review they could not legally plan or coordinate much actual work. There was an off-site at Tom's Fire Island house and a bowling night in Mountain View where Gokul wowed everyone with his skills on the alleys. The teams got along pretty well, other than one Googler whom the Double-Click side termed "Febreze Boy" because of his endless boasting of working on the launch of that odor-reducing spray. Maybe it was a bit *too much* like summer camp.

In a strange coincidence, the two companies' New York headquarters were in the same building but on different floors. While legally employees were not allowed to communicate before the deal closed, they might have shared the elevators every morning. Google was known for giving its employees free food—a rare perk at the time—so Tom arranged a couple of lunches where the Googlers abandoned their cafeteria to avoid any contact and the whole New York DoubleClick office came down the stairs to enjoy the famous gourmet lunch.

There actually was some substantive planning going on, of the cost-cutting variety. DoubleClick had roughly thirteen hundred employees at the time the deal was announced. The Performics sell-off would bring that down to about one thousand, but there was a strong push to trim that down substantially. Tom was paired with the exceptionally poorly named Patricia Severynse (pronounced "severance") to model out where to make cuts and where to retain talent. Part of the rationale for the cuts was a widespread attitude among the Google staff that acquisitions were a "back door" for lower-quality employees to get into the company. At the time, the standard hiring process was heavily biased toward Ivy League pedigrees and 4.0 GPAs.[31] Making deep cuts, Tom would later explain, would give some level of comfort to the Googlers that the remaining talent was up to snuff.[32]

The proposal was that all DoubleClick employees would be interviewed for their jobs and only those meeting the Google quality bar would be retained. This struck Rosenblatt as totally insane. The DoubleClick business was an ongoing enterprise software concern, servicing hundreds, if not thousands, of customers. Between the institutional knowledge and the required operations of the company, cutting head count in this way would have been an abject disaster.[33] This whole experience shed light on how unprepared Google was to enter a customer-centric business like the one they were acquiring. The company's culture of engineering-led innovation, with limited input from the commercial side, was poison to the types of long-term relationships required to sell and maintain enterprise software. The deal had not even closed yet, and it was starting to become clear where the strains would show.

A more orderly process was agreed upon, where managers would be given target cuts, then collaborate with Google counterparts to identify specific people on the firing line. There were almost four hundred people supporting the customers at DoubleClick, and that number was just too high for the tech-obsessed company. The goal ultimately would be to automate and optimize to make the ad serving businesses as close to self-service as possible, despite the facts that customers paid millions of dollars a year for the software and the complexity of the offering really necessitated hands-on help.

Ultimately, only about four hundred Clickers joined Google as full-time employees, with four hundred cut and the remainder kept on short-term contracts.[34] In a foreshadowing of the attitude that eventually dominated Google's approach to customers, the layoffs were born from the belief that the ad serving business was a means to an end rather than a product customers paid for and expected to work reliably.

The cuts did not end with the first integration. There was constant pressure for DoubleClick to fit into the mold of the rest of Google—a company that ran a near monopoly search business with some of the highest margins in the history of business. In early 2009 Nikesh Arora, the chief business officer for the company, would push to cut almost half the support staff in Europe because of his perception they were not efficient.[35] This was a recurring theme in the year or two after the acquisition, long knives coming out for employees or products from those not deeply enamored of the business or strategy, especially after the eventual departure of key advocates like Armstrong and Rosenblatt.

Just a year later, *Business Insider* reported an anonymous client's complaint that "the atmosphere at DoubleClick in these functions is bleak and service to the clients is woeful."[36]

When the deal finally closed on March 11, 2008, the first things DoubleClick employees saw were arrays of snacks and free food being rolled into their offices from Google downstairs. Employees were given primary-colored beanies to mark their first day as Googlers.

Not surprisingly, there was a lot of jockeying for control among the merged management teams. During the federal review period, Gokul had left to start a new company with his brother. This gap made it relatively easy to choose Neal as the lead over all the display products, a role he kept for years before being tapped to lead products at YouTube. Rosenblatt was put in the sales org in a sort of do-nothing cheerleading role and departed less than a year later.

Gokul's multiyear work to build competitive products to DoubleClick's led to some awkwardness. The product that was furthest along and ready for production was the publisher ad server, known as Google Ad Manager (which pretty much everyone shortened to GAM). This product was a simple, free ad server meant for the smaller publishers that typically used AdSense and likely would not be able to afford or even take advantage of the DoubleClick product. GAM had been essentially ready for launch for almost a year, but a decision was made to hold off on releasing the product until the acquisition was completed to avoid muddying the perception of the deal or potentially raising regulator questions.[37] Delaying the release of a completed product caused friction with the product and engineering teams that built GAM, as they wanted to get it into the hands of users and put a notch on their proverbial belt of shipped code. When the DoubleClick deal closed, the GAM team sprang into action and readied a press release to go out literally the same week.

While still trying to locate the bathrooms and log in to corporate Gmail, Neal and the publisher team at DoubleClick were sent a draft press release that essentially said there was a new ad server on the block, it was the future, it was free, and the world was changing forever. This caught them totally by surprise as there had been no coordination during the nine-month deal review process.

The team was not pleased at all. Launching GAM like this, with an ambiguous message about the platform's future, was bound to cause massive confusion among DoubleClick customers who were already skittish. Publishers deeply relied on the ad server. The announcement would give customers the idea that there was a new, untested platform, built by Google without DoubleClick's input, and that they might be forced in short order to switch to it.[38]

From the Google perspective, they had worked their asses off on this new product and it was ready to launch—were a bunch of suits from New York going to stop engineering progress on their first week on the job? After some heated conversations, the language in the press release was softened and there was more of an emphasis on the use cases by smaller publishers. Just two days after the deal closed, GAM launched with new positioning as being focused on "smaller sites." It was an inauspicious start to the integration process and the cultural bonding.

The other products that had been in development under Gokul largely did not launch or were adapted as complements for Google Ads. The GFA buy-side ad server was abandoned, as the effort to sell into demanding agencies was considered just too much work. Instead, DoubleClick's buy-side ad server would be rebuilt on the Google stack. Google Ad

Planner, the Nielsen competitor, was launched to largely confused reactions, then later repurposed to be a tool within Google Ads, with much smaller ambitions.[39] Neal and team were going to have to find ways to navigate this confusing mess of products, personalities, and strategies.

———————

Neal clearly laid out the strategy for the display business at Google and actively communicated it to Susan and the other Google executives: he called it the Three Pillars. Pillar one was the Platform, which would give access to the premium inventory through control of the ad server. Pillar two was the Exchange, which would aggregate the inventory from the platform and make it available for sale. Pillar three was the Network, which would monetize the inventory.[40] This became Neal's mantra for years as he constantly pushed to align internal interests around the vision.

The opportunity seemed absolutely enormous. The business would bring together supply, demand, and data. DoubleClick and AdX were going to—if all plans worked—bring the largest source of quality supply in the world. Google Ads was the largest source of advertising demand (albeit mostly text). No other company in the world had as much useful data as Google, the operator of the largest search engine, the most popular email system, maps, news, and new breakthrough consumer products seemingly every year.

To make the vision into reality, Neal had to ensure he had competent leaders he trusted for each pillar. While there were lots of talented people at Google in the ads group, there was a clear cultural difference between the Clickers and the Mountain View crowd. Foremost, the DoubleClick people were much more commercially oriented—they were comfortable with customers and salespeople, more likely to schmooze at trade shows, and more focused on driving revenue. Google culture valued engineering first, so shipping features was paramount to getting ahead—sometimes without so much regard for customer impact or adoption.

There was also the issue of continuity. The team had managed some of these products for years; replacing them with new folks from Google would have been hugely disruptive to the roadmaps and customers.

The network business would be the biggest challenge, as it was the most underperforming at Google and DoubleClick did not have a corresponding offering to plug in. Since it had launched as the Google Content Network back in 2005, the program had grown to about $200 million in annual revenue, but this was paltry compared to the success of the text network on AdSense and certainly nowhere near the original goals of Gokul, Susan, and other Google executives.

Brad Bender had a long and winding career at DoubleClick, starting in the late nineties as an intern with a desk in the hallway to pay the bills while pursuing a career as an actor.[*] Within the entrepreneurial environment during the early days of the company, he was given opportunities and over time gained increasing product management responsibilities. After a stint running the Abacus business in Europe, he returned to the US to spend time researching and building business plans around data-centric projects and ideas that were floating around at the time. Years earlier Michael Walrath had exploited the ad server's weaknesses and hacked a way to drive performance for his customers. Brad's goal, in a sense, was to retrofit performance into a system that was built for a very different job, ad delivery.

Brad ended up spearheading a new product line called DART Adapt that promised to optimize campaigns in the ad server to performance. It was a tough slog since every change to the algorithms needed to get to the beating heart of the servers and required slow and intensive testing

---

[*] There's a sitcom pilot starring Brad, a bootleg copy of which sometimes gave his coworkers something to rib him about.

and processes. The work, though, gave Brad a level of insight into the worlds of optimization and data that the rest of the DoubleClick team was largely ignoring. During this era, before ad exchanges had become ubiquitous, the primary product focus was on workflow, reporting, and ad delivery. Brad was working on problems that none of the other Double-Click teams outside of Wolf cared about.

DART Adapt had some commercial successes, but ultimately the revenue from this product was inconsequential in the scheme of Google's ambition. Brad was being kept on the team by Google, but he needed a new job. He started working on some of the policy issues around cookies, which were fraught with many conflicting opinions and views. After one such review, Susan Wojcicki came up to Brad and asked, "We have a text network—would you mind taking a look at it?" It was only over the weekend that he realized he had a new job. One that was largely based in California (he lived in New York) and that touched some very sensitive issues within the company.[41]

The network business was struggling, and it was obvious why. The offering was missing key features that advertisers did not just demand but actually were shocked to find missing. Frequency capping, for example, is the ability to restrict the number of times a given consumer might be exposed to your ad within a day or a week. This is a *table stakes* feature in virtually every ad platform, but because the frequency is generally tracked using cookies, it was not allowed on the Google network. This product gap was simply astounding to customers.[42] It was not just frequency management, though. There was a long laundry list of must-have features that were missing or not suited for purpose. The cookie issue also still needed to be solved to get buyers to spend.

Making Brad's job harder, the ability to create and run display ads, and thus the core of the network product, was built directly into Google AdWords, a hugely complex software product that was run by the highly protective (and political) teams based in the Mountain View headquarters. Seemingly every decision about features to build into the network became controversial, as factions within the company would resist using consumer data, search data, or other sensitive assets to benefit this unproven business.

Fixing the network was the top priority for Neal and David[43] and represented the biggest growth opportunity. While AdX was expected to bring in substantial revenue as a marketplace, selling ads directly was always going to have faster growth and higher potential margins. In finance terms, this would be the difference between operating a stock market and running a hedge fund; the stock market gets a small piece of every transaction, while the fund can take outsized returns.[44] There was a risk, though. If AdX took off but the network lagged, the effect might be to hand all the quality publisher inventory to whoever was the best bidder, not Google. This could put into jeopardy a big part of the justification for the $3.1 billion acquisition price tag. Essentially, the Three Pillar strategy could fall apart if Brad did not whip the network business into shape.

The first thing on the agenda was cookies. In and of themselves, there's nothing wrong with cookies. The danger comes with how they can be used and what data they can potentially leak. The DoubleClick cookie, also known as *ads.doubleclick.net*, very well may have been the most ubiquitous one on the entire internet. It had been active for over a decade, and for those users who did not manually delete or clear their browser cookies, it may have been associated with valuable data for just as long. Now Google owned that cookie and decisions had to be made. Would there be a new cookie like *ads.google.com*, and if so, how would consumers think about that? Google's brand was arguably one of its most valuable assets and in fact was judged by a third party to be the world's most valuable.[45] Anything that might tarnish that brand, and potentially convince a subset of users to search less, would be far more damaging than any short-term benefit from ad sales.

The decision ultimately had to be made by Larry and Sergey, with Susan, Neal, and Brad making the case. The company founders were mostly concerned with the consumers and pressed on what it meant for them, how it would affect page latency, and other more environmental issues. The final call was to adopt the doubleclick.net cookie but only launch it once consumer-facing tools like an ad transparency report could be developed. That tool would let consumers see what information the company was collecting about them and opt out or change their preferences.

The cookie debate ended almost exactly a year after the acquisition, heralded by a *New York Times* profile titled "A Guide to Google's New Privacy Controls" with an overall positive spin on the consumer features. The two sides of the coin were captured well in the piece: "Google has moved forward the debate about privacy and Internet advertising, in its typical way, with deceptively simple engineering and a willingness to impose its way on others."[46] This was a huge coup for Brad, Neal, and the whole display organization. Google had made a sensitive privacy policy change that would mostly benefit itself and was able to spin the "paper of record" to give it glowing, positive news coverage. Lessons had clearly been learned from the Abacus disaster a decade earlier.

With cookies out of the way, the network was unshackled. The team built what they called the "parity plus" roadmap, in reference to the set of features that would get the network to parity with other ad networks, like Yahoo's or Microsoft's, but would also be a little better in some cases. In 2010, when Brad felt they had hit that milestone, the network was renamed the Google Display Network, or GDN, to leave some of the bad mojo behind.

Over the coming years, most of the DoubleClick products would be rebuilt from scratch on the Google stack. None of these efforts would be as large as that for the flagship publisher ad server DFP, whose new incarnation became known as XFP. This was going to be a big upgrade for the product but would test the patience of the customers, who had to wait years to see any benefits. The existing DoubleClick ad server desperately needed to be rebuilt. It had been deployed around 2001, when the web was still nascent, and used nonstandard technologies that only worked on Windows PCs using the Internet Explorer browser. The product literally could not be operated in any way on a Mac or using any other browser.

Jonathan Bellack had been the product manager of the ad server for a couple of years leading up to the Google acquisition. Jonathan is a large, loud, and opinionated person. During one of the DoubleClick strategic planning sessions, there was a "war gaming" exercise where team members pretended to be different competitors—there was absolutely no doubt who would be playing Microsoft's Steve Ballmer. Jonathan's strong and sometimes intimidating presence was tempered in the corporate environment, though, as he always coupled it with deep empathy for his customers. He was known for forcefully and passionately advocating for publishers' needs.

Jonathan came to DoubleClick from NYU Business School, and, like Brad, was asked to develop new products in the nascent area of data targeting. This work was not turning into a real job or product, so when the opening for the ad serving product manager came up, he jumped on it. Jonathan had a deep love of journalism and publishing, having done stints at *Consumer Reports* and *SmartMoney*, not to mention as editor of his high school paper. In this new job, he worked closely with global media companies to build products that would help them succeed in the fast-moving digital publishing landscape.

The rewrite of the ad server would not only be the most complex process but also the most politically contentious. Jonathan remembers one member of the GAM team telling him reassuringly, "Don't worry, there are a lot of great PM jobs at Google."[47]

It took a couple of months after the acquisition, but Jonathan was eventually given the nod to continue his leadership of the publisher side of the business, a role that he continued in for about a decade. He would often be a lone voice inside the company expressing the needs of those customers against many other constituencies looking to control, profit, or otherwise manipulate their presence to increase Google's hold on the market. Enterprise software is very different from the kinds of tools Google was used to building. Unlike free tools, enterprise customers are extremely demanding and will not simply do what they are told when features or roadmaps change. The GAM team and their engineering leaders both massively underestimated the amount of functionality and nuance that the DoubleClick system had built over the years and overestimated the willingness of customers to live without some of those features. Google had just launched its GAM ad serving competitor, and the team was proud of their work. There was a natural inclination to dismiss the DoubleClick server as a yardstick for the future product. An email from one engineer told the team that the ad server only had about six major features that GAM lacked and that the migration would start in just six months. At one meeting, when Jonathan expressed his view that "I think you're underestimating how big this project is," the retort was the deeply arrogant "I think you're underestimating Google engineers."[48]

The consensus was it would take about two years to complete XFP. Five years later, the new ad server, dubbed DoubleClick for Publishers, was complete, and the final customers migrated to the new system. Google had expended hundreds of man-years of effort to bring this vital piece of software into the modern era and protect the platform tier from attack by competitors. It was an investment that would pay off.

———————

Almost a year after the acquisition closed, Scott Spencer and Michael Rubenstein had to remake their case for the ad exchange being rebuilt on the Google "stack" as AdX 2.0. Neal would describe this as "rebuilding the engines of a plane while flying."[49] In a detailed presentation to senior executives, including Larry Page, they made the case that the Google Ad Exchange would bring together not just Google and DoubleClick products but also third parties who could bid through an API,[50] probably the earliest hint that the market was going to start financializing and trading in real time. Google CEO Eric Schmidt challenged Neal and Scott to think bigger. He wanted to know how the tiny-at-the-time AdX business could reach $10 billion in revenue (a level it took thirteen years to achieve, likely in 2021[51]).

The presentation also grappled with the question of how "open" the exchange should be. There was a clear awareness that the ad network was not ready and could be boxed out if the exchange let too many competitors in too early. In a follow-up email after the presentation, Eileen Naughton, a senior executive, summarized the reaction: "Larry gave a cautionary green light to proceed on developing the business case. He did not 100% agree to a fully open network—suggested Google set some baseline controls about which exchanges to let in, competitors to restrict, and operating policy." The new Google Ad Exchange, which would not be able to shake the name AdX from Michael's dream, was in motion.

Meanwhile, there was a world of difference between the assumptions underlying the purchase of DoubleClick and the reality of convincing existing Google teams to "play nice" and participate in the vision. Both buy-side and sell-side teams at Google needed to be convinced to participate in the new exchange. The powerful Mountain View–based AdWords team did not necessarily see the point of bidding into the new exchange; they felt they had almost unlimited low-cost inventory from their own network, AdSense. The AdSense team was also skeptical because of the very low amount of revenue currently being sent through the exchange. In the deck presented to the executives, a slide titled "Hot topics we've been dealing with" listed "Integration of AdX and AdSense" as the top bullet.[52]

On the sales front, Google's US efforts were helmed by Tim Armstrong. Like any sales leader, Tim was focused on generating revenue, and while he was an advocate for the deal overall, AdX was so small and theoretical that it had no bearing on his day-to-day job. While Neal and David had expressed a lot of concern about the network holding back the Three Pillars strategy, it was exchange adoption that would ultimately be the most challenging.

All the pieces were falling into place, and the original vision of Neal and David was being realized, albeit slowly and with speed bumps. While the core technologies were being built and rebuilt, and the services team was slimmed down to a minimum, the rest of the industry was moving at breakneck speed to take advantage of the new world of liquid and interoperable advertising exchanges. New companies and technologies would emerge to challenge Google's position and help publishers and advertisers make more money.

CHAPTER 7

YOU CAN'T GET FASTER THAN REAL TIME

All or nothing, use [our ad exchange] or don't get access.[1]
—Scott Spencer

Twelve hundred new accounts overnight. Rajiv Goel realized he must have struck a nerve the previous day when he unveiled his start-up at the TechCrunch 40 start-up showcase in San Francisco in the fall of 2007.[2] It was the public launch of PubMatic, the company he and his brother Amar had been working on in stealth for the past year. The idea was deceptively simple: using algorithms to rotate ad tags on publisher sites to make them more money.

Rajiv and Amar grew up in Silicon Valley with their immigrant parents working in the technology sector. The dinner table conversation could often touch on start-ups and innovation. During the dot-com boom, they founded a golf commerce site, ChipShot, which raised $50 million from top-tier venture capital firm Sequoia, only to succumb to the bust and bankruptcy.[3] Uncomfortably shunted back into corporate life, the brothers would take breaks from their jobs at SAP and Microsoft to try out new ideas and look for the next big thing.

Rajiv recognized there was a sea change coming in advertising. When you could target ads to individual users, it made no sense to buy big, static, direct advertising campaigns where half or more of the audience was wasted. He also felt there were a lot of start-ups trying to solve this problem on the advertiser side but there were not as many trying to help publishers. He wrote the requirements document for what he called the Web Ad Optimizer. It was a way to help publishers to make more money by optimizing which demand source would show on their websites. This would later be called "Yield Management," as it helped publishers to maximize yield on their ads, in the same way airlines did with their seats.

Amar was based in India, where he assembled a team of twenty-nine or so engineers who went to work building the solution, while Rajiv managed all the business side from the Bay Area. For the week after the TechCrunch 40 debut and onslaught of new accounts, he reached out to a dozen each day to better understand how he could help, what products they wanted, and why they had signed up in the first place. From these phone calls he learned some lessons that would largely be true for the following decade. First, the problem publishers had optimizing their revenue was real and was a difficult one. Publishers have many sources of revenue, and they compete for priority along many factors. Second, the "head" was more important than the "tail." That is, the largest publishers had a disproportionate amount of value for advertisers, despite theories about the "long tail" and the democratization of content. Finally, solutions to these problems were hard to automate. There was a robust and complex marketplace between buyers and sellers, and while much could be streamlined, you could not remove people from the equation.

For publishers, the problem of yield management was challenging. Publishers almost always worked with multiple third parties, like Yahoo, AOL, and others, to sell ad space when it was otherwise unsold. They had no idea what these companies were willing to pay on a given day or in a given ad slot, so they had to optimize based on historical results.

Before ad exchanges had fully developed, there was also no way for a publisher to make these third parties compete in an auction.

The existing state-of-the art method of optimization was called the "waterfall." In the waterfall, an ad operations team at a publisher would set up ad networks partners in the ad server in priority order based on their historical prices. If ad network A paid out an average of $3 per thousand ads last month and ad network B was only paying $2.50, then A would get a higher priority and go first. The ad server would serve the highest-priority tag to the webpage, and if that ad network did not have an ad to show, the ad server would then try the next partner on the list, and so on. The ads would "waterfall" downward in priority and in price. This was clunky and inefficient, slowed down the webpage, and often resulted in lost revenue.

The way PubMatic and other yield managers worked was still clunky but much more automated. The publisher would make a single call from the ad server to PubMatic, then PubMatic's system would automatically and dynamically choose which ad networks were likely to pay the most based on the rapidly updated reporting results. It wasn't close to real time, but it immediately generated more yield than the way it was traditionally done by humans. For example, in the old way of doing things, an ad operations person who worked for the publisher might look at the results from their partners once per week and log in to the ad server to change priorities. Maybe they would split up the delivery by country to get better results locally. PubMatic would do all of this plus another five or ten "cuts" of the priorities automatically and pull in the revenue data as fast as it was updated by the ad networks.

There was one source of ad demand that worked differently: AdX. Whenever AdX had a bid that would make the publisher more money than other demand sources, it would simply take that impression, using its information advantage through Dynamic Allocation.

AdX would not allow its tags to be put into the yield management system because it would lose the advantage of Dynamic Allocation and instead would just be bidding blindly like everyone else. This, in turn, left the yield managers with a disadvantage, since they could not use the actual historical prices from AdX and they could only optimize every *other* demand source. It was as if you were bidding for art at Sotheby's but after you sent in your winning bid, the painting was put on a bus to Christie's, where someone could bid one cent higher.

In 2009 Amar emailed Neal Mohan, newly at Google, and asked about integrating. "We were wondering if there might be some ways to integrate pubmatic into doubleclick via your APIs. We are seeing some publishers ask about how to work more tightly with doubleclick . . . and people are looking for some consolidated data around reporting," he wrote.[4] He never heard back.

Neal forwarded the email to his key reports with the note "This seems to be going directly against our dynamic allocation value prop with [AdX] ie, if DFP pubs want to do unsold yield management, they should just use [AdX] and not one of these guys."[5] The subject came up again a couple of months later, and Neal reinforced his point of view, writing that he was not comfortable giving any API access to yield managers.[6] Scott Spencer would write "All or nothing, use [our ad exchange] or don't get access."[7]

This issue of demand from other networks competing on an even footing with Google's demand would come up time and again. Economically, it just seems obvious that a single unified auction would produce more optimal results for publishers than separate, sequentially run ones. Those better results would result in publishers getting paid more and advertisers getting better outcomes. Neal did not necessarily disagree with this idea; he just wanted the single auction to take place in AdX, where Google would take the 20% fee from all participants. This push and pull between the AdX auction and external auctions would define the fight over yield management for a decade, with publishers caught in-between.

Ben Barokas is a charming guy, a born salesman. After university he and a friend set up a cyber café in Tel Aviv so he could happily spend his time schmoozing, flirting, and enjoying the beach air. The first Palestinian intifada put a damper on the café scene, so he closed his shop and looked for a real job. AOL was hiring.

From his first position helping with ad operations through a series of projects working on virtually every ad product at AOL, he felt he knew publishers better than anyone. He had seen firsthand the challenges of managing yield across many ad networks and realized it was an inefficient and time-consuming problem. He partnered with his longtime technology partner Brian Adams, and they founded AdMeld, a company focused on helping publishers manage their yield.

AdMeld's competitive edge was that it really understood the needs of more traditional publishers and was based in New York, giving it a leg up on California-centric options like PubMatic. Barokas knows everyone who matters in advertising and has most certainly hit last call at the club with a sizable portion of them. "They are my people: we ate and drank and slept it every night," he explained as the secret to their early success. The company quickly signed an impressive list of publishers, including *The Huffington Post* and Fox News.[8]

Michael Barrett is an avuncular and well-liked media executive who had extremely successful stints in sales leadership at AOL, Yahoo, and dot-com webpage builder GeoCities. That run of success hit an unmovable wall of bad luck when he took on the problem of being chief revenue officer of Myspace after the pioneering social network was bought by Rupert Murdoch's News Corp. Corporate politics, a difficult-to-monetize user experience, and of course competition from a new start-up called Facebook made the currents treacherous. Michael got fired. Out of that painful experience, he wanted to do something smaller, with more opportunity for innovation.

Ben had worked for Michael at AOL, so there already was a connection. Michael got connected to venture capital firm Spark Capital and partner Santo Politi, who hesitantly pitched him on what he described as the "worst idea ever": Would he consider becoming the CEO of a tiny start-up they had invested in?[9] While no one doubts Ben's sales abilities or charm, one can reasonably question his talent at managing a fast-growing organization. He and Brian were also chafing at each other's desire to set the company's direction, so the investor told Michael he thought it might be time to bring in some seasoned management.

When the company brought in Barrett as a new and quite experienced CEO, the advertising industry took note. While AdMeld was not the first yield management company, it looked to be in the pole position. Its focus on the largest 150 media companies also gave it credibility as the client list included many household names.[10]

Like PubMatic, AdMeld deployed a model where they would manage all the relationships with the ad networks and other demand sources. Just put a single tag into the ad server from AdMeld, and the rest would happen cleanly outside of the ad server. You just had to worry about how to deposit the check. As this came in the aftermath of the 2008 financial crisis, publisher staffing was also a major concern. Not only did yield managers increase publisher yield up to 15%, but they also reduced the need for additional head count in ad operations.

The yield management market was competitive, with AdMeld and PubMatic but also the Rubicon Project and others. To win, they had to keep pushing the envelope to get more yield for publishers. There were constraints to how much they could optimize because they were ultimately dependent on the data coming back to them from the ad networks they optimized. Those networks might only update their revenue reporting daily or might not include a useful variable, like the user's browser or the time of day, in their reporting. Yield managers were trying to optimize in real time, but the data inputs were messy and not provided in real time. This was going to change.

While still at Right Media, amid the chaos, Brian O'Kelley had noticed something striking. The efficiency gain from adding new customers to the exchange had been dropping off. Where the first two nodes to connect created an instant 15% gain, by the time twenty or so companies were connected, there was barely any gain at all from adding the twenty-first. He hypothesized that this was caused by too much similarity among the customers and the fact they were all using the same bidding algorithm (the one he had built!). It was like playing poker when everyone at the table had read the same strategy book and played all the hands the same way.

The solution to the problem would be to allow more bidding diversity, meaning new types of data, new types of customers, and new algorithms. You could try to build all of this yourself, or you could interoperate with other parties. Interoperating was the obvious solution, but it would need to be in nearly real time to work.

Six weeks after being fired from Right Media, O'Kelley started AppNexus, a cloud computing company optimized for use cases that required real-time data: advertising, finance, and health care. This was also a helpful way to ride out his one-year noncompete agreement. Brian had a huge chip on his shoulder after being fired and losing out on tens of millions of dollars from the Yahoo acquisition and, in his own words, was "so fucking angry."[11] For the next year, he invested and brainstormed with numerous advertising start-ups that would host their technology on his cloud. He worked closely with Brian Adams from AdMeld but also a small company called Invite Media that he had largely incubated out of Wharton undergrad. The whiteboard diagrams from these sessions did not use any of the modern terms that the industry had grown up with but got to the gist of real-time connections between systems, showing boxes and arrows moving data between systems and ads in the other direction.

O'Kelley denies it was explicitly in his plan to pivot to advertising after a year. Regardless of his original intent, though, once he was freed from his noncompete, AppNexus did, in fact, compete. It pivoted and quickly started investing in building new forms of advertising exchange technology that worked across systems in real time. Call it "Right Media 2.0," if you will. O'Kelley claims he ran the industry's first real-time transactions in late 2008, when his customer eBay bought test ads on the blog mikeonads.com, which was run by his company cofounder, Mike Nolet.

———————

PubMatic's Rajiv Goel explains the roundabout way he came to the idea for real-time bidding as a method of data preservation. In the waterfall environment, if an ad network chose not to bid on a given ad opportunity, they would pass the ad back to the publisher ad server or yield manager so a different ad could be chosen. Rajiv noticed that the ads passed back had less information available to subsequent bidders than they had originally been given in the first ad call. If the ad got passed back again, it would lose even more information. It was like a game of telephone where something got lost with each connection. At first, he tried to solve this problem by just asking his partners to more faithfully reproduce the original message requests when sending them back, but that was a slog. What if, he reasoned, he could ask all his partners to respond to the same ad request at the same time?[12]

PubMatic wrote up a spec for how they would like to call out to buyers on each ad opportunity and the response they would expect. They created a Microsoft Word document and emailed it out to some key partners, like Joe Zawadski's MediaMath and the kids at Invite Media. Rajeev thinks the first real-time transaction may have been from PubMatic to Invite. OpenX, another early exchange, claims an early transaction with MediaMath as perhaps the first.

AdMeld's first real-time transaction was with one of their ad network partners, a start-up called Turn. Turn was a typical ad network within

AdMeld's system, giving static "tags" to publishers to be optimized based on historical prices. They saw the advantage of moving to real time, since that way they would be able to bid on each impression on its own instead of using crude averages to get a priority. AdMeld's first transactions with Turn were in July 2009, and they immediately generated huge increases in pricing and revenue, as certain impressions could now suddenly be bid at their actual values, which in some cases were much higher. Turn's experience was so meaningful that in the coming months, the company pivoted its entire business model.

It was not just the start-ups, though. Yahoo's Right Media, Microsoft's adECN, and Google's rebuilt ad exchange were all working on real-time implementations. It does not really matter who was first, as seemingly everyone in the industry had the same idea at the same time. This way of transacting would soon become ubiquitous.

———————

Real-time bidding, which quickly acquired the acronym RTB, was obviously the future. Building on the original innovation of the ad exchange, it once again changed the face of digital advertising. While ad exchanges allowed buyers and sellers to have separate business relationships, RTB now allowed the technology to separate. Anyone could build a company to buy ads, and anyone could build a company to sell ads. All you needed to do to gain liquidity was plug into your counterparties. This was a huge step forward as compared to the closed exchange that Right Media had built or the first DoubleClick version of AdX. In both of those early systems, all the participants needed to work within the same technology.

Brian Kane, a former Clicker and now the COO of AdMeld, remembers checking his internal analytics tool, dubbed the Slicer. Every morning he would look to see how the volume was trending, and the percentage of traffic through RTB was just going up and up. RTB demand wasn't just from the ad network partners that AdMeld traditionally optimized but also this new crop of companies representing ad buyers. Interestingly, most of the traditional ad networks only hesitantly made the switch to RTB, since their incentive was to make the most money from their own publisher relationships rather than look elsewhere to acquire inventory. This would be an acute problem at some of the largest companies, like Microsoft, Yahoo, and AOL, where the natural incentives would be to optimize their own properties in a closed-loop system, even as consumer audiences went elsewhere.

In February 2010 AdMeld threw a big event at the Time Warner Center[*][13] in midtown Manhattan and invited hundreds of customers and prospects from the publishing world.[14] This would be the first time many people in the advertising world would hear about RTB. Technology analysis company Forrester Consulting was commissioned to deliver a study on the impact of RTB. A high-definition screen at the event showed a world map with each RTB transaction highlighted in real time. It showed "maybe seven per minute," Barrett would later joke.[15]

RTB was certainly nascent, but the AdMeld conference really opened people's eyes to the potential. Subtly but importantly, the conversation around ad exchange technology was moving from being a way to primarily optimize unsold inventory between ad networks to one where agencies and marketers could participate.[16]

Almost immediately on the heels of RTB adoption, companies solely focused on buying media through this method emerged: Demand Side Platforms, or DSPs.[17] Many of the early RTB participants, like Turn, Invite and MediaMath, adopted this new moniker and became leaders in the category.

DSPs are essentially software tools that let buyers set budgets, rules, and targeting and then bid on the ad inventory from ad exchanges according to those settings. The bidding is entirely on a "spot" basis, meaning

---

* Time Warner had invested in AdMeld and let them use the space cheaply.

every single ad is bid on separately—this is a world away from traditional ways of buying ads in bulk and in advance using contracts. This would be one of the fastest-growing areas of technology over the following years and would attract billions in venture capital funding.

Whereas publishers were used to selling ads to buyers by hand and in large volume, RTB, and the new DSPs it spawned, opened the possibility for buyers to cherry-pick individual consumers they wanted to reach and to do so with rich data profiles. This was a profound change, but at the time it was not entirely obvious how important it was. Letting buyers choose which individual impressions they wanted to purchase would fundamentally tilt the balance of power and deteriorate much of publishers' control over their pricing and sales channels. It was also not lost that the agencies controlled the vast majority of advertising dollars around the world—and they wanted in.

CHAPTER 8

PORK BELLIES AND DIGGING FOR GOLD

We must not trade our assets like pork bellies.[1]

—Wenda Harris Millard

When Michael Rubenstein started making the rounds looking for buyers on Project Wolf, he found surprising interest from ad agencies. The primary motivation for the development of ad exchanges from both Right Media and DoubleClick's AdX was to bring efficiency and automation to the remnant ad networks that bought unsold publisher inventory. Why were the agencies, which controlled most of the premium ad spend, interested in this new technology?

First, there was a sort of envy among agencies for the margins and profits being collected by ad network middlemen. Often agencies were the ones directing the client's spend to the ad networks, and they saw the mechanics of how those budgets were turned into profits firsthand. Even before all the excitement around ad exchanges, several ad networks had seen eye-popping exits, including AOL buying Advertising.com for $425 million in 2004[2] and Yahoo buying BlueLithium for $300 million in 2007.[3]

In a sense, agencies were also responsible for driving outcomes for their clients, though often with a different business relationship and measured on a different timeline. After all, if the client was not happy with the results of their ad investments, they would likely move to a different agency partner.

When RTB came along, the agencies took notice. Unlike the traditional ad network model, with RTB you could buy media without also having to acquire and hold publisher inventory and risk. For an agency representing the buyer, it is problematic to also have commitments to the sell side, so this was a major breakthrough.

Joe Zawadski had spent six months consulting and figuring out how he could build something better than his previous company, Poindexter, which had morphed into just another ad network. Building optimization technology was frustrating. The software was only as effective as the number of variables you could optimize, and working with advertisers was very one dimensional—"If you don't control the inventory, all you're really doing is creative optimization," he would recall.[4] Being in New York was a big influence, and his social set was experiencing the "quant revolution" on Wall Street, where hedge funds like Renaissance Capital were trading automatically, with less and less human influence.[5] With the wave of acquisitions led by DoubleClick and Google, it made sense that all that inventory was going to be made available to buyers in some way and that it would be traded more like stocks and bonds than TV commercials.

His new firm, MediaMath, started as one of the first DSPs. He had rebuilt a friendship with Brian O'Kelley since their falling out at Poindexter, and while the two of them realized they could not possibly work together, they each decided to invest in each other's new firms. Since the expected wave of liquidity from the new ad exchanges was still largely theoretical, MediaMath started by building a system to just optimize hyper granular targeting data within Right Media thousands of times per day on behalf of each of its advertisers. Later MediaMath would be among the first to buy in real time using RTB.

MediaMath played a part in bringing DSPs and what became known as "programmatic advertising" to agencies for the first time. Like search ads a decade earlier, the first buyers to use the new DSP technologies required experience and training that would not be easily distributed within an advertising agency. The solution in both cases was centralization, to create a "center of excellence" for this new way of buying media. These groups were called "agency trading desks" and would spread quickly.

The larger ad agency business is dominated by publicly traded holding companies, like WPP, Publicis, and Dentsu. These companies have tens of thousands of global employees and tens, or hundreds, of partially independent subsidiary groups. Prior to the emergence of ad exchanges, the holding companies were already experimenting with what they called "audience buying," which might involve convoluted ways of buying publisher inventory and sharing it across customers or otherwise acting like ad networks.

For the holding companies, ad exchanges and DSPs were a big opportunity. They opened the ability to replace ad networks on many media plans and take those large margins for themselves. Since the form of buying was new and complex, it necessitated the creation of the centralized agency trading desks, which could then bill clients in nontransparent ways since they were not the entities that had *agency* relationships requiring all work to be done strictly on the clients' behalf. These newly formed entities were a gold mine, operating with much higher operating margins than typical media buying groups.

Joe worked closely with two of the earliest agency trading desks to come to market, Razorfish and Varick Media. These firms in many cases would just take an order from an agency client, then turn around and pass that exact order at a lower price to the MediaMath team, which would execute on their behalf. Even in cases where the trading desk was using the DSP themselves, the fee structure would benefit the agencies, taking higher margins on ad exchange buying and lower on media planning.

Brian Lesser was a product manager and only a couple years out of Columbia Business School when his company, 24/7 Real Media, was bought by Sir Martin and team at WPP. 24/7 had a search agency, a publisher ad server, and an ad network. It was not entirely clear how these assets fit into the future of media buying, but it certainly would revolve around data.

The first step was to assemble as much digital data as possible across all of WPP. Brian pitched Sir Martin, GroupM's CEO Irwin Gotlieb, and other senior executives on the idea and was able to get a $10 million budget to create Project Zeus. It was just a very big cookie database. Brian convinced digital ad buyers throughout the holding company to add Zeus ad tags to their digital direct and ad network buys and thereby create a huge cache of information on where the ads were running, where there was duplication and waste, and how consumers moved across the web.

The next step was to use this data to form an ad network on top of some of the acquired 24/7 Real Media technology. The result was called B3, which quite incredibly stood for Big Black Box. B3 was still not using ad exchanges or doing anything particularly sophisticated; it was simply another ad network that had the advantage of access to a giant cookie database of consumer behavior and pricing. When the B3 ad network was given a chance to serve an impression within the publisher waterfall, it could optimize across GroupM clients to show the highest-valued ad.

When the RTB revolution started, Brian spent time with the other Brian—O'Kelley—and with some of the emerging DSPs. "Literally every week I was learning something new," he recalled.[6] Multiple groups across the global WPP footprint were starting to use DSPs and ad exchanges, and it was getting a bit messy politically. To supercharge B3 and deal with some internal politics, the group was reestablished as Xaxis (think X-Axis) and took on the programmatic media buying from GroupM. The Big Black Box would now have the world's largest media buying group leaning into its growth.[7]

Xaxis, like other agency trading desks, was "non-disclosed," meaning clients did not know how much the underlying media cost, only the amount they were ultimately charged. This became a conflict quickly. By 2012 some agencies and their clients were demanding transparency and would create Programmatic Buying Units, or PBUs, which would work for disclosed and transparent fees. Both models coexisted for some time depending on the customer's needs.

WPP was not alone. Publicis formed a new division, VivaKi, meant to "significantly improve the performance of advertisers' marketing investments as well as boost Publicis Groupe's growth in the context of rapidly expanding digital markets."[8] This group would not have the advantage of a built-in ad network but would execute similar strategies to Brian's at WPP. Havas, a smaller holding company, incubated and retained ownership in technology company Adnetik[9] to enable programmatic trading and targeting. Regardless of the business model, it was clear to the big agencies that this was an opportunity that needed to be grasped with both hands.

———————

The adoption of DSPs by buyers was not an entirely unpredictable result of the growth of ad exchanges, but arguably was the most impactful outcome of this technology. On its face, it was not obvious that buyers of media would prefer to buy on a spot basis instead of locking in big swaths of inventory, like they do in the TV upfronts. Contracting directly with publishers has a number of advantages over DSP buying, most notably control over the premium ad placements like the homepages of Yahoo.com or the *New York Times*. Especially in these early days of the programmatic era, there was no way to buy the "good stuff" using a DSP, simply because publishers were not willing to sell it that way. Programmatic buying was still a path to buying mostly unsold, presumably lower quality placements on the cheap. Many big publishers were not participating in ad exchanges at all, even for unsold inventory. As late as 2013, broadcaster and cable company Turner refused to allow any RTB buying on their sites.[10] Wenda Harris Millard, formerly of DoubleClick and now at Martha Stewart Omnimedia, would warn publishers against selling just to direct response advertisers focused on performance, saying it would commoditize their inventory and famously comparing it to selling pork bellies.

There were two important factors that made the display advertising market deeply different from the TV market or other traditional media like print or radio. First, if you did not control for quality, there was a huge imbalance between demand and supply, in the favor of the buyers. As David Rosenblatt noted years earlier, the supply of websites is virtually unlimited, with little barrier to entry and lots of methods (some shady) for attracting audiences. The web was a lot different from the limited set of channels on TV. If you could place your ads anywhere, why lock in at premium prices?

The more profound issue was that web ads could be targeted on a one-by-one basis according to data collected about each user. This meant that every single impression could, and ideally should, have a different value to each and every advertiser. This fact was in a sense the insight that drove the invention and growth of ad exchanges—the expected value of each impression varied enormously.

Before DSPs, the problem of valuing impressions and matching buyers and sellers was handled by middlemen. The larger these companies, in terms of publisher inventory, advertisers, and data, the more scale they had to efficiently value and match supply and demand. That was why the biggest web portals had taken positions in the market with their own ad networks. With a DSP, a single advertiser could match and pay for only the audience that drove its individual performance without huge scale. Once again, the cookies on the user's web browser play a starring role. As a user takes actions and "surfs the web," their cookies can be associated with those activities. Consider the user who visits an e-commerce site—that fact is associated with their cookie and can be used to reach them with ads later. What happens when that same user chooses to not buy anything on the site? The original profile can now be inferred to indicate a "shopping cart abandoner," and further ads may convince them to close the sale.

Publishers also use cookies, and they have been an inherent part of the underlying technology for ad serving and exchanges. However, there is a critical difference. Publisher profiles are just not as valuable as those collected by advertisers. Knowing that a user spent time in the "Sports" section of your newspaper website is slightly interesting but frankly of little commercial value. Knowing someone was shopping for your product, on your website, just ten minutes ago, on the other hand, is enormously valuable!

This disparity in the value of the user profiles proved to be a critical problem for publishers entering the programmatic era. If a buyer could use a DSP to find the most valuable users on the publisher's site, they could just buy those users and skip wasting money on all the others. Those "other users" were the bread and butter of the publishing business. They were the *majority* of the publisher's audience, and now buyers could simply choose to avoid paying for them. It was as if the ad buyers had a map of your property and could come dig for gold in the one spot they knew it would be discovered.

Fear of this dynamic was exactly the rationale cable conglomerate Turner pointed to as their reason for avoiding ad exchanges. Their sales head, Walker Jacobs, said, "We believe the downside of RTB . . . is that it fragments audiences." He continued, "The mistake that so many media companies have made with RTB . . . is allowing the low end of the marketplace—with this quote-unquote 'remnant' interest—to pick over the audience at the expense of their best advertising partners." His argument was not just that RTB let advertisers cherry-pick; he also felt it hurt direct sales because it caused companies to lose out on the best audiences.[11]

The pressure from ad buyers, especially agency trading desks, to enable programmatic buying proved overwhelming to most publishers. The glut of inventory and the ability to use flexible data would prove both extremely compelling to buyers and painful to publishers. The agencies saw the opportunity and began negotiating, cajoling, threatening, and otherwise pushing their publisher partners to open up more inventory to exchange buying. After all, buyers have the money. Even Turner gave in and announced RTB support the year after Jacobs made his statements and shortly after he left the company.[12]

The team at Google saw the growing importance of ad exchanges to agencies and advertisers as well. The less talked about part of DoubleClick was an ad server sold to the buy side, called DFA. Like its sell-side counterpart, DFA was a clear market share leader and brought in hundreds of millions of software revenue each year. Unlike DFP, the publisher ad server, the DFA product had seemingly limited strategic value to Google other than sharing the same cookie as the ad network, thus allowing for better tracking. The product manager for the product used to joke, "They bought DoubleClick for $3.1 billion and got DFA for free."[*]

---

[*] This book's author was the product manager for DFA at the time of these events and did, indeed, say that.

While DFA had a rudimentary ability to target users based on cookie data (called Boomerang), usage was limited and the functionality was antiquated. In the original Wolf documents, Boomerang is mentioned as a parenthetical on slide 18. In the YMAG presentation used to sell the company, it is also an afterthought on the potential competitive advantages of AdX.

This attitude changed as the importance of cookie-based audience targeting using DSPs started becoming clear. Neal Mohan became aware that eBay was becoming a major customer of AppNexus, potentially putting their ad serving relationship with Google into jeopardy.[13] At the time eBay was one of the largest customers of DoubleClick for *both* ad servers, so this was a wake-up call. It was suddenly seeming obvious that the lack of a DSP was a huge gap in Google's strategy. Having a DSP built into the same system that served all the other ads for the same advertiser customer would be profoundly powerful. The DSP and the ad server could share reporting data, use the same creative assets, adjust delivery based on the frequency of showing an ad to a user, and adjust budgets between different types of buys.

The big agency customers realized this as well and started asking Neal and team about their plan for building a DSP. In what became a repeating pattern, Google decided to buy rather than build. Scott Spencer led the effort, looking at all the major DSPs at the time, including MediaMath, Turn, AppNexus, and the small but fast-growing Invite Media.

Invite Media had an improbable origin story. Wharton undergrads Nat Turner and Zach Weinberg had already run a food delivery start-up together and were working on a new idea for helping small businesses create and run online video ads. Nat had been working as an intern for venture capitalist Josh Kopelman, building his firm, First Round Capital, its first webpage. They pitched the video ad builder to Josh, and it was a "no." First Round had just invested in AppNexus, though, so Josh introduced the kids to O'Kelley, thinking he might give them useful advice.

O'Kelley suggested they pop by his office that Saturday, so they hopped into Nat's car, headed up the Jersey Turnpike, slept on Zach's mother's couch, and got ready for the meeting. O'Kelley, as was his fashion, told the duo that it was the "dumbest fucking idea he'd seen in his life."[14] Rather than just sending them on their way back to Philly, O'Kelley whiteboarded for them how the emerging world of ad exchanges worked and explained how they could potentially build a system to allow advertisers to bid on ad inventory and take control over the money they were sending to ad networks. "He just told us what to do," recalls Weinberg.[15]

A second introduction really set the company up for success. Chris Fralic, another partner at First Round, introduced them to Sam Bloom, who ran a scrappy independent ad agency in Dallas called Camelot. Sam and team were taking a very data-heavy approach to how they serviced clients, bringing in a lot of the techniques from search advertising into display. Their largest customer was Southwest Airlines, and they were using hundreds of different data points and creative ads to customize the consumer's ad experience to the airline routes that might be of interest. If you lived in Tulsa and it was the holiday season, they might show you an ad for discounted fares from Tulsa to Las Vegas. They were executing this strategy in a highly manual way on top of Right Media, and while it was working, it was very hard to maintain.

The timing of the introduction was fortuitous as well since Camelot had noticed an incorrect—or possibly fraudulent—invoice from Right Media and suspected they were getting ripped off in some way they could not figure out. After an initial meeting at Camelot's "seventies western chic" office, Nat and Zach canceled their flights home.[16] They camped out in Dallas for almost a week and coded their new user interface with Sam's suggestions and requirements. By the end of the week, Invite Media had its first customer.

When Google came sniffing a couple of years later, Invite Media had grown but not really matured. The Philadelphia headquarters on 1716 Chestnut Street was actually a three-bedroom apartment sublet from a gay couple who had no idea it was being used (illegally) as a business.[17] The employees were pretty much all young Wharton graduates or dropouts, and the company was being run like a fraternity. Google's corporate development lead, Jason Harinstein,* made it clear in the first meeting with the company that he "was going to buy *somebody* in this space."[18] The implication being that if not you, a competitor.

Nat and Zach were brought into Google's New York office to meet with Scott Spencer and the team. The twentysomethings proceeded to boast to the assembled executives about how to properly build great products, why DFA was a bad product, and the techniques for selling into agency holding companies.[19] It was quite the performance. The Google team wondered exactly what they were getting themselves into with these self-confident, if arrogant, entrepreneurs. The price seemed right, though, as compared to other options like MediaMath or AppNexus, where the entrepreneurs were more seasoned and likely had higher goals for their equity. Even a couple of million dollars in their pockets would be transformational for Nat and Zach. The product at Invite was exactly what Google wanted to complement the DFA ad server and was not too complex or overbuilt. Most importantly, these kids had been successfully selling to Google's buy-side customers, so demand for this kind of product was demonstrated.

Google announced the acquisition of Invite Media in June 2010 for $81 million. The legal team made sure to cancel the apartment lease ahead of time, as the world's largest search company was not in the business of illegally renting residential property. A team was put in charge of rebuilding the technology, working under Scott Spencer. The new Invite

---

* Jason would later team up with Nat and Zach on their next start-up, as the CFO of Flatiron Health, which exited for a reported $3 billion.

would be launched as DoubleClick Bid Manager, or DBM, and then—as is Google's way—would be renamed again as Display and Video 360, or DV360. Within a decade of the Invite acquisition, the Google DSP would be responsible for purchasing over $6 billion in media per year[20] and would arguably become an even more important part of the Google display strategy than DoubleClick itself.[21]

It was around this time that Neal stopped talking about the Three Pillars. Perhaps Four Pillars seemed too predictable, so he got creative and moved on to what became informally known as "the donut." The donut was a diagram where the "hole" was AdX, and it was surrounded by two demand slices, the ad network and the DSP, and two supply slices, the ad server and AdSense.[22] In the world of the donut, all demand and all supply runs through Google products, with AdX taking a 20% slice of every connection. It was a maximal—arguably an arrogant—view of the company's position in the market. With the newly acquired DSP, it seemed within their grasp.

By owning a DSP, Google gave itself even more advantages in the display market. It could acquire customers to the DSP by bundling with both the ad server and with Google Analytics, the free web tool used by millions of websites. The DSP could buy from AdX more efficiently than any other buyer since the two systems could share cookies and were colocated in the same data centers so the bids would get there faster and more reliably. The DSP could utilize the breadth of data available to Google through its consumer products, which included Gmail, Maps, Finance, and the like but would eventually also include the Chrome browser, the Android operating system—really everything other than sensitive search data. The final shoe would drop in 2015, when access to buying YouTube ads would be cut off from all competitive DSPs. If you wanted to buy on the largest video site in the world, you only had one choice—the Google DSP.[23]

In short order the programmatic market had been formed. The innovation of RTB had given buyers power to find just the audience they wanted to reach. The DSPs quickly developed powerful, independent tools to enable this at scale. The big agencies were motivated to move their dollars to the new market to both capture more margin and help clients get better results. And Google was in the middle of it all.

CHAPTER 9

PARKING IT SOMEWHERE

*One way to make sure we don't get further behind
in the market is picking up the one with the most traction
and parking it somewhere.*[1]

—Neal Mohan

At roughly the same time as its yield management competitors, Google AdX had introduced its own version of real-time bidding and launched it with the rebuilt AdX 2.0 in 2009.[2] There was still a lot of work required to make AdX reach its potential, and the yield management companies were taking some of the thought leadership and innovation lead away from Google. The initial ritzy launch of AdX in the *New York Times* started to seem like a distant memory.

By late 2010 Neal and Jonathan were increasingly concerned about the threat of the yield managers to two pillars of the strategy, the platform and the exchange. Publisher ad serving customers were rapidly adopting yield management solutions that included both RTB and optimization of traditional ad network tags. AdX lacked any optimization for ad network tags, so it would only be able to match the demand once those networks migrated to RTB and integrated with AdX, a process that took time and effort.

What if companies like AdMeld made publishers so much more money than AdX that the power dynamic reversed? Instead of new demand coming into Google's exchange and paying the 20% fee, it might start to make more sense for publishers to do the opposite and put the ad network tag into the yield managers, even at the cost of Dynamic Allocation. That possibility would dismantle all Three Pillars at once. In an email Neal laid out his concerns to Jonathan: "The reality is we missed the [Yield Management] threat—both on the AdX side as well as the DFP side."[3]

Google feared a world where most of the indirect revenue was coming through yield management, leaving AdX as an outlier, primarily representing the Google ad network's demand and not other third-party demand. If AdX became less important to publishers, then so could the ad server. You could even imagine what might happen if a company that owned a competitive ad server decided to acquire one of the yield managers!

There was also the threat that yield managers would disintermediate Google's access to publisher inventory—the very rationale for the Double-Click deal. In one example that was particularly alarming to the sales team, revenue from an AdSense publisher declined by 70% after the Google tag was placed in a yield manager and optimized against other ad networks.[4]

In a presentation about the plan to compete with yield managers, Jonathan and other team members laid out the case to senior executives within Google's ad business. The executive summary plainly stated, "Yield Managers are disintermediating our access to inventory, inhibiting our overall display strategy."[5] Sixty percent of Google's paying ad server customers were using a yield manager. The proposed solution was to build a competitive solution to allow publishers to manage and optimize their ad network relationships with just one click. The plan was approved with the consensus of Neal, Susan, and revenue lead Henrique de Castro.*

---

* Henrique de Castro would later become infamous for an eye-popping $58 million severance package after only fifteen months of work at Yahoo.

The final slide of the deck asked whether Google should buy one of the yield managers. The slide asks whether the technology was relevant and whether the customer relationships were "elastic," meaning publishers could swap out other solutions post acquisition. These questions became relevant quickly.

Google was planning on building yield management itself but also wanted to think about shopping for a solution. Neal and Scott Spencer's vision was that all demand was going to move to real-time bidding and that yield management of ad tags would go away. That vision was taking too long, and the publishers were getting restless. Neal suggested "picking up the one with the most traction and parking it somewhere."[6] It is very unclear what the verb "parking" means in this context. A generous interpretation is that Google would build its own solution while the existing solution that was acquired would continue to work and keep customers satisfied. A less generous reading, and one that would be used as evidence in later lawsuits, was they intended to effectively neuter a competitor.

Jonathan responded to Neal's parking comment with an equally ambiguous statement: "If we bought one and parked it, it would let us solve the problems from a position of strength (market share, knowledgeable team members)." Once again, you could read this in many ways.[7]

Regardless of the motivation, AdMeld was clearly their desired target. When Neal asked his corporate development partner Jason Harinstein to set up a call with "their CEO," he did not even have to specify which company "their" referred to.[8] An initial approach in the $150 million to $200 million range was rebuffed by Michael Barrett at AdMeld and likely leaked to *Business Insider* as a negotiating ploy.[9]

A couple of weeks after the initial deal conversations had broken off, Barrett and the company's CTO, Brian Adams, were attending an annual industry conference in Palm Springs. In a strange coincidence, Google

CEO Eric Schmidt gave the keynote with the banal title "People vs. Data."[10] The AdMeld executives were feeling great about their business and its progress, but they could not help but notice all the competition. Rivals PubMatic and Rubicon were present, but also the invention of RTB had produced a Cambrian explosion of companies trying to grab a piece of this seemingly limitless opportunity. The market was getting crowded, Barrett thought, so maybe they should take Google a little more seriously.

On the spur of the moment, Barrett and Adams caught a plane from Palm Springs to the Bay Area, where they could meet with Neal in person and see what was possible. A partnership was out of the question, Neal indicated firmly. Google was either going to build its own solution or buy a company in this space. Since AdMeld had rejected the offer, they were looking elsewhere. Barrett did not want to let the opportunity slip out of his hands—he made it abundantly clear to Neal that AdMeld was not rejecting any offer, just the low one! They were back at the negotiating table.

The company had hit almost $100 million in revenue the previous year and was projecting over $260 million in 2011. Internally Google compared the AdMeld opportunity with PubMatic and felt AdMeld was the preferred choice based on its more advanced RTB offering and slightly more attractive price.[11] The official rationale for the deal was a mixture of publisher needs and time to market with a yield solution, along with a new team and fast-growing revenue. Importantly, another reason was to avoid disintermediation.[12] With huge engineering efforts being dedicated to the new ad server, XFP, there was a real fear Google was going to lose its grip on publishers. Spending a couple of hundred million dollars was a good insurance policy against the $3.1 billion already invested.

In June of 2011, four months after Barrett and Adams flew up to meet Neal, Google announced they would be acquiring AdMeld for $480 million.*[13] A week later, Ben Barokas had too much rosé while celebrating on a yacht

---

* As a strange side note, Google became AppNexus's largest cloud customer, with both Invite and AdMeld hosting their servers with O'Kelley's firm until their tech stacks could be rewritten.

at the Cannes Lions festival and broke his femur in a jet-skiing accident.[14] He was going to have a lot of money to console himself and recover.

Wary from his last experience being acquired by Google, Brian Kane steadied himself for arrogance and layoffs. When the first integration meetings between the companies took place, he was surprised to see Neal, Scott, and Jonathan on the other side of the table. The DoubleClick crew was clearly in charge, and things would be different this time.[15]

The deal cleared government scrutiny quite quickly and closed before the end of the year. Still in their old offices on Park Avenue, AdMeld threw a lavish "roaring twenties" themed holiday party that featured Barokas wheeling himself around in a wheelchair and wearing a fancy top hat.

By March 2012 AdMeld was fully absorbed. Barokas departed for a cushy expense-account-fueled job in Google's European organization. Brian Kane had one foot out the door after "spending three months eating the free food,"[16] and Barrett stuck around for six months before becoming the CRO of rival Yahoo. Brian Adams and the other AdMeld engineers were tasked with improving Google's early RTB technologies and closing the gap with the other yield management competitors, a contribution that probably ended being of more importance than anything else to come out of the deal.

Like the management team, the product pretty much disappeared. Google announced the yield management features of AdMeld would be built into the ad exchange the following year while the real-time features would be shuttered.[17] In a customer-facing presentation, Google touted the control and revenue benefits that customers would enjoy. The features being migrated would include ad network optimization, private exchange capabilities, and flexible price floors at the buyer, advertiser, and agency level.[18] Over time, these pricing floor tools were extensively utilized by publishers but would also end up being a major sticking point in the relationship between Google and its customers.

According to the former AdMeld executives, many of the yield management features that moved over were not very impactful to customers.

In the short time between Google identifying the need to own a yield management company and completing the deal, all the energy in the industry had moved to RTB. The RTB revenue running through AdMeld had exceeded ad network revenue in the third quarter of 2011, right after the deal had been announced. By the time the AdMeld features were being implemented by Google, the percentage of RTB volume was up to 66% of the total.[19] Further, Google intentionally limited which new customers would get access to the yield management tools they were building, calling them "AdMeld Legacy Features," with the rationale that RTB was the future and these features were perceived as expensive to support.[20] Neal would later testify that he felt comparing RTB to yield management was "like comparing streaming music to CDs."[21]

Most customers did not seem to care very much. While AdMeld had grown based on loyal relationships with publishers and had generated them much-needed revenue, by the time they shut down, it was basically yesterday's news. After all, the publishers had choices and could move to another yield manager, another ad exchange, or even stick with Google for their yield management needs. The point that the demand was "elastic" turned out to be prophetic as publishers simply moved elsewhere.

Nevertheless, the threat from AdMeld has been neutralized. Google had bought a direct competitor and effectively shut it down, and no one seemed to have noticed. The leading yield manager was effectively neutered, and while it was "parked," Google bought itself more time to move everything onto its ad exchange.

CHAPTER 10

YAM, MAY, AMY

If you grow share, you get promoted; if you lose, you get fired.
And it works like this for TV and print.[1]

—David Rosenblatt

The years after the wave of advertising acquisitions saw intense competition between Google and the Big Three. Despite them having a head start and many natural advantages, the changing fortunes of these companies and corporate politics would stand in the way of building a viable counterweight to Google.

Yahoo's Right Media remained the largest exchange with the most liquidity for some time, despite the indifference or hostility of the company's senior management. In the same way DoubleClick had looked askance at the performance ad network Sonar, the Yahoo senior ad team saw little to gain from this ad exchange filled with companies they had never heard of and inventory from smaller, second-tier websites. In an especially ironic twist, in both cases the head of sales was the same exact person, Wenda Harris Millard, of "pork bellies" fame! As it turned out, Wenda departed Yahoo shortly after their acquisition was announced. Regardless of who was in charge, raising the revenue from their Tier 2 inventory, like email, was a much higher priority than running an ad network or exchange on third-party websites.[2]

While Yahoo did not have the platform of Google, it was highly engaged with the open web in one area, newspaper websites. As early as 2006,[3] Yahoo had developed what it called the "newspaper consortium," a series of partnerships with local papers that gave them more exposure in search results along with ad sales through a network. They would invest heavily in this effort for the better part of a decade, and it would serve as an example of how tech giants could gainfully work with traditional publishers.

In hindsight, they should have capitalized on their success with newspapers and looked further outside of their portal to grow their footprint. Yahoo was losing consumer market share as more modern products like Gmail stole consumers from their older offerings. Yahoo had lost its leading search engine position to Google sometime in the 2000s and thus the ability to direct consumers to other monetizable properties. Despite a series of small content acquisitions, like Flickr, Upcoming, and JumpCut, Yahoo was not able to stem its slow and steady decline in traffic. Without a network play, the company's advertising market share was bound to decline as well.

Tim Armstrong left his position at Google and joined AOL as CEO in 2009. AOL was in the midst of a multiyear transformation from a dial-up business to a web content and advertising portal. On the content side, it had bought *TechCrunch* in 2010[4] and *The Huffington Post* in 2011[5] and was investing heavily in journalism, content, and video. On the ads side, it owned AdTech, the second largest publisher ad server, with a very strong presence in Europe. The real gem, though, was the ad network Advertising.com. A former employee estimated that excluding the legacy dial-in business, 95% of the profit for all the rest of AOL came from the ad network.

Adverising.com gave AOL the strongest offering of any company, including Google, in the market for indirect publisher ad sales. Ad.com, as everyone called the division, was the largest and most successful ad network, with tens of thousands of sites under its umbrella. Like the Google ad network, Ad.com was really a buy-side business, selling to advertisers and developing data and technology to optimize the outcomes they were willing to pay for. Unlike Google, though, Ad.com acquired its publisher inventory directly through business development relationships with guaranteed fees paid, instead of a real-time exchange with variable rates. As exchanges grew more popular, Ad.com kept up with the changing marketplace and diversified its publisher inventory by bidding into AdX and other exchanges.

Although Tim was a big advocate for the DoubleClick acquisition at Google, he never really warmed up to ad exchanges and indirect sales. Members of Neal Mohan's team would complain that Tim was more interested in selling big deals to agencies than signing up buyers and sellers to AdX, and former AOL executives expressed similar sentiments about his time as CEO.[6] What Tim really liked was "big, shiny, high impact, visible opportunities," and video was a big part of that.[7] AOL made significant moves into video, launching the On Network in 2012, which reached a reported thirty-five million consumers, and acquiring a specialist video ad exchange, Adapt.tv, in 2003 for over $400 million.[8] Between the huge ad network and the leading position in video, AOL was in a stronger position than its cohorts, despite not having an open ad exchange until much later. Like Yahoo, AOL also had declining attention from consumers. Tim's bet on video, and the underlying strength of its ad network, would buoy the company and maintain more value while not exactly stemming the overall decline.

Microsoft had acquired both an ad exchange, AdECN, and an ad network, aQuantive. Despite using these assets to launch its own ad exchange, there were few signs it was making a big difference in the software company's positioning in the advertising world. They also did not have any technology on the publisher side of the business, other than the homegrown ad server that supported MSN and other sites. In 2010 Microsoft sent out an RFP to the various ad exchanges, asking for bids to support the company's yield management and monetization efforts.

Brian O'Kelley's AppNexus was in an awkward position at this moment. Brian had recruited Michael Rubenstein, the founder of AdX, to be the company's president, running the business side. While the platform was built to support both the buying and selling of media, it had little traction with publishers and did not offer a solution like PubMatic or AdMeld for optimizing ad networks. The company tried to eschew any categorization to keep its options open, until finally capitulating and accepting the label DSP.[9] Their largest customer was eBay, which used it to buy media, so "DSP" was closest to the truth. Brian's vision was bigger. He wanted to do everything—to essentially complete what he had started building at Right Media on both the buy and sell sides of the market.

When Brian saw the RFP from Microsoft, he was upset—partially because they were asking for the types of yield management tools his company did not offer and partially because he felt they were missing the point entirely. The RFP, he told his Microsoft contact, was dumb and shortsighted. It only focused on optimizing ad networks and unsold inventory, while Google, post the AdMeld acquisition, was building a stack to allow all types of ads to compete in a unified auction. Microsoft needed to get into the game and commit if it wanted to win.

Microsoft was not speaking with one voice at this point. Dave O'Hara, the corporate development lead, was interested in doing something bigger with AppNexus, potentially including a big investment. He told Brian the rest of the team needed convincing—perhaps if there was some competitive interest, he could make things happen. Brian went to AOL and quickly received a term sheet to sell his company for $100 million, which was then leaked to the press. This was really a stalking horse bid and was far too low to take seriously. It had the desired effect and got Microsoft to move, however. After some grueling negotiations in Bellevue, Microsoft agreed to an investment of $40 million in AppNexus and, more importantly, to putting all their ad inventory into the company's ad exchange.[10] This was a transformative deal for both companies. Microsoft now had a smart and aggressive proxy to fight Google, and AppNexus was instantly anointed as the most important and valuable independent in the market.

———————

While Google had the advantage of the ad server platform for accessing inventory, the Big Three had the advantage of owning and controlling huge amounts of inventory themselves. In 2011 the companies combined had about 22% of the US ad market, compared to Google's 9%.[11] Google's strategy to grow was based around control over the ad server, but this had not yet borne fruit.

Each of the Big Three was selling to advertisers and agencies separately, losing out on the scale advantages Google had in terms of data, engineering, and sales capacity. With AppNexus anointed by Microsoft, O'Kelley started spending time lobbying AOL and Yahoo to join some kind of grand alliance.

The ideal solution for O'Kelley would be to have AOL and Yahoo switch over to the AppNexus technology, then let the sales forces of each company sell each other's inventory and potentially use each other's data. Yahoo and Microsoft had already partnered in 2009, when Bing replaced Google search results on Yahoo's properties.[12] This came after Microsoft had tried to buy the company for $44 billion (a transaction Yahoo shareholders certainly would grow to regret leaving on the table).

In perhaps a sign that the companies might not be willing to go all in on their partnerships, each of the Big Three had their own code name for the project. Yahoo called it YAM, Microsoft called it MAY, and AOL called it AMY. A careful observer might note that each acronym started with the respective company's initial in front.

The alliance, whatever it was called, was announced in November 2011 but was not exactly what had been hoped. Yahoo and AOL were not going to use AppNexus's technology, and instead the three companies would have loose interoperability. The alliance was also limited to just the resale of unsold ad inventory, repeating the pattern from the Microsoft RFP and avoiding a unified auction. "The goal was a combined go-to-market that would leverage each company's strong sales force and brand, but the end result was watered down," according to AOL's SVP for publishers, David Jacobs.[13]

At the AppNexus Summit conference in New York that year, Interactive Advertising Bureau (IAB) head Randall Rothenberg moderated a panel with Dave O'Hara, who had led the Microsoft investment; Jim Heckman, the SVP for ads at Yahoo; and Jacobs. It was quite a coup for AppNexus to get these companies on stage at what was effectively a promotional event for its customers. Randall introduced the panel by joking, "Your alliance is one of the worst-kept secrets in the business," reflecting the aggressive outreach that the teams had been doing to get the market ready for the announcement. Randall's questioning was fairly skeptical and mostly focused on the big question of why this alliance was limited to unsold inventory and how it would really help advertisers. Jim from Yahoo made the case that by combining inventory, it would give advantages in data, scale, and brand quality. Ultimately buyers were still going to need to buy through one of these three companies; it was just that each would have access to a little more inventory from the others to offer. There was not a lot of meat on the bone.[14]

Technology was a limiting factor in expanding the alliance beyond unsold ads. While Right Media was optimized by price and the expected value of ads, the Tier 1 inventory from Yahoo's homepage and news content ran on a different ad server that could not optimize by price. Put another way, Yahoo's ad server did not have anything like the Dynamic Allocation feature that let AdX bid into the Google ad server. As a result, Yahoo could only allocate ad inventory to the alliance from the bottom of their priority stack, essentially still a waterfall. AOL had similar issues.

O'Kelley would continue lobbying over the next year in an attempt to strengthen the partnership and give advertisers a single auction across all the premium supply. He felt it was the only way to compete with what Google was building on top of DoubleClick. He started pressing Yahoo on their technology problems and making the case that they should sell Right Media to him and switch the rest of their business over to AppNexus technology. For Brian, this would be the ultimate victory, reclaiming his lost prize while putting his new company at the center of the anti-Google alliance.

At the time Ross Levinsohn, a media executive with a background at Fox and News Corp, was the interim CEO of Yahoo. He was put into the position after the firing of Carol Bartz and was also up for the permanent job once the board made a final decision. O'Kelley and Levinsohn were close to a deal. Selling Right Media seemed like a smart move. It never really fit with Yahoo's strategy of optimizing O & O properties, it was not helping with the grand alliance, and the company was shifting more overall focus to media and advertising, rather than technology.

The AppNexus product and business teams were set to fly to the West Coast for a final set of diligence sessions before signing a letter of intent. Brian and Jim Heckman were making progress in a working session at the AppNexus office in New York when Jim checked his phone. He read the news that Marissa Mayer had been named Yahoo's new CEO[15] and that his boss Ross had been passed over.[16] The meeting ended abruptly, and the whole partnership would soon as well.

Marissa was a tech celebrity, having overseen Google Search and many of the other consumer products that had made that company a household name. Magazines embarrassingly hailed her as the "Googirl."[17] The news of her appointment to Yahoo was shocking and most certainly not going to be good for this deal. Marissa was not an ads person (her counterpart Susan ran all the ads products), and her closeness with Google seemed like a very bad sign. As a former Googler, she also felt like good engineering could solve any problem, so a divestiture of a technology asset would not sit well. Predictably, she killed the Right Media deal on her first day.

Marissa spent most of her efforts on the consumer side, with an ill-advised billion-dollar acquisition of Tumblr. By 2014 she was admitting on an earnings call that she needed the company's ad tech stack to get to "parity" with others.[18] It took a couple of years to capitulate, but in early 2015 Yahoo officially killed Right Media.[19] Moving forward, Yahoo would offer the Yahoo Ad Exchange, which was primarily their own sites, plus some limited inventory from other publishers. Other than its foray with newspapers, Yahoo was never committed to doing business with the open web publishers, and as David Rosenblatt predicted years earlier, their revenue dwindled hand in hand with their audience.

Yahoo and AOL would eventually come together, but not as originally planned.

———————

It was not just the Big Three in the US that wanted to gain scale and fight off Google. Publishers in Canada, France, and many other countries formed alliances to pool their inventory and data and give advertisers better outcomes. In France, two consortia were established, La Place Media and Audience Square. Both operated by making their ad inventory available on a single exchange and gave advertisers a "one-stop shop" for reaching their audience within the country. A contemporaneous quote lays out the sentiment clearly: "A lot of publishers are starting to see how Google is their enemy, not necessarily *L'Equipe* or *Le Figaro*."[20] These regional consortia continue in various forms to this day. In the UK, the Ozone Project has had success with a newspaper site co-op.

The co-ops made more sense as a bulwark against Google because they immediately add value to the buyer. Media buyers were likely already looking to buy ads through DSPs that match the footprints of the leading publishers in each country and now could transact with a single seller to get broad reach within a region. In contrast, the efforts by the YAM companies were just bulk reach without much differentiation.

Despite billions in investment, Microsoft failed to become a meaningful counterweight to Google in the advertising market. The Bing search engine remains in the single digits of market share. The AppNexus partnership was plagued by distracting demands to add support for ads on the Xbox, to Windows Phones, to Nokia phones, and to Skype.[21] Microsoft even had a "call option" in its contract with AppNexus, allowing them to acquire the company for a cool $1 billion, but they let it expire, unexercised. The aQuantive acquisition would turn out to be the largest corporate write-off of all time with virtually no value extracted by Microsoft. AdECN was shuttered in 2011.[22] Microsoft's efforts to counter Google in the ad world would be a persistent story of expensive frustration.

In 2015, just a year into his tenure as the new CEO of Microsoft, Satya Nadella was saddled with a complex set of businesses that had been assembled during the Steve Ballmer era. One area he saw as an opportunity to slim down was advertising. Project Coleridge was named after the poet behind "The Rime of the Ancient Mariner" in a nod to the local Seattle baseball team. The plan was to outsource all the global ad sales for the media business and remove twelve hundred employees from Microsoft's books through layoffs or transfers.

Rick van der Kooi, Microsoft's VP for advertising and a board member of AppNexus, approached O'Kelley and team with the opportunity to absorb the business. It was just too big a bite for the company to take and would have come with large dollar commitments that could jeopardize the whole enterprise. Instead, they signed a deal to outsource the entire advertising sales in the eight largest markets to AOL. AppNexus took sales responsibilities in secondary markets, like the Nordics and Eastern Europe. The *New York Times* quoted AOL's president saying, "Think about me being able to sell *The Huffington Post* and Xbox together," which does, indeed, make you think.[23] It was a radical slimming down of Microsoft's ambitions in advertising and the final nail in the coffin of the company's effort to build a counterweight to Google.

PART III

MONOPOLY MONEY

CHAPTER 11

THE PLATFORM, THE EXCHANGE, AND A HUGE NETWORK

Is there a deeper issue with us owning a platform, the exchange, and a huge network? The analogy would be if Goldman or Citibank owned the NYSE.[1]

—Jonathan Bellack

Financial markets are heavily regulated. Banks have internal compliance officers with fiduciary duties to protect not just the firm but also the market. In the years since the emergence of ad exchanges, the advertising market had adopted the structure of finance markets without any meaningful oversight or controls. This gap in accountability would allow Google, but also its many independent competitors, to manipulate the market for their own gains. The actual customers, the advertising buyers and publisher sellers, would largely be afterthoughts and would have little insight into what was happening in the middle of their transactions.

Five years after the transformative DoubleClick acquisition, Google found itself in an enviable position within the fast-growing and dynamic display advertising business. The ad server had not just maintained its enormous market share but substantially increased its footprint with publishers like the *New York Times* and *CNET* abandoning their home-grown technology and moving to Google. AdX was thriving and was a clear leader against independents like PubMatic and AppNexus. The threat from AdMeld has been neutered. On the advertiser side, the DSP built from the Invite acquisition was quickly becoming a market leader. The ad network continued to grow on the back of Google's dominance in the search market and the work of Brad Bender and team to transform it into a performance-generating machine. By 2013 the display network was a $6 billion dollar business while AdX was transacting $4.6 billion per year, both exceeding expectations.[2]

Google effectively had strong—or arguably dominant—technology in every corner of the digital advertising business. That meant that for many available ad auctions, Google technology, and Google customers, were on both sides of the transaction. In many cases, Google systems would set both the price the advertiser was willing to bid and the price at which the seller was willing to sell. They also controlled the ad server that determined which ad ultimately would serve and the exchange that saw all the demand for each ad, yielding nearly perfect information on every transaction. In what would become an iconic—and quite infamous— comment in an email discussion, Jonathan Bellack laid it all out, asking, "Is there a deeper issue with us owning a platform, the exchange, and a huge network? The analogy would be if Goldman or Citibank owned the NYSE."[3]

In 2012 a New York–based quantitative team called gTrade was formed. Their mission was to develop, test, and implement changes to the display advertising systems to improve Google's profits, particularly on the buy side, meaning the ad network and DSP. This was a proven model within Google, as the innocuously named Ads Quality Team had been regularly tweaking and influencing search ads results for some time in order to increase revenue, sometimes generating enormous returns.[4] gTrade took on some projects that would result in improvements in the ad products themselves, such as better fraud detection. They would become better known for a series of changes to the auction mechanics that in some cases would become quite controversial. The outside advertising community would not hear about the projects with code names like

DRS, Bernanke, Poirot, and Bell for many years, but they would feel the results. Google would use these projects to grow its revenue at the expense of competitors, and in some cases at the expense of its own customers.

The key to understanding any optimization problem is to identify the constraints. With Google's ad business, the key constraints were not legality, as this area of commerce was unregulated. Technology was rarely an issue, as the excellent Google data scientists and engineers seemingly could solve any engineering challenge. The main constraints were contractual promises made to the customers of AdX, AdSense, and the DSP.

The revenue share to publishers from AdSense had not been revealed in the early days of the program, resulting in speculation and paranoia among participating publishers as to what Google was taking on every transaction. One early action from Neal after taking the reins at Google was to dispel this confusion by revealing in a blog post that the overall take rate was 32% and that publishers would get 68 cents of every dollar spent.[5] The public declaration of the AdSense margin acted as a sort of public promise limiting any future changes without notice. Similarly, for AdX, there were negotiated and signed contracts with publishers, specifically agreeing to take rates, which were almost always set to 20% for open auctions.

There were two fairly large loopholes in these commitments. It was not stated that the revenue share would be calculated evenly on every single impression. Really there was not any detail given at all about how these shares might be implemented. Google would take actions to make these take rates *averages* over many impressions rather than a specific calculated rate to give it more flexibility per auction, which it would then use to advantage itself.

The revenue shares also excluded any mention of the calculations on the advertiser side. AdSense only really received demand from Google

Ads, so the 32% total take rate could be allocated between buyers and sellers in a nontransparent manner, as suited the company. AdX was a sell-side product, so again, the buy-side fee could be manipulated as desired without breaking any contractual pledge. Buy-side fees do not really matter to sellers since they only generally care about the net revenue they are paid. Google could thus raise or lower these buy-side fees to win more auctions, even when using competitive publisher data from the ad server and the auction. Winning more auctions helped grow market share for Google's products, which gave them more data and more scale, which then fed further advantages. It was a feedback loop no one else could match.

────────

Knowing that the ad network business aimed to achieve fast growth in a competitive sector, the gTrade team's first focus was on increasing the volume at the expense of profitability. A program called Buy Side Dynamic Revenue Share (DRS) was implemented where the network would lower its bid and take lower margins (as low as zero!) to win auctions on AdX. This was possible because AdX shared the minimum price needed to win with the ad network and the bids could be reduced only to the extent necessary to win. For example, suppose the highest bid from the ad network was $1 and the typical fee was 14%, leaving a net bid of $0.86. If the highest bid in the auction was from an external DSP and came in at $0.87, the ad network bidder could change its bid to $0.88, win the auction, and take a reduced margin of 12%.* The external DSP would lose the impression, and Google would make more money and take more market share. This was only possible because AdX shared the information about the other bids in real time, like an auctioneer who is in cahoots with a bidder. This program rolled out in 2013 and increased

────────

* This simplified example leaves out the calculation of AdX's fee.

the network's win rate on AdX by 4.6%. It also increased revenue for publishers by single digit percentages, given the slightly higher bids.[6]

When there was only one bidder in a search auction, Google just unilaterally imposed a minimum price: starting at $0.05 per click and gradually rising over time. In display advertising, though, the minimum amount was left up to each publisher, called a "floor price." Publishers could set floor prices in each exchange they worked with and could choose whether or not to disclose these floors to the buyer. This resulted in a sort of cat-and-mouse game where publishers would frequently change floors to get higher levels in auctions without many bidders, while buyers would try to compensate by bidding as little as possible while still winning.

On the sell side, the gTrade team realized that with perfect information about each auction, AdX could afford to take slightly lower fees from their publisher customers in order to win auctions they might not have otherwise won. AdX almost always took 20% by contract, and this fee was calculated as a bid reduction, meaning a $1 bid from a DSP or other bidder would be evaluated by the exchange at $0.80. Suppose the publisher-set floor price for an auction was $0.81. In this case AdX would not win the auction and the publisher would serve some other ad, perhaps from an ad network or maybe a public service ad for free. The gTrade team built a second system, confusingly called *Sell-Side* Dynamic Revenue Share, that would allow AdX to reduce its revenue share to 19%, 18%, or whatever was needed to win the auction.[7] This was new revenue to Google that would otherwise go to a competitive exchange or simply not clear the floor price. From the publisher perspective, they would get their floor price, which by definition was what they were willing to accept. This program increased Google's revenue by an estimated $250 million and likely gave publishers more money, though at the expense of competitive exchanges.[8]

With the success of the sell-side revenue share manipulation, the gTrade team got to work on a second version of this product that would not just reduce AdX's revenue share but also allow for much higher than

20% shares so long as the average remained 20%. This was obviously a bit more sensitive, since publishers had agreed by contract to a certain rate and now that rate would be exceeded on certain auctions. In an internal slide presentation discussing these changes with the commercial teams, the program is listed as "Still confidential —no external mention at all" and the rationale for the communication strategy lists "Legal risks" and "PM/Eng would like to explore further optimizations that contracts allow for."[9] Unlike the first version, which only reduced fees, the newly expanded feature would launch in June 2016 with a checkbox in the AdX user interface to allow publishers to opt out of the feature.[10] This opt-out would also apply to the original DRS, so publishers would potentially make less money if they did not participate in the expanded program. Google defended this decision on the basis that it gave publishers a choice before having their revenue shares increased.

One of the critical problems with running a second-price auction is the ambiguity of what to charge when there is only a single bid. In search, where Google cut its teeth with auction mechanics, there is "bid density," meaning there are typically multiple bids for a given search term. In the web advertising market, on the other hand, bid density and bid prices vary enormously.

Advertiser demand for web display ads has a great deal of variance and does not converge onto single valuable targeting criteria like a consumer searching for "new car." Advertisers use cookie data about users to determine their bid, and it is possible, or even common, that much higher bids come from one advertiser over another. If a user visits a car dealership website to check out the latest models, that dealer might bid extremely high to show ads to that specific person (or browser, really), whereas no other advertiser has any idea they were shopping for a car. It is also common for one auction to be hugely competitive and profitable while another—just milliseconds later—might have no bids at all.

In practice, the process of reducing bids in second-price auctions was rife with corruption and manipulation, not just by Google but by pretty much all the players in the market. A stock market had organically grown, and the "banks" were put in charge of their own regulation.

One common practice was for exchanges to change their floors dynamically so they were as high as possible relative to the bids that were expected from a given advertiser. Imagine you knew that bidder A was relatively unsophisticated and instead of varying their bid using advanced technology, they just always bid $2.00 no matter what. Well, you could set your floor price to $2.00 for that advertiser and maximize the amount of money you collected from the "dumb" bidder. This type of dynamic flooring could be done as well across different kinds of inventory, times of day, or geography, or any other variable that was likely to predict either excessively high bids or a lack of bid density.

Google rolled out its dynamic flooring product in the ad server in 2015.[11] In 2016 they rolled out Reserve Price Optimization, a product that would automatically increase auction floors in AdX without any publisher involvement. In an internal FAQ relating to this release, the question "What if my publisher wants to know the impact?" is answered with the curt but illustrative "No! We don't share any data."[12]

Another concept popular with AppNexus and some other exchanges was the idea of a "soft floor." In this scenario the publisher would set a floor below which a bidder could not win the auction but then set a second, higher floor that would be used to reduce second prices in the case where there was no bid density. In a normal auction, if you bid $2 and there was a $1.50 floor, you would pay $1.50, and if you bid $1.49 or less, you would lose the auction. If instead there was a floor of $1 and a soft floor of $1.50, then the higher bid would still get reduced to $1.50, but the $1.49 bid would be allowed to win and not be reduced. Of course, the presence of this auction methodology was not disclosed to the advertiser.[13]

Google, being on both sides of the market, could use the ambiguity around second-price mechanics to benefit itself. Some of the changes they made improved the results for the advertisers on the ad network and some generated more revenue for publishers, but Google always won, growing revenue and increasing its power and dominance.

Google wanted to solve the problem of lack of bid density, since more bids in AdX meant less bid reduction and thus higher prices. The simple and effective solution to this problem was to force the ad network to always send the top two bids into AdX, while most other bidders sent just one. Instead of just sending AdX a really high bid on behalf of an advertiser with valuable data, like a car dealership in the earlier example, the network bidder would also send a second bid from a different advertiser, solely for the purpose of limiting the bid reduction and making the car dealership pay more. On its face this seems like egregious behavior, since the second bid could not possibly win. The network was systematically overcharging its advertiser customers in order to make more money and market share for AdX.

In a presentation from the gTrade group, the problem and solution are outlined: "If Adwords submitted only 1 bid, the publisher will not be monetized well. The simplest solution was adopted—Adwords would submit 2 bids to Adx to prop up publisher payout."[14] The ad network ultimately would "second price itself" on over 80% of winning bids,[15] artificially reducing the buy-side margin from 57%(!) to just 15% and overpaying publishers by an estimated $500 million annually.[16] The ad network subsidizing AdX may have seemed like a great idea early in the evolution of Neal's Three Pillars strategy, since it bolstered the fledgling ad exchange. Over time, however, the ad network's growth slowed and bolstering margins became a priority. The gTrade team took on this challenge with Project Bernanke.

In an instance of uncharacteristic flair for a Google presentation, the cover slide of the launch presentation for Project Bernanke included a photo of former Fed chairman Ben Bernanke along with the seal of the US Federal Reserve System and the subtitle "Quantitative Easing on the AdExchange." The cover sheet also claimed, "Attorney Client Privileged," perhaps indicating concern about how the contents might be seen in the wrong light.[17]

The ad network bidder was already accepting lower take rates to win more auctions. Under Project Bernanke the gloves would come off and the ad network could now bid either lower or higher—sometimes much higher—on auctions to maximize winnings. To avoid breaking the constraint of contractual commitments, though, the Bernanke program kept a "pool" of revenue for each publisher, averaging out to the correct rate.

Imagine the ad network was planning on bidding $2.00 into a non-competitive AdX auction where the only second bid was from Google as well. The second bid could be set to any amount above the publisher's floor price,[18] and the ad network's margin could be manipulated from the bare minimum to an outsized amount well higher than average. Under Bernanke, when the auction could be manipulated to overcharge the advertiser, the excess amount would be put into a virtual bank account for that publisher. Then, on auctions from the same publisher sometime later, there might be a very competitive auction that the ad network would normally lose at its standard margins. Instead, the ad network would increase its highest bid to win while taking its desired margin using funds from the pool collected earlier. With the network algorithm calculating both the first and second bids and knowing the landscape of other bids in the auction, it was quite easy to raise or lower the second bid and thus manipulate the final price.[19]

Testing and simulations of Bernanke showed the auction manipulation would increase Google's profit from the network into AdX in the range of $50 million to $65 million per year. Publisher revenue also increased, by an estimated 6% per year, due to additional winning bids. The losers were the competitors, with 23% fewer wins on AdX from external bidders.[20] The original estimates were actually modest—in the first year after launch, Bernanke increased revenue by $230 million.[21]

———————

Not satisfied with Bernanke, Google undertook additional implementations called Global Bernanke and Project Bell. These programs crossed a line in the evolution of Google's approach to publishers because they broke the key constraint, the requirement to match the contractual take rate. In Bernanke and the various flavors of DRS, the publishers were made whole with their expected 20%. Competitors were harmed and, in some cases, advertisers overpaid, but there was a balanced approach overall. Now, Google started working in its own naked self-interest and acted forcefully toward publishers that did not play by its rules. Instead of a pool of funds per publisher, Global Bernanke instituted a "global pool" that could be allocated unevenly by Google to its preferred publishers. Bell further focused this effort to systematically punish publishers that gave other parties like Criteo a "first look" at inventory instead of putting the Google ad tag directly on the page.

Nothing was more important to Google's overall strategy than maintaining their code on the publisher's pages. Having the tag on the page improved the quality of the impressions they were allowed to see and allowed for better fraud detection, among other benefits. Having another tag ahead of them diminished the value, partially because some other company could grab the best impressions before AdX even had a chance to bid. Google spent time trying to accurately detect which publishers were giving the prized first look to other companies and added an indicator to its buying tools in order to allow lower bidding and thus drive spend away from inventory that was not direct.

The publishers who put a competitor ahead of Google were called "Passback pubs," and under Project Bell, the ad network's bids to those publishers would be systematically reduced. The savings from these bid reductions would be added to the global pool "without any constraints," meaning the ad network was allowed to bid as low as possible to win these impressions while bankrolling the maximum amount. This pool would then only be used to increase bids on "First Call pubs," those that put the Google tag directly on their webpages. The impact, according to an internal presentation, was to "effectively shift spend from Passback pubs towards competitive First Call situations, giving the ad network better access to good inventory."[22] By Google's estimates, 60% of publishers using multiple calls stopped as soon as they were subject to this treatment,[23] yet another example of the power Google had to get publishers to do what they wanted. Those that played by Google's rules would get more of the spoils.

The internal Bell presentation offers a point of view for publishers that reads a bit more like a gangster's "offer you can't refuse" than a typical corporate set of talking points. In a slide titled "Bell, from a publisher's point of view," it suggests that buyers do not want to be intermediated and that to maximize yield you should put the Google tag on the page, then ominously says, "If you don't, you will get lower yield."[24] In addition to punishing publishers that did not do what Google wanted, Project Bell would also add an estimated $140 million in revenue for the company.[25]

Google was not the only company playing games. For those closely following the growth of programmatic advertising, there seemed to be a new scandal every month, where some party was taking margins in unexpected ways. The agency trading desks were early advocates of "nondisclosed" margins, and many just assumed they were ripping off their advertiser customers in some way. As programmatic became more mainstream, these centralized groups were disbanded and there was a gradual demand for transparency from clients.[26]

Many ad exchanges took more money than they deserved by leveraging a "buy-side fee" on every transaction. This was a bit of semantic nonsense that allowed companies to more or less double their take rate on every transaction. An exchange like Rubicon would contract with a publisher to act as their ad exchange and institute a rate of 15%, for example. From a publisher's perspective, a 15% rate would mean they should expect to get $0.85 for every dollar bid. When auctioning the inventory to buyers using DSPs, however, Rubicon would institute an additional fee, which could be 15% or 20% on the inbound bids before running the auction. A $1 bid would be reduced to $0.85, then the publisher fee would apply, reducing it again to something like $0.72 (calculated as 85% times 85%). This is a bit like the "resort fees" at some hotels—they are not part of the daily rate, but they are also not optional and increase the cost of your vacation. Buy-side fees were common until the late 2010s.[27]

In one particularly egregious example, Index Exchange was caught operating a scheme to win more auctions by misusing bids from advertisers across auctions they had not intended to bid on. Called "bid caching," this technology would hold on to a losing bid from an advertiser and then use that same bid on a totally different auction the advertiser would not have otherwise won. It was sort of the poor man's version of Project Bernanke and caused a huge stir when revealed in 2018.[28]

The difference between Google's manipulations and those of some of their competitors was that Google could pursue theirs within their closed-loop system without anyone knowing better or having any way of definitively testing.

Procter & Gamble is the world's largest advertiser, so what it says matters. The company's chief brand officer, Marc Pritchard, took the industry to task in a 2017 speech at an industry conference. He did not hold back any punches, saying, "We serve ads to consumers through a non-transparent media supply chain with spotty compliance to common standards, unreliable measurement, hidden rebates and new inventions like bot and . . . fraud." The advertising supply chain, he asserted, was "murky at best, and fraudulent at worst."[29]

The opaqueness and lack of regulation of the ad exchanges world made detection of these many anomalies quite difficult. Google was the only company that had all the data on what was going on within its auction, and they were not willing to provide customers with the detail needed to suss out what was happening. For the other market participants like customers of a DSP, the raw data would only include half of each transaction, making it quite difficult to ascertain where the money might have gone. There were some advertisers who tried to do the legwork and collate all the raw data from all their trading partners— but critically, without transparency from Google you could not get the full picture.

In later years, the ad industry would come together to conduct end-to-end studies showing that large portions of the advertisers' dollars did not travel safely into the publishers' hands and that waste could be up to 25%.[30] Even when studies were conducted by forensic accounting firms, not all the waste could be identified or isolated—essentially, no one could figure out what exactly was going on.

The more pragmatically minded participants in the market used experimentation to get a sense of what was happening. Even if you could not figure out why a phenomenon occurred, if it could be predicted and acted on, then maybe that was good enough.

By the mid-2010s one of the chief rivals to Google's ad network was publicly traded Criteo. Criteo had expanded from its French roots and was now a global giant, with over $1 billion in revenue.[31] Criteo had direct integrations with many publishers but also bought through exchanges like AdX. Maintaining a team to establish and nurture relationships with publishers was expensive. At one point Criteo had over one hundred people dedicated to this business. There was always a thought that perhaps there would be a business advantage to acquiring more of the inventory through exchanges and less direct.

Ultimately, the advantage of being directly integrated with publishers proved to be more than a theory; it was tested. Criteo ran tests where they took a set of user cookies that had high value and bid both through their direct connections and through AdX to see how efficiently they could buy the inventory even accounting for AdX's fees. AdX would consistently underperform, even at very high prices. It was time for a more radical experiment. Criteo tried bidding only $10 into their direct integration but $100 (!) through AdX. One would expect the AdX bid would always win, yet the direct integration continued to outperform. Clearly there were things going on in the AdX black box that were not well understood and likely gave Google secret advantages.[32]

Another way that Google's auction would be empirically probed was by manipulating floor pricing. As a publisher raises its floor price, they expect the buyer's win rate to trail off since there should be a somewhat elastic relationship between demand and price. If the buyer is willing to buy a certain amount at, say, $1.00, then raising the price to $1.50 should reduce demand. Even if the advertiser's bidder is able to adjust, there should be a time lapse between the publisher's change and the bidder's reaction. This relationship would not always hold for AdX, and instead floors could be raised and more money could be made. This might seem like good news for publishers, and in the short term, it often was. But for smart observers, it implied that all was not right in the AdX auction. Perhaps Google was bidding the lowest it could to win on any given auction because of its information advantage, and by raising the floor, you were just temporarily reversing that advantage. One ad operations expert explained this phenomenon as follows: "When we would raise floors on AdX, we could almost always make more money because their bids were modeled to pay just above what everyone else was paying, and they almost couldn't decision without pricing data of all the rest of their competitors. Because of this, I would almost always recommend publishers floor AdWords differently than the rest, because their informational advantage drove prices down for pubs."[33]

Many media companies suspected things were awry within Google's advertising system based on their own experiments and data, but there was no smoking gun. The litany of secret manipulations of auction mechanics by the gTrade team would shock the advertising world when it became public in court documents in 2024, almost a decade after the group had been formed. Allison Schiff, writing in trade publication *AdExchanger*, summed up the reaction perfectly: "Guess it's not paranoia if they're really out to get you?"[34]

Even with sensationalistic headlines and pointed fingers, the impact of Google's auction manipulations remains somewhat a matter of perspective. If a given auction change, like DRS, benefited both Google and its customers, then is it a matter of deep concern? There was clearly a loss of trust, a feeling that a business partner had not been honest. At the market level, in almost all the cases of auction manipulation, the real losers were competitors, so AdX's 50% or higher market share in the ad exchange business was built at least partially on anticompetitive tactics. There's also the question of whether contracts were broken. In most cases the letter of the contracts with publishers was followed, but with Global Bernanke and Bell, there seems to be evidence that some publishers were paid less than their contracts indicated, potentially opening issues of fraud and breach.

Every observer seems to have a different view on these abuses. In the eventual Department of Justice antitrust case, these issues were excluded from the evidence, perhaps reflecting a belief they were too complicated to explain to a jury. In the state case brought by the Texas attorney general, they are front and center and there is a heavy emphasis on business fraud in the allegations. Within Google there was also friction. One former senior executive drew the line at Global Bernanke, saying, "That program was fucking evil."[35]

While it seemed like every aspect of programmatic advertising was under Google's control, they were about to lose their firm grip as some surprising innovations would start to level the playing field.

CHAPTER 12

AD TECH URBAN LEGENDS

We just did it, and it was new money.[1]

—Jana Meron

By 2010 Aly Nurmohamed was a veteran ad network operator based out of London, having managed publisher relationships at AOL. He wanted to try something new and joined Criteo, a small French company that was growing quickly in its home market. His job was to try to help them break into the UK market where Aly was based.

Criteo did not invent "retargeting," but they were one of the first companies to make it scale. Criteo would set cookies on the consumer's browser to identify when someone had shown interest in a product but not yet completed a purchase—called an "abandoned shopping cart." Criteo would show that user ads for the product they had not purchased. Obviously this user was interested in the product they viewed, and it was likely the consumer could be persuaded to buy the item with a little nudge of advertising, generating spectacular results. If you've ever seen ads that seemingly follow you around the web, that was likely Criteo. This method of advertising was extremely effective and lucrative, and eventually it was also sold by Google's ad network, though under the more subtle moniker "remarketing."

In Criteo's home country of France, they had locked up supermarket giant Carrefour and several other large retailers as advertisers, giving them a great deal of power to ask French publishers to do whatever they wanted to get a piece of those budgets. The standard operating procedure was to ask the publisher for a "first look" at all the ad inventory on their site, meaning Criteo would be called for an ad before the ad server or anyone else, then only if Criteo did not choose to buy the ad would it be passed back to the publisher's ad server. This was a very powerful position since Criteo could effectively choose any impression to buy without any competition. Publishers tolerated this intrusive method because the prices Criteo paid were so high, given the effectiveness of the retargeting approach.

Aly approached the leading publishers in the UK with the same offer, but without a roster of major spending advertisers like Carrefour, there was little interest. Publishers were not willing to rework how all their ads would serve in the vague hope of additional revenue once some local advertisers eventually signed up. The only other option would be to put Criteo's ad tags in the publisher ad server to try to get inventory as part of the waterfall. But the waterfall was not going to be a winning strategy since Criteo's model depended on seeing a large number of user cookies and skimming off only those that had abandoned their shopping carts. In the waterfall, it would be pure luck if their ad tag was called on a page that had the right user.

They needed a hybrid approach, one that would identify the user on all ad calls, then only show their ad when it matched. Along with technical counterpart Nicolas Messelet, they devised an ingenious solution. Criteo's code would be placed on the publisher's page and would quickly look at the user's cookies to see if there was a match. Instead of showing an ad immediately and jumping in front of the ad server, the code would instead insert a special signal into the ad server's tags on the page, like "criteo=true."* This type of signal was an existing ad server feature called a key value, and it was normally a way publishers might characterize their content to better sell ads. Key values might indicate the location searched on a weather site (zip=90210) or the demographics of a visitor (gender=female). In this case Criteo was piggybacking on the publisher's other key values, like jumping on a freight train. Then, inside the ad server, instead of putting the Criteo tag at a low priority in the waterfall with the other ad networks, the publisher would put Criteo at a very high priority along with all the sponsorships and best paying ads but only target the ad to show when the magical "criteo=true" signal was present. When the key value was missing or "criteo=false," nothing changed, and the ad server would act normally.

This implementation allowed high value demand to break through from the waterfall without interfering with the normal ad server flow supporting the rest of the publisher's website. Most importantly, it was a way to balance risk and reward for the publisher. Publishers would make a lot more money when their users turned out to be valuable to a buyer without incurring the opportunity cost of losing or interrupting other sources of demand. Advertisers could find the rare user who could be convinced to buy their products without waste. The implementation that Aly and Nicolas developed was one of the earliest instances of a massive movement that would come to be known as "header bidding."

Dynamic Allocation, the innovation that enabled much of the exchange era, allowed Google to compete in real time with waterfall demand, while other ad networks and exchanges would only be called when nothing else was sold. The growth of retargeting, as proven by Criteo's workaround, had shown there were high-priced, valuable opportunities for indirect

---

* Not the actual code used.

demand to compete with even the most premium ads sold by the direct sales force. In fact, user cookie data could be so valuable that Google later estimated 80% of publisher revenue was generated by just 20% of impressions.[2] This validated some of the "digging for gold" concerns that publishers had about making their inventory biddable, since the buyers could only "mine" those impressions they wanted, leaving the remainder—the majority, perhaps—unsold. From the buyer's perspective, though, it was becoming increasingly obvious that programmatic tools like DSPs could be applied to the entire landscape of publisher ad inventory and should not be relegated to just the unsold bits in the waterfall.

The challenge with allowing premium demand to compete with direct publisher ad sales was assuring that the direct deals did not underdeliver against what was promised. This was the concern that Michael Rubenstein and Scott Spencer had encountered in the very earliest days of Project Wolf, the apprehension that machines were going to replace or interfere with human sellers. It was sort of a mantra of the ad serving world that on-time delivery was paramount, as Michael Walrath had discovered—and hacked—using the Satisfaction Index.

With a couple of years under their belt running an exchange, it was time for Google to take on the problem of competing with direct sales. Scott and the AdX team solved this problem for Google with a new feature called *Enhanced Dynamic Allocation*—which, like many other innovations, would both help publishers and further lock them in. Enhanced Dynamic Allocation, or EDA, would allow an AdX bid to preempt even the most premium ad sold directly if it offered a higher price and, critically, it was also estimated to not reduce the likelihood the direct ad would deliver on time. The system essentially weighed the price being bid against the Satisfaction Index and made a judgment. In a sense this was like an expected value calculation but calculated against on-time delivery rather than a specific economic outcome. This comparison was done against the actual bid from AdX, while other demand sources remained in the waterfall, hoping to get lucky with their demand. This development would make Google an estimated $150 million per year as its ad network cherry-picked the best impressions for itself.[3]

The opportunity that Criteo had unlocked for high priced, premium "spot" demand was too big for other ad exchanges to ignore. EDA only allowed Google's AdX to compete with top-tier direct inventory, and other exchanges were not going to sit still, given how much value could be unlocked. EDA was an advantage that only Google, as owner of the ad server, could deploy—but the imperative to compete with it would ironically undermine Google's hold on publishers entirely.

———————

Andrew Casale was a young teenager living in the Toronto suburbs with his parents. He was also making over $100,000 per month. Like many kids in his generation, he picked up HTML and coding at home and realized he could create websites and make money. He created websites like 3bigshows.com, which would quickly summarize what happened on the previous night's episodes of *Survivor*, *Boot Camp*, or whichever reality TV shows had become popular. A typical post might cover why a contestant was kicked off *The Mole* and give an episode summary.[4] By turning around the summaries quickly, he benefited from search traffic, which then fueled ad revenue from an array of ad networks.

A teen could not exactly be the face of the company and probably could not even sign contracts legally. Andrew's dad, Joe, became CEO of the company, which became known as Casale Media. The experience of running websites and managing ad networks showed Andrew how much opportunity there was to build better solutions to help publishers. The reality TV business was getting played out, so with Andrew's brother Jordan also on board, Casale Media became a family business operating an ad network.

Casale Media grew quickly but ran into the same problems that other networks experienced: a struggle to get publisher inventory. They were stuck in the waterfall like everyone else, without any control over when they could bid. Andrew recalls that when the first agency trading desks emerged, in meetings he was told that his business model was obsolete. Kurt Unkel, an early executive at Publicis's Vivaki, told him that over time they were not going to use ad networks and all buying would migrate to DSPs.[5] A phone call with Nat and Zach of Invite Media just confirmed the way the wind was blowing—Invite was never going to place orders to buy ads from a network like Casale Media; they would only bid in real time.

Andrew was seeing the underpinnings of his family business quickly erode, but he was also really excited about the prospect ahead. The idea of bidding in real time just made so much sense. "This was going to win," he recalls thinking. The part of the ad network business he hated was selling to advertisers and agencies—at heart he was a publisher guy. The company pivoted and put all of its engineering efforts into enabling real-time auctions from its publisher customers into DSPs like Invite. While other ad networks like Advertising.com saw ad exchanges as a new way to get inventory to support their buying customers, Casale went the opposite direction and worked on behalf of publishers to make them more money. CafeMom, a network of websites for moms, was one of them.

Paul Bannister ran ad operations and technology for CafeMom. Kellogg's, the cereal company, wanted to buy ads on CafeMom's inventory through a relatively new concept, the private marketplace deal, or PMP. Private deals allowed a publisher and advertiser to arrange business terms outside of an ad exchange, then transact the ads through RTB. These types of deals were becoming popular because they allowed publishers to build and maintain relationships with their partners, but then allowed the advertisers to utilize the advanced capabilities of their chosen DSPs, including cookie targeting and frequency management. They were also a compromise between the "pork bellies" approach, where buyers would cherry-pick only the best inventory, and the old-fashioned methods of buying media manually.

AdX had introduced private deals after acquiring AdMeld, one of the few innovations from the acquired company that ultimately was integrated into the Google stack. With Enhanced Dynamic Allocation, this was a powerful combination. Sellers could offer a premium-priced deal to buyers and then allow them to bid on the best ad inventory on their sites in competition with direct deals. This was one of the breakthroughs that would move ad exchanges from being just the domain of "remnant" or unsold ads to encompassing the entire digital advertising world.

CafeMom at the time was mostly selling their ads directly and used AdX for unsold inventory. Paul's sales team brought him the big, high-priced deal from Kellogg's at $8 per thousand impressions, a price much higher than you would ever generally get on an ad exchange. But Kellogg's was insisting that instead of a direct deal, they wanted to execute using a private deal through an ad exchange and buy it using their preferred DSP. AdX could do this because of Enhanced Dynamic Allocation, but Paul was not willing to pay a 20% fee against such a rich deal. Paying a $1.60 fee in overhead for every thousand impressions was highway robbery. If he executed using a different exchange, the campaign would likely underdeliver since Google's ad server would prioritize all his direct sales above the exchange tags in the waterfall. The only way to give a non-AdX exchange access to all his best inventory was to somehow make the exchange bid before the ad server had a chance to decide on the impression.

Paul called Andrew Casale, who he knew was technical and entrepreneurial and willing to be flexible. Andrew assured him he could make it work. He and his brother whipped up a JavaScript-based solution for the CafeMom website that would ask Casale Media's exchange for a bid first, then insert the winning bid into the Google ad server as a key-value pair. Instead of the Criteo solution, which was essentially a Boolean true or false, this more flexible solution would also include the price in the bid, like "bid=800" for the $8 order. Within the Google ad server, instead of a single very-high-priority order like the Criteo implementation, Paul would insert hundreds (later thousands) of orders, each targeted to just a single stratum of pricing found in key value in escalating ten cent increments (e.g., bid=810, bid=800, bid=790, etc.). In this way, the bids would be priced properly against all the other demand. The $8 Kellogg's order would win if the next best order was $7.90 but would lose if there was an order for $8.10. The whole thing was a massive hack that gave Casale Media the same benefits that Google had kept for itself with Enhanced Dynamic Allocation.

The Kellogg's campaign went live on January 6, 2014, and everything worked immediately. Paul and Andrew had hacked the system to deliver a premium ad campaign, working around Google's advantages. It would not be the last time.

Andrew Casale would learn from the experience to build a repeatable product to run auctions in the "header" of the webpage and insert the results into the ad server. This would be the final transformation of his company from ad network to ad exchange and would be reflected later when his father Joe announced his retirement and Andrew took the reins at the newly renamed Index Exchange.[6]

The first mention of "header bidding" for most people in the advertising community was a June 2015 article in the trade publication *AdExchanger*.[7] For an obscure new technology, it already had quite a bit of adoption. In fact, it was being propagated across the media landscape at a scorching pace. According to the article's author, Sarah Sluis, over two hundred publishers had already bought in to this totally new, and frankly bizarre, method for improving the yield on their websites.

It was no wonder that header bidding would take off given the amazing results it generated. Like a miracle cure given to dying patients, implementing header bidding would generate huge improvements in revenue for long-suffering media companies. Matthew Wheatland of DMG Media (operator of the *Daily Mail)* worked with competitive publications to test various header bidding solutions. They were shocked to see 50% to 100% increases in revenue when they moved a demand source from the waterfall to the header.[8]

Word traveled fast, and a movement was born. Header bidding spread through the publisher community as word of its effectiveness passed from one publisher to the next. For many publishers with a lot of unsold ad inventory (and thus a higher reliance on ad exchanges), it was worth jumping in with both feet. For many mainstream publishers with big sales teams and conservative views about adding new technology, there was hesitancy.

Latency was a key concern. By running an auction on the webpage before the content loaded, you were slowing everything down. Maintenance was also a big problem—it can seem easy to put some code on your webpage, but what happens when it breaks? Header bidding was also just strange. It upended the way advertising technology was supposed to work by evaluating bids outside of the ad server. It was akin to your accountant calculating some of your company's finances on a napkin, then typing in the results manually to the official finance systems.

Then there was the FUD factor: fear, uncertainty, and doubt. Rubicon Project, an independent exchange that was considered a leader in the market, pushed a narrative that header bidding was a "race to the bottom," meaning that giving bidders more access to publisher inventory would allow buyers to bid lower and devalue publisher inventory. The real problem was that Rubicon was the biggest independent exchange, so they benefited from the current state of the inefficient waterfall, and header bidding was giving competitors a leg up. Google also pushed the narrative that header bidding was a "hack" that increased latency and would increase its attacks—both rhetorically and technically—over the coming years.

Different publishers got religion about header bidding in different ways. Jana Meron of *Business Insider* brought up the idea to her development teams and senior executives and was rebuffed; they thought it was too "far-fetched." She knew it was a big opportunity, but she needed to do more homework, and she admittedly was not the most technical person in the conversation. When Rubicon invited her to a resort getaway with other publisher customers, she took the opportunity to learn more. Cooling off in the pool, Jana found a Rubicon engineer willing to talk, and she spent an hour interrogating him about the inner workings of header bidding and wrappers until she got comfortable making the case. (Either that or they were both too waterlogged to continue.) When she finally got the team at *Business Insider* to execute the header, "We just did it, and it was new money."[9]

Not surprisingly, Brian O'Kelley would again play a role. As the creator of the ad exchange years earlier, it seems a strange twist of fate that he would be forced to invent a hack to allow bids to flow freely into a competitive exchange. In order to keep Microsoft happy after its big commitment to AppNexus, it became a priority to get more publisher supply into his exchange to bolster liquidity and earnings. He was hindered by the same problems as all the other exchanges—publishers made less money than they did with Google's exchange since the ad server would not let bids compete on a fair basis.

The first header bidding implementations developed by AppNexus were mostly one-offs for particular customers and certainly predated Casale's work with CafeMom. Once customers caught on to the value of implementing in this fashion, a code library was deployed on the AppNexus cloud that would take in parameters and make a call to the AppNexus ad exchange to get bids using JavaScript.

While integrating a single header was a manageable task for many publisher technology groups, it became quite unwieldy to implement code for every ad exchange that wanted to bid. If a website like usatoday.com wanted to use four exchanges, they would have to implement four different sets of header code, any of which could cause latency and quality problems. If header bidding was going to take off, it needed some structure and management.

One of AppNexus's sharpest product managers, Arel Lidow, teamed up with engineers Matt Kendall and Paul Yang to whip the nascent header bidding technology into shape. It seemed obvious what was required: publishers needed an easy-to-implement solution that managed multiple headers and minimized latency.

Out of this work, prebid.js* was born. Prebid was a so-called "wrapper" solution that bundled any number of header bidding solutions into a single package that could be implemented and managed by publishers. On August 6, 2015, the first public release of prebid was posted to the code-sharing site GitHub. It had six integrations, two of which (Criteo and Amazon) are listed in the notes as "not well" supported.[10] The documentation does not exactly exude confidence, claiming "the script is decently tested and live"—good enough for many publishers to take the plunge.

Arel and Matt took it to Brian and told him their plan to make it open source. It's not clear if they told him before or after the meeting that the code for prebid was already posted to GitHub and marked as open source. Brian reasoned that if his company's greatest challenge was Google, then open source made a ton of sense, since it would align all the independents. If their greatest challenge was competing with companies like PubMatic and Rubicon, though, keeping it proprietary to their own ad server would be the most advantageous. After some discussion, the plan was clear—open would win.[11] If this turned into an AppNexus-only solution,

---

* .js indicates it is a JavaScript implementation.

it would defeat the whole purpose of evening the playing field with Google.

Matt Goldstein was an old hand in the publisher world. After sixteen years at Viacom and some misadventures in the start-up world, he came to realize that his key talent was connecting people and talent. A fast-talking downtown New Yorker, Matt knows everyone and everything in the New York digital media community. His loose and informal monthly newsletter, titled *What I Saw Happen* can run into thousands of words and sometimes feels like a diary of everything that crossed his desk in the past month in bulleted text form.

Matt felt that publishers could learn from each other and cooperate to better get leverage over all the forces that were working against them. In late 2015 he decided to take action and brought together the first of what now are quarterly roundtables of publishers. These off-the-record and invite-only meetings typically take place on Friday mornings at a host company's office and address key issues of interest to the leaders of the New York media sales and operations circles.

One early topic that publishers wanted to talk about was header bidding. While many publishers were experimenting with implementations, there was so much unknown about the ways to manage the process, and so much FUD coming from interested parties, that Matt felt his roundtable was the perfect forum. There was also a growing set of vendors who were offering wrappers, and the whole thing was so complex that it was difficult for publishers to figure out what to do.

The agenda for Matt's second-ever roundtable, in January 2016, was titled "Wrapper Wars."[12] Matt had invited six ad tech vendors to stand in front of the assembled two dozen publishers and explain how their technologies worked, answer questions, and generally shed light on what was going on. AppNexus's prebid team was there, as was Andrew Casale and his brother. Andrew now refers to this meeting as "the grilling." The publishers in this setting, he recalled, were "fucking savages," asking question after question about performance, security, ease of use, and all other minutiae that could be interrogated in a short fifteen-minute session.[13]

There was not one immediate "winner" of the Wrapper Wars. This meeting, more than anything else, opened the door for widescale adoption of header bidding and wrappers. It had accomplished the real goal of making the "mafia dons" of New York's publishing community comfortable with the implementations and dispelled any remaining questions or doubts about how it would all work.

A dark horse in the Wrapper Wars was cloud computing giant Amazon. Amazon had slowly and steadily been building a sizable advertising business. At first most of the revenue came from ads that would appear in search results on its shopping site. It seemed obvious that the company's enormous data footprint would eventually be used to build a substantial ad challenger to both Google and Facebook. Google's data about "intent" from its search engine had proven incredibly valuable for advertisers, so there was little doubt that the site on which the most shopping searches took place would have an equally compelling story in advertising. Amazon started letting advertisers use its data and technology to buy ads on other sites in late 2012 and built its own header solution to get access to publisher inventory a couple of years later.[14]

Amazon has a habit of doing things a little differently, or unexpectedly. Jumping into the Wrapper Wars without offering an ad server, exchange, or ad network was one of those things. The company's header bidding solution for its own ads worked directly with publishers, and they refused to bid into wrappers from other companies like AppNexus or Index, on the grounds that their bids could be collected and used to profile valuable users or otherwise leak data.[15] The way around this was to build a wrapper themselves. In late 2016 Amazon made a big step and announced the Transparent Ad Marketplace, or TAM. It was basically a cheap, fast, easy-to-install wrapper for publishers, with one important difference—all the bidding took place server side in Amazon's cloud, instead of in the browser while the user was waiting for the page to load.[16] This meant that latency could be tightly controlled and the biggest drawback for header bidding was manageable. It also meant that Amazon would get all the data on all the bids from other parties.

———————

Ashton Kutcher played a strange supporting role in the development of header bidding. The popular actor and tech investor was involved in various aspects of the internet business and in 2014 decided to enter digital media directly with a new start-up called A Plus. With a similar zeitgeist to media wunderkind BuzzFeed, A Plus intended to be a data-driven content play with contributors getting paid based on the volume of page views.[17] By 2016 it was in the top fifty most popular websites in the US despite some allegations of plagiarism and generally low awareness among consumers and advertisers. *Business Insider* archly commented, "Ashton Kutcher owns one of the most important media companies in America, and almost no one even knows it exists."[18]

A Plus's contribution to journalism may remain limited, but it remains critical in this history of header bidding.

———————

Steph Layser had graduated from Penn State with a degree in marketing and women's studies when she improbably took a position at Rupert Murdoch's *New York Post*. She was working as an account manager, but rather than the more glamorous books of business, she focused on what were at the time called "indirect" channels, meaning mostly ad networks. Her work was effectively yield management—trying to get the ad networks to generate additional revenue for the *Post* through optimization. In what would become a pattern in her career, she dove in deep into the details and became an expert. Whether she cared about the journalism of the *Post* or about the right ways to fund journalism were secondary. She was motivated to solve an interesting challenge—generating the maximum advertising yield.

By the mid-2010s Steph was an expert in yield management. She moved on from News Corp and climbed the career ladder within ad operations. She ended up at A Plus with the impressive title "VP ad operations & programmatic strategy." Her title did not exactly reflect the day-to-day reality that she worked at a small, struggling media company that could not get the attention of the largest advertisers with the largest budgets. Her job was more or less to squeeze every bit of juice from the fruit that Ashton had plucked.

Steph's counterpart at A Plus was engineering manager Nick Jacob. She and Nick were looking for ways to increase yield when they stumbled across the new prebid.js release from AppNexus. They implemented prebid and saw an immediate 40% increase in revenue—it was amazing. The problem was there weren't enough companies participating! Only six integrations were present, and two of them were tentative. A Plus was already dependent on a much larger list of companies, and as each of them adopted prebid, they would surely generate far more revenue. The list had to be expanded.

They went to work. Along with friendly partners from Magnite, Criteo, and others, Steph and Nick became the Johnny Appleseeds of header bidding. They worked with competitors, vendors, and everyone who was willing to build out the prebid adapters. They planted the seeds, explained how to harvest, and got their hands dirty. All on Ashton's tab.

In a follow-up to the *AdExchanger* article introducing header bidding, reporter Sarah Sluis interviewed Steph about her work on prebid and other wrappers. In a seemingly offhand comment, she complained that Amazon wasn't playing nice with header wrappers. "They told us no way, they don't touch anything that's open-source."[19] The lawyers at Amazon were not pleased and promptly sent a cease and desist letter to A Plus. Already on the rocks from a questionable business model and financial troubles, Kutcher and team abruptly fired Steph. Her header bidding adapters lived on. A Plus did not—it was acquired for an undisclosed sum by Chicken Soup for the Soul in 2016.[20]

The open-source prebid.js wrapper did not instantly come to dominate the publisher market. For years after its launch, the Wrapper Wars continued, with the technology from Index Exchange as a leading proprietary solution. Since these technologies were built by ad exchanges that competed with one another and had a lot to gain by tilting the playing field in their own favor, there was skepticism and distrust between the parties. In one example, six competitive exchanges and several publishers accused Index of biasing its wrapper to favor the company's business interests.[21]

The advertising industry had a history of success in developing open standards and technologies, including the OpenRTB protocol, which normalized the way all the RTB signals were passed between buyers and sellers. Prebid.js, as an open-source wrapper built and maintained by the industry, seemed to many people the ultimate and likely winner when everything shook out.

It was not enough for prebid.js to be open source. It would also have to have transparent governance to gain the industry's trust. If the primary contributor, AppNexus, could change the code at a whim, then having the open-source code was merely a fallback and not a real reassurance of continuing independence. The obvious candidate for governance was the IAB Tech Lab, the nonprofit technical standards organization associated with the IAB. The Tech Lab managed OpenRTB and was a forum for developing and managing many standards used within the industry.

AppNexus representatives brought prebid to the Tech Lab and proposed in committee that it be managed by the organization. The move was vehemently opposed by Google, which argued it was inappropriate for a standards organization to bless a technology that was really meant to only work within one specific vendor's technology, in this case the Google ad server. The obvious flaw in this argument was that this specific technology, the Google ad server, was a monoculture, deployed across the entire web.

Regardless of the arguments for or against the Tech Lab taking prebid, the result was a schism. An observer of the events would later say, "Google squashed a lot of things; they ran the IAB."[22] A new nonprofit organization, prebid.org, was founded with funds from AppNexus, PubMatic, and Rubicon as "an independent organization dedicated to open-source tools that drive publisher monetization."[23] This dispute caused a rift in governance between prebid and the rest of RTB, which would remain at the IAB. The prebid board would include many leading technologists from advertising companies, and membership would grow to over one hundred companies in just several years.[24] More than anything else, it galvanized and funded an anti-Google coalition of independent companies and publishers.

By the end of 2016, less than a year after the Wrapper Wars meeting and eighteen months after most people first heard the term, *AdExchanger* was offering the headline "The Year Header Bidding Went Mainstream."[25] As an final proof point on this theme, publicly traded Rubicon's stock crashed 35% when it blamed poor earnings on slowness to adopt header bidding.[26]

There are many claims for who created header bidding, and the technologies varied as well. What they all had in common was that they solved a common problem, the inability for publishers to get all their revenue sources to compete with Google on an even footing. Header bidding was the first crack in Google's decade-long hegemony over media companies. With some JavaScript and some creative use of ad technology, publishers could finally optimize yield on their own terms, without Google's permission. If that wasn't enough, the eye-popping revenue improvements were the icing on the cake.

Google was not about to take this development lying down, though. Inside the company something close to a panic was brewing. They were rushing a project to market to regain their hold on publishers and displace header bidding.

CHAPTER 13

SOMETHING SLIGHTLY BETTER

The problem is that Header Bidding exists :)[1]
—Payam Shodjai

Jonathan Bellack forwarded the seminal *AdExchanger* article introducing the world to header bidding to his broader team, and in this one email chain we can see the mixture of dismissal, negativity, arrogance, and internal conflict that would characterize Google's coming approach to this rapidly spreading innovation.

Aparna Pappu, VP of engineering, offered a quick take: "The fight for the tag on the page continues, and suboptimal setups continue."[2] This comment reflects Google's obsession with keeping their tag on the publisher page as a way of avoiding disintermediation. While header bidding participants certainly liked having their tags on the page, it was not the primary impetus for the movement; it was much more about getting access to inventory.

Drew Bradstock, a product manager on Bellack's team, dismissed the revenue effects and offered that "pubs are gambling and can't actually see the opportunity costs of doing this."[3] Drew seemed to have taken the point of view that latency or other problems with header bidding have hidden costs that publishers are ignoring. While this might be accurate, it also reinforced the parochial attitude toward publishers that existed inside Google at this time, that publishers did not know what was good for them.

Nunzio Thron, an engineer on the team, got to the heart of the matter that others were trying to avoid: "Publishers are doing it because their ad server doesn't do what they want (e.g. getting inventory to compete on both Rubicon and AdX). It's very rational for publishers to want to integrate all possible demand sources, and if our answer is 'you don't need those demand sources' rather than 'here's how to integrate those demand sources smoothly with high yield and low latency' I believe we'll lose publishers."[4]

Tellingly, the more customer-facing team members diagnosed the problem accurately as well. Michelle Sarlo Dauwalter, a specialist in the support organization, offered bluntly, "If we are committed to competition, and we believe competition drives revenue, we should allow for all sources of demand to compete fairly, in real-time (or as close to real-time) as possible. While I can help our Sales team build a story around latency and lost impressions . . . the fact remains that if we allowed for real-time competition across all demand sources, we wouldn't even need to have that conversation!"[5]

And finally, bringing to the fore some of the optimistic and visionary spirit that originally pervaded Google but that seems to have dried out, Dauwalter concluded, "If all demand sources competed fairly, we could start stripping away the waterfalls, would immediately gain more access to inventory, make more money for publishers, increase ad viewability and engagement, and ultimately make the internet a better place."[6]

"If" indeed.

The dislike for header bidding at Google was not entirely commercial and self-interested. For the engineering-led culture of the company to see publishers running their advertising business on what was perceived as hacked-up JavaScript just felt deeply wrong.

The biggest actual problem with header bidding was increased latency. Every time a publisher page would load, a bunch of different vendors would load their own code, each of whom would then make a call to their servers, wait for a response, and then finally submit their bid into the ad server. In a worst-case scenario, this process could add up to a full second or two to the page load. From the earliest days of the development of Google Search, founders Larry Page and Sergey Brin were obsessed with optimizing the speed of their pages. Until very recently, Google searches still included the number of milliseconds it took to deliver results.*

The latency argument had validity but was also self-interested. One publisher executive complained that the Google ad server was actually the slowest part of his entire stack. "Given the latency of [the ad server], I don't think they have a leg to stand on talking about header bidding latency," he added.[7] Another example of latency hypocrisy related to the ad network bidding into AdX. While other bidders, including DSPs, were given strict time-outs on every auction, when the ad network bid into the exchange, it would get extremely loose time-out restrictions, a fact that was not disclosed.[8]

Header bidding was also wreaking havoc on Google's ad server infrastructure. Instead of a single ad for each source of demand, you might have thousands or tens of thousands of ads from each source to allow for the use of key values that reflected each ten-cent increment of targeting. Even for the vaunted Google engineering systems, the software was simply not built to sustain this use case. Early adopters of header bidding would often run into limits on the number of "line items" allowed in the ad server and had to struggle with their account management teams to get the limits raised.

---

* The internet is unclear about exactly when the search milliseconds were removed from Google results.

Jonathan raised concerns about billing and reconciliation.[9] There was no way, he argued, for a publisher to audit whether the bids coming into the header (and thus winning the auction) matched the payment the publisher got at the end of the month. There was no real evidence this was happening, but it was a real concern at the time.

In addition to Rubicon and others being disadvantaged by header bidding, FUD—fear, uncertainty, and doubt—was also coming from Google. While everyone agreed that latency was the main problem with the technology, Google execs would frequently bring up ad quality and fraud as a drawback, even though there was no evidence to back that up. Payam Shodjai, a product leader for the Google DSP, suggested "a carefully crafted marketing campaign . . . primarily targeted to buyers and couples spam + [header bidding] into a single story."[10]

In November 2015, at a conference focused on advertising operations, Jonathan Bellack got on stage with Tom Shields from AppNexus to informally debate header bidding. Tom was a legend in advertising, arguably one of the inventors of the first ad server (even before DoubleClick), and had recently sold his company, YieldX, to AppNexus.[11] It was a cordial and gentlemanly conversation among erstwhile rivals, with Tom emphasizing the revenue to be made and Jonathan bringing up the anti-header talking points of latency, bad ads, and financial reconciliation. The video remains on YouTube but cuts off before audience questions.[12] According to witnesses, the most interesting part was after the debate, when Joey Trotz from Turner confronted Bellack. Joey was a longtime and loyal customer of the DoubleClick ad server and regularly attended client events to provide feedback on the products and generally build bridges with the team. His question was simple, asking more or less, "This is all nice, but your customers are making more money from this and need your help. What are you going to do to help us?"[13]

Jonathan is at heart a publisher guy, and by all accounts he really cared about the well-being of his customers. While he worked under Neal in the same organization as Brad and the ad network team, as well as the newly ascendant DSP team, he had to look out for his customers to feel like he was doing his job. There was no doubt that he was still constrained and conflicted, as the rejection of prebid from the IAB illustrated, but he had to do something. He reframed the problem as not how to kill header bidding but how to make something better. His customers were doing something that made them more money, they weren't going to stop using, and they wanted his product to support. Whether it was distasteful, or against the interests of another Google team, was secondary.

Not everyone agreed. The internal debates over header bidding were fraught and seemingly endless. One option would be to build a wrapper themselves or adopt prebid in some way. This was not appealing to the Google teams since it would perpetuate the things they did not like about header bidding, the latency and lack of control. The next obvious solution was to allow direct bidding into the ad server by other exchanges for a fee significantly lower than AdX's 20%. This was essentially an echo of the exact same debate that led to the AdMeld acquisition years earlier when the yield managers were not allowed to optimize AdX against the other sources of demand. In both cases, doing what publishers wanted would result in more yield, while AdX would lose out on its exclusive integration and the advantages of Dynamic Allocation.

Google could not just ignore this problem either. With header bidding, suddenly a big part of the value of an ad server was being commoditized. If publishers were making many of their most important ad decisions in JavaScript on the webpage itself, it was not that big a leap to imagine putting the rest of their ad decisions through that mechanism and dropping the ad server entirely. The ad server was the linchpin of Google's publisher strategy, so any threat to its dominance was taken very seriously. If you squinted just hard enough, you could imagine a competitor like

Facebook or Amazon teaming up with a header bidding solution to peel publishers off Google.

Lisa Lehman, a partnerships director at Google, imagined just such a scenario. In a long 2015 email, she saw the writing on the wall given the growth of header bidding, writing, "In a world where (nearly) everything that currently happens in [the ad server] today can be executed via RTB pipes, ad exchanges/SSPs really truly can replace the ad server."[14] By January 2017 Google estimated that 50% of its large publishers were using header bidding.[15] There was no putting this genie back in the bottle.

Ultimately the Google response to header bidding was Project Jedi, a new ability to accept bids into the ad server directly, in exchange for a lower fee, generally 5% to 10%. Jonathan had pushed to make this product good enough to entirely kill off header bidding but was directly told not to do so by more senior executives in the group. He was told to make Jedi just "slightly better than header" so it didn't entirely remove the advantages of AdX. Later efforts to improve the offering, called Jedi++,* were ultimately only partially funded.

To have any chance of success, Google had to make some concessions. The most obvious was to kill its so-called Last Look capability. Last Look was a funny concept: because Google never built a product with this name, there was never a press release or blog post with this name, and depending on how you looked at it, either it always existed or never existed. Simply put, many customers interpreted the original Dynamic Allocation as a "First Look" because AdX could outbid other ad networks or exchanges before they were called in the waterfall. Once those same demand sources moved into the header and were bidding first, the

---

* Adding two pluses to the end of something makes it larger, or better, in engineering speak. For example, C++ is the expanded version of the coding language C.

exact same Dynamic Allocation product morphed into a "Last Look" that would let AdX bid *after* competitive exchanges. Nothing had actually changed on the Google side, but the net effect was that AdX could bid one cent more than the winning header bid and snipe auctions from competitive exchanges. There was no way these competitors were going to agree to be a part of the new Jedi system, which would give Google *even more* information about their bids if Google still retained this key advantage.

In an email, engineering leader Jim Giles explained, "Both publishers and exchanges have very strongly complained about the fairness of it" and maybe this could "earn a little more trust in the industry."[16] Crucially, though, the plan was to only remove Last Look for the new Jedi product, where Google took a fee, while Last Look would live on when the winning bid came from header bidding.

In an unusual move for Google, the Jedi product was announced in advance of general availability, likely to get industry feedback and adjust the plans before launch. It was given the unsexy name Exchange Bidding Dynamic Allocation, later renamed Open Bidding.* The original name was meant to show that participating exchanges would get the advantages of Dynamic Allocation. The innovation of header bidding had so damaged Google's defenses that they had to trade off the breakthrough feature that generated so much of its success to get adoption of their header replacement.

There were advantages to Open Bidding. The product worked entirely on the server, so there was no code on the page to slow things down or increase complexity. The setup process for making new connections between publishers and exchanges was very easy, literally the click of a button. The system also knew when certain ad auctions were not winnable, because they were set with an especially high priority in the ad

---

* This product name was changed multiple times in short order. To keep it simple, we are going to refer to it by the current, easier-to-remember name, "Open Bidding."

server—by not auctioning these at all, the system was saving everyone the hassle and expense of bidding on things they could not win.

The industry reaction to Open Bidding, though, was lukewarm. The 5% to 10% fee struck many exchanges as unworkable. If an exchange like PubMatic was taking 15% from the publisher, by bidding into Open Bidding, they were increasing the net fee by 33%. Open Bidding restricted which companies could participate in order to protect AdX, so buy-side companies like DSPs or Criteo were not allowed in, only exchanges representing publishers. Open Bidding also handled the billing and reporting, which many competitors felt separated them from their publisher customers.

A big flaw in the strategy for Open Bidding was an underlying assumption that it would replace header bidding. Commenting on the initial release, Bellack noted that if buyers bid in multiple ways on the same impression, they might experience higher prices, since they might "second price" themselves. This is exactly what you would expect if the publisher maintained their existing header setups while also adding Open Bidding to the mix: the duplication of auctions would—and did—go through the roof!

Another way this assumption shows up is the claim that Open Bidding reduces latency since it gets bids directly from the ad server. That might have been true if the publisher replaced their header setups with Open Bidding entirely. If the publisher left both in place, though, which almost all of them did, you ironically increased overall latency since you were adding another whole auction to every ad call. It's like trying to make your relay race team faster by adding an extra leg. The main argument against header bidding was made worse by Open Bidding!

———————

There was a realization that Google, as the operator of the biggest DSP, was contributing to the growth of header bidding indirectly. When the

Google DSP bid on other exchanges, those bids were being inserted into the Google ad server using header bidding and then potentially beating the bids from AdX. Jonathan laid out the problem in an email: "I think you know this, but I am told regularly that [the DSP] is the top buyer on every other ad exchange, so a huge chunk of publisher [header bidding] revenue is Google demand going outside our ecosystem and then coming back."[17]

Payam Shodjai, the product lead for the DSP, responded, while shortening header bidding as "HB": "The problem isn't so much that [the DSP] is buying HB inventory—the problem is that HB exists :)" and then added in a more serious tone, "Since [the DSP] is the largest buyer on many exchanges, we are also the largest buyer of HB inventory."[18]

Jerome Grateau, a Google executive working with European publishers, laid bare an aggressive competitive response. Confronted with price competition, he suggested the right strategy was to "dry out" header bidding by making sure the ad network and the DSP only bought through AdX.[19] In a subsequent email, Grateau showed he understood how radical this suggestion was and the likely blowback, acknowledging that publishers are rational to diversify their revenue sources to "keep Google at bay."[20]

One solution being considered was to stop the DSP from buying any inventory except through AdX. Chris LaSala suggested as much in an email about competition from taking share from AdX. He suggested, "With my Google hat on, the right answer is . . . [to] suggest that [the DSP] stop buying on [third party exchanges] when they know they can see the impression in AdX."[21]

Had this been pursued, it would have been another way in which Google would radically transform the advertising landscape—in addition to publishers only getting Google ad network demand through AdX, they would also lock in the largest DSP's demand to the exchange. The product teams actually ran this experiment and found that it would result in a significant, 30% to 40%, loss of impressions for advertisers and so was not worth pursuing.[22, 23] They would find other, less radical ways to "dry out" the header bidding movement using their control over the demand in their DSP.

———————

Tim Cadogan knew something was up. He looked at the numbers again, and it was pretty clear to him that things were heading in the wrong direction. After years of steady growth, the ad exchange he ran, OpenX, was seeing a precipitous decline in transactions. It didn't take a lot of digging to find the problem. Google had abruptly started to bid less—a lot less—for the same ad inventory. Google's DSP was the largest buyer on ad exchanges, so a change in its bidding strategies would send ripples, or really waves, of change to the sellers and the publishers they represent. This wasn't good at all.[24]

Across the LA freeways from OpenX's Pasadena headquarters, rival ad exchange Rubicon saw the same phenomenon. Zooming out from the typical cycle of ups and down throughout the workweek, the graph of Win Rates was showing an unusual and distinct downward trend. Matthew Brown from Rubicon emailed his account manager at Google the downward chart, noting, "We believe this is about ~$100K/day opp loss due to this change."[25]

It wasn't getting better. The reduced demand coming to OpenX continued as they headed into the fourth quarter, when advertising revenue typically peaks. Tim emailed Google AdX product manager Sam Cox with graphs showing the precipitous decline in revenue but never heard back.[26] Tim was in the midst of a nine-figure deal to move all his technical infrastructure to the Google Cloud, and he still could not get any meaningful response from the company.[27] Tim felt he had no choice. OpenX was forced to lay off one hundred employees (later increased to two hundred) and regroup in the face of this new reality.[28]

———————

Inside Google, the project was named Poirot, after Agatha Christie's Belgian detective. The problem, as framed by Google, was one of *detection*, not punishment. The product teams at Google, led by Payam, believed that exchanges like OpenX and Rubicon were not always conducting fair auctions and were overcharging for the inventory Google's customers bought. The question was how to detect this and what to do about it. If in the process they bought less non-AdX inventory through header bidding, that would be a nice side effect.

The gTrade team characterized the effort as "defensive bidding" and intended to "neutralize" the ability of non-Google exchanges to manipulate the second-price auction. The team analyzed the ratio of the clearing price of auctions to the bids. If the auction was truly second price, you would expect a low ratio, maybe 20% to 30%. If the auction was "dirty"—a word the gTrade team used—the ratio would be closer to 1 to 1, as bids would not be reduced very much. The findings showed that some exchanges seemed "dirty" by these standards. The "cost/bid" rate was 65% for AppNexus, 82% for OpenX, and a whopping 90% for PubMatic![29]

Project Poirot formally launched in July 2017 under the name Optimized Fixed Bidding and was defaulted to active for all DSP customers. Within a year, the product brought the percentage of bids that the DSP made on non-Google exchanges down from 50% to under 39%.[30] PubMatic saw a 40% reduction in spend from Google, and OpenX saw a 35% reduction. Meanwhile, Google's profit from its DSP was up 12% because of the revenue shift to AdX (i.e., they were getting paid twice when the DSP bought AdX instead of another exchange).[31] What really bothered people in the competitive exchanges, besides the obvious loss of revenue, was the silence. Google never made any public statements but also did not respond to the direct inquiries of their partners. When Rajiv Goel of PubMatic was asked what Google could have done differently in this whole incident, he answered, "Make a phone call."[32]

Poirot only applied to non-Google exchanges; bids to AdX were unchanged. As we have learned, Google used tricks like sending two bids to manipulate the second-price auction in AdX, but these only came from the ad network's bidder, not the DSP. It also offered a feature called Reserve Price Optimization that would move around publisher floors to maximize revenue and reduce bid reductions. Chris LaSala admitted as much in an email, citing these features as reasons why "our auction acts as a modified 2nd price auction."[33] When Poirot was actually used on AdX, it produced an under-10% price benefit to advertisers, so it was not ultimately turned on despite the lack of a true second price auction.[34] Bids on all other exchanges were subject to the Poirot treatment, but AdX was exempt.

Poirot was both a body blow to third-party exchanges and the final straw for second-price auctions. The shenanigans second-price auctions made possible were becoming clear to teams at many DSPs, not just Google's. Header bidding also was inherently a first-price phenomenon since it did not make sense to reduce a bid in an auction when that price was going to have to further compete with other sources of demand in the ad server. It is not hard to illustrate this phenomenon. If you bid $2 into an exchange like PubMatic running a second-price auction, that bid might be reduced to $1 before being inserted using header bidding into the ad server. The ad server might have direct deals or bids from other headers above $1 but below $2, where your bid loses even though you were willing to pay more. In a header environment, the buyer just wants their best bid to compete.

As Poirot rolled out, the majority of exchanges were already experimenting with first-price auctions,[35] and by the following spring, almost half of impressions were sold on a first-price basis.[36] Just as Google's Enhanced Dynamic Allocation has spurred the adoption of header bidding, Google's Poirot accelerated the change to first price auctions, which would render useless many of the auction advantages that had helped build its dominance in the first place.

CHAPTER 14

GARBAGE IN, GARBAGE OUT

Google and AdX are the worst purveyors of
made for advertising sites in the ecosystem.[1]
—Jed Dederick

A long with latency, CPU and bandwidth usage were key concerns of web publishers, and ads certainly played a part. Susan Parker was growing tired of complaints that the websites she managed were heating up users' laptops or causing their fans to go crazy. Unlike many ad operations professionals, Susan had a computer science degree, and as a result, she could be quite methodical in her approach to finding issues on her sites. More than once she isolated the problem as a bad ad that was loading a whole bunch of junk and making multiple additional calls for more ads. When the code behind these ads was examined, it would prove intentionally obscured and unreadable so automated scanning processes would not easily detect the behavior ahead of time. It was becoming clear that what Susan was confronting was not just a technical problem with ad creatives, it was a widespread problem of fraud.

Susan worked for media conglomerate Hearst, and in addition to slowing her site down, these ads would sell ads to other buyers by misrepresenting themselves as legitimate. She would be informed that sfgate.com, for example, was the single most common domain to buy on all of AppNexus, despite being a medium-sized local Hearst newspaper website that did not actually sell through that exchange. "I was obsessed," she said. "I yelled at everyone my industry was turning into a criminal enterprise, a cesspool."[2]

The most egregious form of fraud common in the mid-2010s was the phenomenon of "domain spoofing." This is when a low-quality site misrepresents itself in the ad exchange as another site and gets the benefit of the stamp of quality without the effort. Publishers like Hearst saw their inventory sold by sellers and ad exchanges they did not work with and did not get paid by.

There was the related phenomenon of "ad stuffing," where a single "good" ad would appear on a publisher's site but behind the scenes, the ad code would load ad after ad into invisible placements on the page, far off to the right of the content or behind the visible ad. Every one of these "stuffed" ads would be sold on the exchange as appearing on the original site—like sfgate.com—and would appear legitimate to buyers, yet none were visible and the actual publisher would not get paid. Very often these auctions would be misrepresented as a more valuable video ad slot, giving buyers the incorrect idea that you could get video impressions from legitimate sites at unrealistically low prices.

More devious fraudsters would develop code that would appear totally normal and harmless when inspected, unless it was served under particular circumstances like on sfgate.com and viewed by a user in Des Moines, Iowa, at which time it would unload its terrible payload. This type of behavior made detection done by exchanges or DSPs useless since they would observe the ad locally, when the key conditions were not met and the ad's payload would remain cloaked. One of the only ways publishers would realize these ads were running was when they would receive complaints from users that the webpages were making their cooling fans go crazy as the ad loads abused the available CPU of customer laptops.

No one knew how pervasive these practices were, and complaints from publishers like Hearst often fell on deaf ears—or just resulted in individual ads getting banned, hardly a comprehensive solution. When buyers pored over their log files, they might find disturbing data, like mismatches between the sites they had targeted and the sites on which their ads actually appeared. Publishers who wanted to investigate, meanwhile, would have to find ads "in the wild" on their site and isolate the code and try to decipher which buyers on which exchanges were responsible.

Susan ended up doing just that and traced many of the bad ads she found to buyers using the MediaMath DSP. She was fed up. She sent a long, detailed, and angry missive to her contact at the company, Sam Cox, who later referred to it as "the Molotov email," for the explosion of reactions it generated. The DSP quickly responded by firing many clients and publicly apologizing in a blog post.[3] This was just the first skirmish for Susan and Sam in the war on ad fraud.

AppNexus found itself smack in the middle of many of the fraud problems. In 2014 *AdExchanger* reported they had "come to be seen as a major point of entry for invalid impressions in the programmatic space."[4] Later that year they would announce a supply certification program to try to get ahead of what seemed like a growing problem.[5]

The company was the epicenter of certain types of fraud for a confluence of reasons. Among the major exchanges, it had always been the most lax in signing up new ad network customers, including no-name middlemen based in Israel.* The ad networks were part of the origin story for the Right Media exchange, so the early strategy for AppNexus largely

---

* It is not clear why so much of the low-quality and fraudulent ad business is based in Israel. The country has also produced numerous advertising successes, such as EyeBlaster and Innovid, both of which went public.

focused on poaching those customers and making the technology appealing for their specific arbitrage-like use cases. The tech stack O'Kelley built was also probably the most flexible in the industry, allowing sellers to pass whatever data they wanted to buyers to enhance their inventory. Unfortunately, flexibility in the wrong hands allowed for more easy misrepresentation and fraudulent inventory. Finally, since the technology included both a buy-side DSP and a sell-side exchange, fraudulent customers could trade a single impression among themselves multiple times until a real ad buyer placed a bid and everyone got paid.

To the company's credit, they decided to purge their bad business partners. In 2015, at a conference in London, Chief Data Scientist Catherine Williams announced that they had removed the fraud and a whopping 65% of transactions on the system had disappeared. Brian and team positioned this as a victory lap, saying, "AppNexus has the scale and mandate to solve a challenge that the entire industry confronts."[6]

The industry's reaction was not as congratulatory. One competitor summed it up in a tweet: "Did Appnexus just admit to ripping off buyers for the last 8 years?"[7] In their defense, the headline did not match the reality. Since most of the transactions were buyers and sellers on the same platform, potentially selling the same impression multiple times, the actual number of bad ads was an order of magnitude lower than 65%. As part of the purge, they fired a full third of all their customers.

The incident, though, was a black eye for a company that saw itself as the savior of an industry plagued by problems. Cleaning up AppNexus only took care of a single bastion of fraud. Plenty of others still proliferated. The industry needed a more comprehensive solution across publishers and exchanges, and surprisingly (and secretly) it would come from Google.

———

Sam Cox had a long career in advertising technology and can credibly make a claim to have invented an early version of header bidding. Sam had big hair, a big personality, and a big dog, Pickles the Labradoodle, who might sometimes be seen at industry events. Jonathan Bellack knew he needed more talent on his team that knew the ins and outs of the publishing world, to help balance out the more naïve, "Googley" people who thought every problem could be solved with an algorithm. After Scott Spencer moved on to other opportunities within Google, Jonathan aggressively recruited Sam from MediaMath to the ad exchange team at Google. Sam eventually relented and took on the parts of the exchange that interfaced with buyers.[8]

From his time at MediaMath, Sam had seen a lot of the exchange challenges from a buyer's perspective. He was receiving a constant stream of complaints from his MediaMath customers about the quality of the ads being bought on exchanges and the problem of deceptive packaging and labeling. Facebook.com, for example, was commonly targeted on exchanges, despite the fact that Facebook the company absolutely did not sell ads through exchanges since the shutdown of its own exchange, FBX. There was also a persistent problem where banner ad slots were being mislabeled and sold as video ads. If any random website or exchange seller could claim they were the *New York Times*, how could the real *Times* ever catch up and survive?

Sam concluded that you could determine whether an impression was authentic or fake using three signals—the exchange, the domain, and the publisher ID. The last of those, publisher ID, was just a string of numbers of letters that uniquely identified the account of the seller, in much the same way a brokerage might identify the sellers of securities on a stock exchange. Since the publisher ID was unique and consistent, it could serve as the forensic key needed to figure out who was the real nytimes.com and who was fake. After all, you could just ask the *Times* which publisher ID they sold through on a given exchange and if it did not match what you saw in your reporting, you had found a problem. The question was how to do this at scale and not just try to block potentially thousands of bad publisher ids across dozens of exchanges by hand.

Sam was having a hard time convincing people inside Google that this was a real problem that had to be addressed. Some of the buy-side product managers actively discouraged this way of thinking, since they feared that cutting off any substantial portion of inventory from their bidder would put them at a disadvantage against other competitors who might bid more freely. This is a prisoner's dilemma—if a single DSP took the stand that it did not want "bad" inventory, it would achieve lower results and would lose against the competition; if every DSP stood against this fraud, it would be wiped out and the whole ecosystem would be better off.

Sam had a crazy idea to demonstrate how bad a problem this really was. In this instance, Google's presence on both sides of the market would come in handy. What if, he thought, he could trace the ad exchange auctions from Google's sell-side ad server to Google's buy-side DSP and show how many auctions were fraudulent? All he needed was a willing volunteer.

It just so happened that just as Sam had changed jobs to work at Google, the thrower of the Molotov email, Susan Parker, had changed jobs and was now a customer of Sam's at the *New York Times*. He knew how obsessed she was with this problem, so he made a crazy proposal to her: "Let's shut down all your ads for fifteen minutes and see what happens."[9] He would not tell her exactly why, but she trusted him and was game. Shutting down the ads was not actually that hard. Using the vaunted priority system in the ad server, Susan could just set up blank ads in every size available on the *Times* website to run from 4:00 a.m. to 4:15 a.m. and set them all to priority 1, which means "serve ahead of everything, no matter what."

No one stayed up overnight to watch the ads blank out, but it seemed to work as planned. The next morning the analytics group at Google, led by David Goodman, looked at the auctions seen by the Google DSP and reported back that there was no real difference in volume during the shutoff period. That did not make much sense. They reran the analysis but this time pivoted the data by exchange and publisher ID. What they saw was shocking. The publisher ids owned by the *Times*—the legitimate ones—all went to zero. Those were a tiny minority of all the publisher ids in the data, however. The data showed tens of thousands of publisher ids representing counterparties that just kept on selling nytimes.com inventory despite having no business relationship with the company.[10] The fake traffic vastly outweighed the real traffic.*

It was time to expand the net to see how widespread this problem really was. Sam expanded the scope of his experiments to include *Business Insider*, Weather.com, and other leading publishers. Jana Meron, the head of operations for *Insider*, was game, and this time she did not even have to get in the pool. She just really wanted to see how bad a problem this was. Similarly to what was found with the *Times*, the results Jana saw were ridiculous. There were twenty-seven million available video impressions in the fifteen minutes she shut down the site, when there should have been zero. That was more video traffic than the site would have in total in fifteen minutes if they were still serving ads.[11]

With the evidence in hand, Sam wanted to create a sustainable solution. He knew that if it came from Google, it would be seen as some kind of power grab or manipulation—the other side of the coin for being a dominant industry player. He hired an outside consultant, the well-regarded advertising technologist Neal Richter, and they brainstormed and whiteboarded a solution. The requirements were simple: it could not require any coding, and it could not come from Google. The idea came up to model the solution on the ubiquitous technology known as robots.txt, wherein a publisher can post a simple text file that tells search engines and other web crawlers whether they want their content to be indexed. Why not do the same thing for ad sales? From this insight was created the spec for ads.txt, a simple text file that allowed publishers to declare on their own

---

* Because header bidding participants were not aware their ads would not serve, there were legitimate auctions that were unwinnable, but that continued during the blackout period.

websites which exchanges and publisher ids on those exchanges were authorized and official. It was surprisingly simple and easy to implement.* With ads.txt, DSPs and ad networks could easily know which auctions were fake and should be avoided, and which ones were authorized.

Sam and Neal met with Alanna Gombert, the general manager of the IAB Tech Lab. They wanted to donate the spec to the trade group but were worried that if it was put through the committee process, it would be watered down by some members who might be financially benefiting from the current state of things. Alanna put the spec on a fast track and got it out for public comment quickly. She described the spec as a "no-brainer" and realized that even though Google did not want its name involved, the fact that it was supporting the effort would make everything a lot easier. The Tech Lab posted their press release on May 17, 2017, and included quotes from Alanna and other industry leaders but not Sam or Neal or anyone from Google. The release noted that the spec was developed by the "IAB OpenRTB Working Group,"[12] which was really not the case.

Business Insider became the first website in the world to put up an ads.txt file. Within a year of the standard being published, more than half of all publishers had adopted it.[13] Even Facebook published an ads.txt file, in their case just an empty one to prove the inventory was not available for sale. The ubiquity of this simple tool has largely stamped out spoofing and brought millions, or maybe even billions, of ad dollars back to the publishers that deserve them. Google made this happen and did not even take the credit.

---

* These files are ubiquitous on the web even though you may never see them. You can go to any ad-supported publisher site and look for a file in the root directory called ads.txt. To see one, try www.nytimes.com/ads.txt.

Beyond avoiding outright fraud, there is also a lot of debate about variations in content quality. There have always been two points of view about media buying. In the first camp are the traditionalists like Wenda Harris Millard, arguing that ad inventory should not be bought "like pork bellies." That is, the quality of the content matters and the relationship between the publisher and the advertiser matters.

In the second camp are the optimizers, who care only about advertiser performance and will buy the cheapest media possible to get those outcomes. The premise of ad exchanges, in a sense, is that ad inventory is fungible and that it is better to only buy the individual spot impressions that work rather than committing to specific publishers in advance for blocks of inventory. Rob Norman, the former head of GroupM, noted that "publishers are in the business of bundling very valuable users and impressions with much less valuable ones" and that ad exchanges allow advertisers to only buy those most valuable impressions.[14]

The ascendance of the optimizers was bad for mainstream publishers with expensive newsrooms and fixed costs. If advertisers do not inherently care about quality, then that investment is for naught. This straw man of quality versus optimization breaks down, though, when you get into some of the specifics. Mainstream advertisers do not want their ads next to pornography or hateful content, no matter the outcomes. Where do you draw the line on quality, and how do you do so at scale, in milliseconds? This debate would have huge implications on the economics of the open web.

Quality goes beyond the content, extending to the audience. Imagine you are trying to make money off web viewership but do not want to spend money on journalists or any of that pesky content that drives real engagement. You might produce low-quality sites with cut-and-pasted content and get a domain that sounds legitimate like holidaygiftsforfamily.co.us or celebritynewsyoucanuse.net. The ad industry calls these Made For Advertising sites, or MFA, and there are millions of them, with more created every day. They proliferate because they are cheap to spin up and inevitably some money from the ad exchange ecosystem filters down to them, whether advertisers want it to or not. The confluence of Made For Advertising sites and media buying algorithms that do not prioritize content quality can create a giant sucking sound of advertising dollars away from legitimate news outlets. After all, if you are buying pork bellies, do you care that some of them have a *New York Times* brand name?

Google's role in the proliferation of Made For Advertising sites is conflicted at best. AdX, as the largest ad exchange, is the most common way these sites make money,[15] while the Google DSP, as the largest buyer, spends the most media dollars on these sites.[16] The traffic generated to these sites is also commonly acquired through ads placed using Google search ads or through Facebook, and other ad networks are also acquisition channels. Google's ads team has an enormous number of policies about which sites are allowed to advertise and which types of ads are appropriate. Enforcing all these policies is inconsistent and can be difficult. For example, there are policies against using a trademark without authorization, but if Google or Facebook were to proactively scan every ad or site for known marks, they would have no basis to know whether they were authorized or not and would find millions of false positives. Instead, they wait for complaints from the rights holders and react.

Google is very conservative with enforcement against sites on their exchange and ad network. After all, if there are no complaints, then removing a site does nothing in the short term besides lose the company money. The bureaucracy stands in the way of enforcement as well. A site that hosts pirated manga content can be banned from search results but still monetize using the ad exchange. The decision to ban requires several senior-level people to agree to an action. "The policy and bureaucracy are maddening and should be run by product and engineering," offered former Google and Facebook policy lead Rob Leathern.[17] To cherry-pick one example, Facebook kicked a scammy Chinese mobile app developer—Cheetah Mobile—out of their system in 2017,[18] while it took Google until 2020, three years later, to do the same.[19]

Google also has a policy of allowing both buyers and publishers on AdX to remain anonymous in log files. A buyer looking at log files may see they bought ads on publisher "1234," but they will not see the company name. This policy has long exacerbated the desire for transparency and quality in the ad exchange ecosystem and indirectly hurts legitimate publishers at the expense of fly-by-night scammers.[20] On the DSP side, the lack of transparency also prevents exchanges from finding fraud. When companies sell inventory to Google's DSP or ad network, they receive a monthly report of "clawbacks" based on fraud. These clawbacks are for sites Google has determined, in its own judgment, were against policies in some way. The clawback report fails to disclose which actual sites were found to be in violation! There is no way for non-Google exchanges to use this information to improve their quality and remove bad content; they just lose money every month and indirectly subsidize the bad guys.

It's not just Google but also some mainstream publishers themselves who undermine their own business interests to profit in the short term. According to an investigation by advertising analytics company Adalytics, *Forbes* was running a parallel, shadow website, chock full of ads, that was intentionally designed to not be easily found by casual web consumers. Instead of the standard www.forbes.com site, a special site, www3.forbes.com (notice the 3), would only be viewed by consumers who clicked on a traffic-generating ad and would then be overwhelmed with low-quality experiences like slideshows filled with ads.[21] Advertisers, meanwhile, thought they were buying the normal *Forbes* experience, but their ads were showing in a significantly downgraded environment. They were certainly not the only offender, as many other brand-name media companies quietly stopped the practice once *Forbes* was outed.

One of the side effects of the growth of ad exchanges and programmatic buying was "ad creep." This was described by a publisher executive as "increasing revenue by playing the volume game."[22] Once the market for ads became liquid and buyers used algorithms in their DSP to target ads based on cookies, a publisher could almost instantly make more money by just adding another ad slot to the page. The new ad slot would attract the same cookie-driven campaigns as the existing slot. Of course, this had long-term negative effects on the publisher's brand and user experience. Advertisers, too, might see diminishing outcomes from the ads placed in a cluttered environment. This is another example of the collective action problem, or prisoner's dilemma. In digital advertising, being the "good" publisher that limited the number of ads on its pages would not necessarily make more money.

One way the ad industry tried to control the proliferation of ads was through the adoption of "viewability" as a measurement standard. Led by the IAB and other trade groups, the concept was to measure whether the ad was not just *served* to the page but also *visible to the user* on the page. First adopted in 2014, this movement would attempt to reduce ad creep and rationalize the value of high-quality web ads against tiny banners at the bottom of scrolling web pages.[23]

Google, as the largest source of traffic for many websites, has an outsize influence as well. Not only can Google choose how to monetize ads on a publisher's site, but they can also change their search algorithm to punish cluttered sites, which they have done multiple times through the years.[24]

These quality issues prompted the emergence of third-party "verifiers" like Integral Ad Science and DoubleVerify, both now large publicly traded companies. These companies got their start by promising brands and agencies they would monitor where their ads showed and prevent them from appearing next to bad content, like pornography or violence. Now they measure viewability, brand safety, fraud, and other factors.

Off the bat, the verifiers rubbed many the wrong way, using tactics like sending chief marketing officers screenshots of their ads next to porn and thrusting their agencies into crisis mode. Over time the companies have matured, but the criticisms have not necessarily eased. Since the use of verifiers is ubiquitous among large advertisers, their data on which sites and content are "brand safe" can have a huge impact. These companies have been accused of systematically rerouting advertising dollars away from quality journalism, especially during the COVID crisis, when some advertisers wished to avoid showing ads on "hard news."[25] They have also been criticized for missing actual pornography on some sites[26] and mischaracterizing innocent content as unsafe. Even *TIME* magazine's Person of the Year profile of none other than Taylor Swift was incorrectly marked as "unsafe" because the article included phrases like "she fights for women's rights."[27] The verification software that acts as the ultimate judge of content is so unsophisticated it cannot distinguish between "fighting" involving violence versus pushing for social change.

Putting the problems of fraud and spammy content into context, we might see it as another facet of the Rosenblatt problem, that the web is an infinite ocean of content. An individual publisher trying to capture advertising dollars is often like the builder of a sandcastle fighting an inbound tide. The value of the content can be like sand escaping between your fingers.

CHAPTER 15

GOOGLE'S VERSION OF THE WEB

The phrase "pivot to video" has become a joke,
shorthand for a media company's last-ditch effort
to turn things around before the layoffs begin.[1]

—Nieman Lab

While many traditional publishers jumped into the nascent web publishing world in the 1990s as an experiment, the sustained growth of consumer usage became the impetus to build real businesses around the emerging medium. Consumer behavior did not stand still, and as technology progressed, media consumption did as well. Just as web adoption eclipsed print, the dual trends of streaming video and smartphones would challenge the assumptions underlying the web. Google would be joined by rivals Facebook, Apple, and others in trying to capture consumer attention—and advertising dollars—in these emerging media.

The big tech companies would drag along traditional media companies from both print and broadcast video into these new arenas, with decidedly mixed results. In particular, the advertising revenue media companies rely upon would be significantly challenged as consumers enjoyed their content on different types of screens in different environments.

American households crossed the key threshold of 50% on broadband in the late 2000s, and that opened the door to richer websites, ads, and experiences. Combined with the ubiquity of the Adobe Flash player and its support of streaming video starting in the aughts, many advertisers and publishers began investing in video as a viable form of digital media, rather than a tiny thumbnail-sized player based on the antiquated Real Player technology.

The first publishers to begin making money on video content were traditional broadcasters, like CBS, that had both the content and the advertisers willing to pay for it. Video ads could command far higher pricing than banner ads and, in a repeated mantra, could offer advertisers the "sight, sound, and motion" needed to build brands.

Where ad dollars go, ad networks and technology companies follow. Companies like BrightRoll, Tremor, Adapt.tv, and others entered the business of powering and selling ads on publisher video inventory. It also became quite lucrative to have video to sell, leading to a proliferation of low quality, often pirated video content across the web.

In October 2006 Google jumped into this emerging web streaming area with both feet by acquiring YouTube for $1.65 billion. YouTube at the time only had sixty-five employees and operated out of a tiny office in San Bruno, near the San Francisco airport, but the site had grown to over one hundred million videos and an estimated 45% of all online video viewership.[2] The video site was hemorrhaging money as bandwidth bills for all that viewership came due each month. It was also under threat by content rights holders for copyright violations. Shortly before the acquisition, YouTube had settled a dispute with NBC over unauthorized uploads and then started promoting clips from the broadcaster—an early illustration of the push and pull that the site would have with media companies.[3]

Despite the headwinds, YouTube had caught lightning in the bottle and was growing at an astronomical rate. Google had been trying to create its own competitive product, Google Video, but it failed to take off, ironically because they took pains to review every uploaded clip before setting it live instead of throwing caution to the wind like YouTube.[4]

Copyright infringement on YouTube was rampant, and rights holders were growing restless as the viewership dwarfed what they were achieving on their own sites. In 2007 Viacom filed a billion-dollar lawsuit against YouTube claiming over 150,000 clips from their library had been illegally uploaded without license or compensation.[5] Under the Digital Millennium Copyright Act, sites like YouTube are obligated to respond to requests for content removal, which YouTube did. However, Viacom's suit alleged there was "willful blindness" to the abuses on the site and that YouTube was a "repeat offender."[6]

At the root of the tension between publishers and YouTube was not just copyright violations but also money. Publishers make money on YouTube but not as much as they do on their own sites. On YouTube, Google tightly controls the monetization and shares a portion of the revenue. YouTube was an early innovator in creating ads that balanced the user experience with monetization; adding the "Skip" button to many ads reduced the annoyance factor but also lowered prices significantly. While YouTube has more aggregate demand from the Google ad network and DSP than pretty much any other media property, it also spreads that demand across billions of videos ranging from premier content from major broadcasters to kids' videos created by solo entrepreneurs. The end result is less revenue per view. Google also preferences YouTube in search results, driving traffic to their own site over others, even for the same content.[7]

Around the same time the Viacom lawsuit was filed, there was a flurry of activity among broadcasters and technology companies to help control and monetize web video. The broadcasters and studios had seen what happened to the record labels when Napster almost wiped them out. They were determined to proactively bring their content to consumers in a paid manner, rather than stick their heads in the sand and hope the digital world would go away.

Hulu, a joint venture between NBC and News Corp, was formed in 2007, with Disney later joining, in the hope of creating a premium, licensed video portal to compete with YouTube.[8] Joost, an ambitious start-up founded by the team behind Skype, built a video viewing app that was "peer-to-peer," which meant it used less bandwidth than centralized websites like Hulu or YouTube. Almost at the exact time they were suing YouTube, Viacom invested in Joost and licensed its content, also in the hope of building a sustainable and revenue-generating video experience for consumers.[9]

The year 2007 also saw the debut of the biggest technological threat to Google's hold on web video, the advertising technology company FreeWheel. The company's cofounder Doug Knopper was the general manager for much of the ad serving business at DoubleClick prior to the acquisition by Hellman & Friedman. Along with fellow DoubleClick alumni Jon Heller and Dianne Yu, the team identified a major problem with the emerging video space. The traditional ad servers, like Google's, were fundamentally ill-suited to match the business practices of broadcasters. Ad servers meant for web banners assumed that every ad call was atomic and could be chosen on its own, without regard for what might show on the next page or even ad slots on the same page. In a broadcast environment, each commercial break might have up to five ad slots, and they needed to be selected carefully to avoid duplicates from the same advertiser, competitors adjacent to one another, differing ad lengths, and many other aspects specific to this "linear" environment. Broadcasters also had complex business relationships with their distribution partners. Cable companies like Comcast negotiated with programmers to retain two minutes of ad space every hour for their own sales teams. The ad server would need to allocate ad inventory between the parties in the digital video realm as well, even if the exact deal terms might differ.

FreeWheel was rapidly adopted among traditional broadcasters, at the expense of Google's video ad serving option.[10] Despite its growing popularity, the FreeWheel technology did not solve the problem of generating revenue on YouTube, since Google would not allow publishers to use their own ad servers on their channels on the site. Google even made a not-so-serious attempt to acquire FreeWheel for $95 million but after a quick rejection did not pursue at a higher price.[11]

This situation loosened up as Google became more anxious about growing the content of the site beyond the stereotypical "dogs on skateboards." The company hired a team to work directly with content owners and encourage them to license their quality material. Companies like NBC and Turner were willing to play ball, but they needed to control their monetization. In the face of potential competition from Hulu and others, the YouTube team blinked and allowed FreeWheel to serve ads on their site for these premium broadcasters. It would not last.

In 2014, after a series of rulings and appeals, Viacom and Google came to a settlement of their long-running suit.[12] While it was not disclosed at the time, part of the settlement required Viacom to move off of FreeWheel on to the Google ad server.[13] FreeWheel was thriving but also saw that the video market was going to be a brutal battle between enormous media firms looking to control the future of television. Perhaps with this in mind, they made the decision to sell out to one of the world's largest traditional media companies, Comcast, for $360 million.[14] Comcast was not going to let Google do to TV what it had done to the web—they wanted to do it themselves! With NBC as the "anchor tenant" and the FreeWheel system allowing most of the major broadcasters to interoperate, this seemed like a viable ambition.

By 2018 FreeWheel under Comcast was firing on all cylinders. They had won Viacom back from Google on the merits of their product and had locked up the ad serving for most of the market for premium video. Two things would put a damper on the vision, however: GDPR and Disney.

GDPR, the General Data Protection Regulation, is a broad set of privacy requirements put in place by the European Union. The regulation particularly impacted digital advertising since it required specificity about the data collected by every party in every transaction, along with the legal basis for doing so. These requirements represented a huge difference from the loose way companies were used to doing business in the advertising sector, where cookies and pixels were strewn about without much thought or legal protections. The lawyers at YouTube looked at their processes for serving ads and sharing data and decided the relationship with FreeWheel could no longer be supported. They decided, unilaterally and without any communication to the team at Comcast, to send out letters to all customers saying they would have to switch ad servers to Google's to continue serving ads on YouTube. Left without any recourse, Comcast brought this issue to the attention of Congress and European antitrust authorities.[15]

The second blow to Comcast's ambitions came from its archrival, Disney. While the two companies compete against each other on a wide number of fronts, they had peacefully coexisted within the FreeWheel ecosystem. That ended when the House of the Mouse swapped to the Google ad server, delivering a critical blow to the anti-Google coalition.[16] While Disney claimed this move was made for technical reasons, it was widely perceived as part of a complex chess game, possibly involving the acquisition of Fox.[17] The Google ad server turned out to just be a way station, as Disney built its own ad server a couple of years later.

It was not until 2022, with YouTube already dominant in streaming television, that FreeWheel was allowed back in for ad serving.[18] For four years, broadcasters and other video publishers lost control over their ability to monetize their content on their largest distribution partner. It is not even clear if Google did any of this out of malice; it seems more likely it was a mixture of indifference and fear of a privacy backlash. Regardless, as was usually the case, Google came out on top.

YouTube remains the top streaming destination, and the majority of its monetization comes from Google's own ad network and its DSP, which is the only way advertisers can buy ads on the site programmatically. The fact that Google's ad server is not dominant in the video market and FreeWheel continues to hold significant market share has ended up having little effect on the outcome. FreeWheel, meanwhile, remains a healthy business within Comcast but has not achieved the strategic goal of creating an independent video ecosystem out of Google's control. On the web Google's Three Pillars strategy was intended to capture the ever-broadening and fragmented set of publishers. In video, the market remains concentrated among YouTube and the large broadcasters, so exchange and network liquidity matter much less. The thing that matters the most in video is scale, and YouTube has that. In 2024 the site made up over 10% of all TV viewing in the US,[19] and in the prior year, it generated over $31 billion in revenue.

YouTube was not alone in its video vision. In 2015 Facebook issued a blog post stating, "We're increasingly seeing a shift towards visual content on Facebook, especially with video" and claiming that over the previous six months, they had averaged more than one billion video views per day.[20] Mark Zuckerberg predicted, "I wouldn't be surprised if you fast-forward five years and most of the content that people see on Facebook and are sharing on a day-to-day basis is video."[21] Along with the continued skyrocketing growth of YouTube, this was the start of a stampede toward video. There was a sense in the publishing world that video content was going to save them in a way that no amount of programmatic banner revenue ever could.

Over the next two years, there was a kind of mania among news and media organizations to create more video and reduce the focus on written work. In 2016 Mashable fired its whole news staff and would "focus on producing lots more video about 'digital culture.'"[22] Venerable media outlets like *Sports Illustrated* and the *Washington Post* would invest heavily in creating more video and publishing to YouTube and social.

It would later turn out that Facebook was massively, and disastrously, wrong. They had overestimated viewing time by up to 80%, according to a *Wall Street Journal* investigation.[23] The company settled an advertiser lawsuit for $40 million in overcharges, and the case revealed they had known about the errors for over a year.[24] The media companies that had hired studios to create short-form content for the platform were almost uniformly failures, and the phrase "pivot to video" became a gallows humor punch line among the media elite. Another chance for survival had slipped from the grasp of anxious—and arguably desperate—publishers.

The shift of consumer attention from desktop web browsing to smartphones was another area where there was uncertainty about how publishers would cope and how their destiny would be intertwined with technology. There were big adjustments to be made when creating content for smaller screens, with less bandwidth and lower tolerance for latency. The big technology companies sought to solve this problem with new, lightweight ways of presenting content to consumers. But their interest was always primarily to lock in consumers to their platforms, not necessarily to benefit publisher business models. As a result, they systematically underestimated the importance of advertising and monetization in their solutions, leading to a series of failures.

First out of the gate was Facebook Instant Articles. This was a new format for publishers to create web pages rendered to look native to the Facebook app. In their blog post announcing the initiative, they claimed that normal news articles could take an average of up to eight seconds to load. Publishers on board included the *New York Times*, *National Geographic*, BuzzFeed, and others.[25] While Facebook did not demand a revenue share on ads within their format, they sharply limited the load and did not permit any ads "above the fold," where a user would see them right away. The format also did not support header bidding or other more advanced monetization techniques.

Not surprisingly, the Instant Articles did not monetize well and lost favor with publishers.[26] In a *Digiday* piece in 2017, an anonymous publishing exec summed it up: "It is not Facebook's job to fix publishers' broken business models . . . the fact that anyone even contemplated it indicates the desperation with which ad-supported publishers will jump on new revenue opportunities."[27]

The relative merits or problems with Instant Articles was also a bit of a sideshow compared to the much greater impact Facebook's algorithm changes would have on publishers. In early 2018 the social app made a major overhaul to its news feed algorithm to emphasize articles and content from friends and family and de-emphasize news and viral content. Facebook knew this change would have a broadly negative impact on traffic to news sites, with the worst impact to sites like BuzzFeed and *The Huffington Post* that had learned how to get attention on social media. While Facebook has made other changes to the algorithm intended to help news publishers, the net result has been continued and painful declines in traffic. In 2024 some estimates showed traffic from the social network down 50%.[28]

A couple of months after Instant Articles launched, Apple debuted its News app. News would ingest and format publisher content and make it available to consumers in an app available across all Apple devices. Like Facebook's format, Apple restricted ad load and capabilities significantly and did not allow cookies or other identity data to be used. While Apple News does support a robust subscription capability, which in some cases makes publishers meaningful revenue,[29] ad monetization is consistently poor.

Following its rivals, Google jumped in later that same year with their typical strategy of being technology first. Instead of a reader app, like Apple, they designed an open-source technical specification, Accelerated Mobile Pages, or AMP. AMP was designed to "dramatically improve the performance of the mobile web."[30] From the start Google gave AMP pages advantages in search results, showing a "Top Stories" carousel featuring content in the new format.[31] In 2018, when Google launched a dedicated news app, AMP support was a requirement for publisher content to be shown and was also required to be featured on the Google News web experience.

Publishers did not find great success with AMP. The pages did not monetize as well, and the benefits of traffic acquisition were questionable.[32] When it launched, AMP did not support header bidding, and it has been alleged that Google intentionally slowed down non-AMP pages and ads to benefit its own monetization.[33] Whether through malfeasance or just the nature of the specification, AMP pages just did not produce as much ad revenue as typical mobile web pages. AMP also brought regulatory scrutiny, as it appeared to be a way to gain control over the entirety of the mobile web. "There is a sense in which AMP is a Google-built version of the web," said Joshua Benton, director of the Nieman Journalism Lab, as quoted in *Politico*.[34]

AMP grew in adoption in the second half of the 2010s alongside the steep growth of the mobile web, but as publishers and technologies grew more skilled in this environment, the utility diminished. In 2021 Google News removed the requirement for content in their app to use the AMP format.[35] In the early 2020s, Twitter, DuckDuckGo, and other platforms ceased support, and publishers like Vox and BuzzFeed publicly disavowed the format, claiming their own webpages were 30% faster and monetized better.[36]

Ultimately, none of the attempts from the tech giants to speed up and standardize the mobile web would halt the inexorable decline in viewership, as consumers moved to mobile apps and social media. By trying to standardize and improve the user experience, the big tech companies found publishers unwilling to sacrifice ad revenue and suspicious of the control they would give up to companies who quite naturally put their own interests first.

––––––––––

The efforts from the tech giants to create mobile formats were all inexorably linked to their distribution mechanisms. Publishers need visitors to monetize through advertising, and the fragmented nature of the web has always made capturing and retaining them like fighting a receding tide. The big tech companies have played a key role in content distribution, one that has from the beginning had mixed impact on ad-supported publishers.

As soon as Google News launched in 2002, publishers worried that it would disintermediate them from their audience. A single news story would have hundreds of versions from every news outlet, flattening out each publisher's unique reporting, design, and perspective. It did, however, drive traffic to news websites, which was what those publishers ultimately wanted. This uneasy balance between having the content commoditized and generating value from the distribution would cause publishers to vacillate and produce erratic responses to the product over the years.

European publishers sued Google multiple times for copyright infringement, believing that the snippets or initial paragraphs of their content were being used improperly. Rupert Murdoch testified in front of the US Congress, calling news aggregation "theft."[37] Despite the fact that Google, and later Facebook, was distributing content for free and driving traffic to their websites—also for free—the "big tech" companies were blamed for the overall decline in the media businesses. An editorial in the Canadian *National Post* railing against the companies was typical red meat: "Facebook and Google are true monopolies destroying a public good, not the water or air this time, but our democracy."[38]

The weapon publishers used to exact some measure of control was politics. The tactic was a "link tax." Since the invention of the World Wide Web, linking from one page to another has been the connective tissue. There has never been permission required, or payments required, from the linker to the "linkee." Just the idea of charging to get linked seems absurd on its face. Nevertheless, publishers and their lobbyists have successfully imposed these laws.

In the European Union, the EU Copyright Directive required Google to build licensing arrangements with over fifteen hundred publications.[39]

Australia passed a law in 2021 requiring payments to publishers for links, which prompted Facebook to cut back any promotion of news on their apps.[40] In 2023 Canada passed its Online News Act with a similar link tax requirement. Facebook promptly shut off all news in Canada,[41] and Google soon after threatened to do the same.[42]

Tech industry pundit Benedict Evans has railed eloquently against the absurdity of link taxes but summed it up best in a LinkedIn post asking, "Is it really so hard to admit you want a subsidy and make an honest argument for that?"[43] Given the dire situation among publishers, it is not entirely hard to understand this approach.

CHAPTER 16

ACTS OF GOD

Nothing has such high switching costs . . .
takes an act of God to do it.

—David Rosenblatt

N ews Corp and its nonagenarian chairman Rupert Murdoch had a long and uncomfortable relationship with Google across many fronts. Murdoch frequently peppered his speeches with accusations that Google used his content without proper licensed rights. He used his tabloids to highlight scandalous revelations ("Big Brands Fund Terror" read a headline from the *Times of London*[1]). He pushed legislation demanding direct payments to publishers and later accused the search giant of anti-conservative bias.[2]

Murdoch and his senior leadership team were looking for counterweights to Google's hegemony in news and media. One potential pawn in his game was AppNexus. In 2016 News Corp made a $10 million strategic investment in the Google rival.[3] The press release announcing the investment tiptoed the line on details, coming up short on a major commitment by News Corp to the AppNexus product, and instead indicated a weaker statement that "AppNexus products would be made available to News Corp."[4]

AppNexus was clearly positioning itself as the independent alternative to Google. Through product innovation and acquisitions, Brian and Michael had been steadily building a Google alternative for almost a decade and AppNexus had become the platform of choice of the company's enemies worldwide. By the mid-2010s, AppNexus had representatives of Microsoft, News Corp, and WPP on its board. The deal with WPP partially reversed Sir Martin's post-DoubleClick strategic bet and spun out the 24/7 ad server to AppNexus in the hope it could gain momentum as part of a company dedicated to technology.[5]

It proved more difficult to move ad servers than anyone might have thought. The team in charge of ad revenue at News Corp's New York headquarters was asked to review whether they could move some or all their operations off Google's ad server and onto AppNexus's. Project Cinderella was the internal code name for the project and was run by Chris Gunther, the SVP of the company, reporting directly to Robert Thompson, the chief executive of News Corp.

After a couple of combat tours in the Wrapper Wars, Steph Layser had returned to corporate life, running much of yield and ad operations at News Corp. She had started her career at the *New York Post* and now was returning to the company in a more senior role. She was put in charge of the technical analysis of Cinderella.

Steph's goal in the Cinderella analysis seemed achievable. She wanted to quantify the amount of revenue at risk if they were to change ad servers. There were effectively two parts to the analysis. First, there was the type of analysis anyone might do when considering a switch of software vendors. Would the new vendor be able to support the same activities and outcomes the sales team had grown used to and relied upon for revenue? While Google's ad server was arguably the most full-featured product available, AppNexus had acquired the ad server assets of 24/7 Real Media and had also completed an acquisition of YieldX, a specialist data company for publishers. The technical comparison was close overall.

The second risk, though, was much harder to quantify. The problem was that switching off the DoubleClick ad server also meant switching off AdX, and switching off AdX also meant losing all the demand from the Google ad network. The network, with its millions of advertisers, was not allowed to bid on any other exchanges in real time; it would only provide a rudimentary true or false bid, as was common in the preheader bidding days. It was a safe assumption that all the other demand on AdX, other than the ad network, could be recouped by working with the myriad of other ad exchanges, but the Google ad network demand was special.

Steph knew how to do this analysis, but to really get to the heart of the matter of how much demand she might lose, she needed log files.

Log files are digital advertising's ultimate source of truth. When an ad is bought, sold, bid on, displayed, or really does anything at all, a text record—a log—is recorded with all the details. As a customer of a given advertising system (say, an ad server), you could rely entirely on the fancy graphs and charts you see in the vendor's user interface, or you could go deeper and look at the raw data in the log files. Logs are not for everyone; you need a minimum level of technical sophistication and know-how to get useful insights from millions (or billions!) of rows of data. If you want to operate in digital advertising at the highest level, though, logs are a requirement.

As the largest advertising technology company in the market, Google certainly was no stranger to log files and had established processes for aggregating and distributing them to customers. Over time, though, there were changes to which data points the logs should contain and where to draw a line for reasons of consumer privacy, competitive advantage, or contractual obligation. Logs provided before the Google acquisition of DoubleClick, for example, all contained the raw DoubleClick ID, which could allow an enterprising customer to combine logs from multiple customers to help them cooperate on reaching certain consumers or enhancing their data profiles. These techniques raised privacy questions, since the same users could be tracked across websites and had not necessarily consented to this kind of data use. Visiting a medical website might mean one thing, but when combined with data showing a visit to a life insurance website, this might imply something much more personal. The Double-Click ID was hashed—making cross-customer use impossible—shortly after the company was acquired.

What about when Google's own conflicts of interest get in the way of raw data delivery? A log from the ad server might tell you what ads you sold and to whom and for what prices. A separate log from your ad exchange might tell you what bids were present for a given auction and who won at what price. If you combine the two, you might be able to infer when and where the ad exchange was able to win and at what prices. This data could then be used to audit the ad exchange and better understand how they were taking fees, which in the case of Google was a highly nontransparent process they were not interested in sharing.

Google refused to provide Steph and News Corp with detailed logs showing the amount that AdX was bidding and winning against their inventory or the identity of the advertisers doing the bidding. Steph's requests for more detailed logs were rebuffed time and time again by her Google account team. She wanted to figure out how much of her ad exchange revenue was coming from the ad network versus other buyers so she could evaluate the risk of switching ad servers.

The logs status quo was pretty much useless. Google would provide separate logs for ad serving and AdX, but the most important data was missing. In particular, the bids from the ad network were missing from the ad exchange logs. This struck Steph as absurd—Google was bidding into her account; she should have the right to know what the bids were and who they came from. Google insisted that they could not provide the data due to "advertiser privacy," which was also absurd since the publisher certainly had the right to see who was bidding on their inventory. The reality was they did not want Steph or anyone else to see under the covers. With full log transparency, Steph might learn about the multiple bids from the network, the non-20% bid reductions of Bernanke, or the fact that the majority of the value of AdX was from the ad network rather than DSPs and other bidders.[6] This type of data was critical to the Cinderella project.

Steph was confronted with two uncomfortable facts. Removing the ad server would certainly hurt AdX revenue, and Google policies prevented her from getting enough data to estimate by how much. The AppNexus ad server was $500,000 cheaper than Google. AppNexus's open exchange rate was only 5.7%, compared to Google's 20%. But News Corp generated $83 million in programmatic revenue, and 53% of that was from AdX. The risk to that $44 or so million vastly exceeded savings on technology fees.[7] She simply could not guarantee to the senior executives at her company that they were not going to lose significant money if they switched. Cinderella did not get her glass slipper, and the transition to AppNexus—despite the $10 million investment—would not happen.

The internal News Corp summary of the analysis, after recommending they stay on Google's stack, prophetically states, "AppNexus is the only real alternative to the Google publisher product suite, offering a partial hedge on Google's power and influence; the only other real hedge is government intervention."[8]

———————————

In 2019 Richard Caccappolo, the chief operating officer of DMG Media, asked Matthew Wheatland to build a business case for getting off the Google ad server. Matthew had gotten into the advertising industry a decade earlier, and somewhat unexpectedly, when as a young economics graduate in London a recruiter convinced him there were interesting problems to solve in the sector. He was fascinated by all the data available and the ability to make money by manipulating the priorities and timing of ads on websites.

The relationship between DMG and Google had been slowly deteriorating. In 2016 a product change to the rules relating to mobile apps selling through AdX had a disproportionate negative impact on DMG's revenue, and their complaints were arrogantly rebuffed by the Google product managers. There were suspicions that Google was manipulating search results in ways that would punish Mail properties, though these were never proven. The team was also keenly involved with header bidding and Google's frosty—and later outright hostile—reaction to the technology.

Like Steph at News Corp, Wheatland had to confront the key issue of an ad server switch. It was not a question of whether there was a better product in the market but rather how much revenue would be in jeopardy from losing direct connection to AdX.

While under the same log constraints, Wheatland did something clever and looked at the auctions that AdX had won, then compared that to the next highest non-AdX bid from his header data. This would give him an inexact estimate of how often AdX was the only bidder for an auction, which indicates unique demand that cannot be replaced. He also was able to deduce how often the winner of the AdX auction came from an outside advertiser (a bid that could be retained after switching to another ad server) versus from Google (a bid that would likely disappear). He ultimately estimated that switching ad servers would cost them 28% of their exchange revenue[9] and that 55% of AdX impressions were being won by the ad network, meaning they would not be retained on another system.[10] Like their competitor News Corp, DMG would not be switching any time soon. Later he would bemoan the process, saying, "Publishers just want ad tech that works in their best interest."[11] Tim Wolfe, the SVP of revenue operations for newspaper company Gannett, did a similar analysis to Steph's and Matthew's. He found that the company would stand to lose 50% to 60% of its indirect revenue if it left the Google ad server. Given that indirect was 60% to 75% of his business, those numbers represented far too high a sacrifice for regaining control over yield and monetization. They had to stick with Google.[12]

The competitors to Google also felt helpless to make progress in ad serving. Advertising start-up Kevel spent over a decade trying to compete with Google's ad server before effectively giving up and moving into a different niche. CEO James Avery summed it up in an email to *AdExchanger* reporter Sarah Sluis: "Almost every ad server has gone out of business because of this integration between AdX and [the ad server], publishers may want to use another ad server, but they would end up giving up a chunk of revenue from AdX. It turns out monopolies are pretty effective. :D"[13]

Tim Cadogan's OpenX had started as an ad server company, with an open-source alternative that was used by thousands of long-tail publishers. Despite continued investment, OpenX shelved their ad server in late 2018.[14]

AOL's ad server, the Oath Ad Platform, which had been built on top of their AdTech acquisition, also could not compete and was shuttered in 2019.[15]

Even with a solid ad serving technology stack, plenty of cash, an integrated ad exchange, and a reputation for innovation, AppNexus was only able to make small inroads with publishers. In Europe, where many publishers had very strong opinions about Google's dominance, AppNexus was able to rack up some wins for its ad server. German publishing giant Axel Springer switched to AppNexus but continued to use Google's ad server in a convoluted setup built to capture as much AdX demand as feasible.[16] Norwegian publisher Schibsted also made the plunge.[17] The Europeans could only take this chance because of the relative weakness of the Google ad network in Europe. While Google was a major player in display advertising in the US, it was not nearly as large in other regions where local networks and telecom companies played a larger role.

AppNexus never won an ad serving customer in the US market. Michael Rubenstein remarked about the fight to win ad server deals from Google, "Their advantages were overwhelming."[18]

While DoubleClick's ad server had been dominant before the Google acquisition, at an estimated 60% market share, the combination with AdX and the ad network made it the only game in town; it grew to occupy over 90% share in the US and a slightly lower share in Europe.

CHAPTER 17

ARPU

The end of an era.[1]

—Ryan Joe

A recurring tragedy in the fight to control digital advertising is the failed efforts of telecom companies to build successful businesses and act as viable counterweights to the tech giants. Billions—if not tens of billions—of dollars have been spent acquiring and building advertising divisions within both legacy voice and cable television conglomerates with nothing but pain and loss as the result.

The first wave of involvement from telecom companies was based around the thesis that the consumer data going over their pipes could be used to enhance the value of publisher inventory through better targeting. Instead of relying on a cookie, which could be deleted or blocked at any time, the telecom operators could append data at the network layer, potentially on every internet request that went through their infrastructure. While this might sound at first like a good idea, it quickly runs into concerns about privacy. Verizon learned this the hard way when it was pilloried for its practice of adding a "super cookie" to the traffic on its network, leading to an FCC fine and lots of embarrassing PR.[2]

Verizon was not the only one to stub its toe. Singapore-based SingTel acquired advertising assets for upward of $600 million, only to divest for $239 million.[3] Even telecom equipment manufacturer Ericsson made a play with its eModo group, which it later shuttered.[4]

The growth of video consumption changed the attitude of telecoms to content and advertising opportunities. The goal was not simply to leverage subscriber data behind the scenes but to engage with the end users and offer them content and pricing bundles that would grow the Average Revenue Per User, or ARPU. The thesis went, if the consumer is buying a cell phone package, why not upsell them with a subscription to HBO or give them an app that displays content from *The Huffington Post*? That was the theory, at least.

The first move came from Verizon, separately from their earlier privacy episode. In May 2015 Verizon announced that it would be acquiring Tim Armstrong's AOL for $4.4 billion. The press release claimed the acquisition "further drives [our] LTE wireless video and OTT (over-the-top video) strategy,"[5] which is a pretty vague endorsement of the synergies of AOL's business. While certainly experiencing headwinds from Google's growth and the long-term move away from the "portal" businesses, AOL was able to retain strength as an advertising technology player, with the strong foundation of the Advertising.com ad network. Despite the telecom speak, the press release did put advertising front and center: "AOL is a leader in the digital content and advertising platforms space, and the combination of Verizon and AOL creates a scaled, mobile-first platform offering directly targeted at what eMarketer estimates is a nearly $600 billion global advertising industry."[6]

Verizon followed-up on AOL by acquiring Marissa Mayer's Yahoo in 2016 and combining the companies into a new company called Oath.[7] The acquisition price of $4.83 billion was a giant step down in valuation for the former leader. The company had turned down Microsoft's offer of $44 billion in 2008 and as a public company had a peak valuation of approximately $125 billion. Unlike AOL, Yahoo continued to lag in advertising monetization off its portal, while efforts to stem the tide of consumers were hardly effective.

The Oath name was abandoned in favor of Verizon Media, but that was not enough to make the division fit within the telecom environment. Tim Armstrong departed in 2018, and it was reported by the *Wall Street Journal* that one factor was the telecom's unwillingness to give its subscriber data to the division.[8] The combination of AOL and Yahoo certainly could have pulled off a Three Pillars–type strategy, but declining O & O audiences, corporate politics, and just a general problem executing would make it impossible. Despite the belief in synergies, the fact was that the core telecom ARPU was so much larger than the potential from the advertising business that it made little sense to continue investing in an area dominated by Google, Facebook, and other tech giants. The combined AOL-Yahoo was then purchased by private equity firm Apollo for $5 billion, a fraction of the market capitalization of all the companies that combined to form that entity.[9]

Brian Lesser's career had taken off alongside the growth in programmatic media. Since his first entry into the business as part of the 24/7 Real Media acquisition by WPP, Brian had a string of successes, most notably the development and leadership of the Xaxis trading group. He springboarded from Xaxis to a role as CEO of the Americas at GroupM, one of the most powerful positions in the agency world. When a recruiter called about a position at AT&T, he was skeptical. The recruiter pressed on and offered him the opportunity to fly to Dallas for one day and spend time with the telecom CEO Randall Stephenson. Brian was game.

Randall laid out a huge vision for AT&T, including content, advertising, and more. The company had already announced the acquisition of Time Warner, one of the largest media and content companies in the world. When this was combined with their subscriber relationships and the ongoing trend of consumers purchasing streaming services, the whole strategy made sense.

Brian joined and became the CEO of AT&T Advertising & Analytics. He knew that one of his first moves was going to be to acquire an advertising technology company. The company would have premium content and audiences from HBO, CNN, and the rest of Time Warner's properties. It would have the paid subscription user base and telecom data to power advanced targeting. It needed a powerful platform to execute the vision.

Brian had served on the board of AppNexus since the WPP investment in that company, but when he changed jobs, he relinquished the seat back to the holding company. Despite his closeness with AppNexus, one of his first moves at AT&T was to look at a different company as a potential acquisition, The Trade Desk.

The Trade Desk was a company filled with surprises. It was a DSP that was founded years after all the other major competitors had already staked out their places in the market. Unlike many other similar companies, it eschewed any acquisitions and only grew organically. When other DSPs were trying to go direct and sell to marketers, The Trade Desk made very clear its allegiances and sold only to agencies. The strategies had worked, and now the company was publicly traded with a multibillion-dollar valuation, while early pioneers, like Joe Zawadski's MediaMath, were struggling.

Jeff Green, the company founder, was an early pioneer of ad exchanges, serving as the COO of AdECN through its acquisition by Microsoft. He also had run the exchange at Microsoft prior to the reins being handed over to AppNexus. It had only been a year or so since Jeff took his company public, and he was willing to hear what AT&T had to offer. After a meeting at the Rosewood Mansion on Turtle Creek hotel in Dallas, Project Rosewood was born and The Trade Desk was in play.

Unfortunately, the Time Warner acquisition was getting delayed by politics. Time Warner owned CNN, and President Trump was not a big fan of that channel.[10] As a result, a lot of time passed where Brian was stuck, unable to complete a deal to build the advertising platform the company needed to execute its strategy for fear of getting swept into the regulatory drama. When Time Warner was approved in June 2018, The Trade Desk's stock price had skyrocketed out of reach and its market capitalization had soared into the tens of billions. Rosewood was dead, and Brian needed a backup plan.

Brian made a call to Jon Hsu, the CFO of AppNexus. John was from 24/7, and the two had worked together closely before he left to join O'Kelley's company in anticipation of an eventual IPO. Growth was tepid at AppNexus, and competition with Jeff at The Trade Desk was brutal. A deal was made, and AppNexus joined AT&T for a reported $1.6 billion.[11] It would later be renamed Xandr, as a tribute to Alexander Graham Bell.

Neither Brian was happy. For Lesser, it was an "imperfect fit." AT&T's strategy would heavily focus on video advertising for brand advertisers, areas that were not strengths of the more data-driven and programmatic AppNexus. For O'Kelley, it was a lot of money but not the "win" it rightfully should have been. The effort to vanquish Google in ad serving was a bust. The DSP trailed competitors. Public companies like Magnite and The Trade Desk had significantly higher valuations than his company had achieved at exit. It did not surprise anyone when O'Kelley left the company a couple months later after disagreements with Lesser. *AdExchanger*'s Ryan Joe called it "the end of an era."[12]

Lesser was not able to overcome the telecom curse. He left in 2020 after his boss, Randall Stephenson, announced his retirement. Under the face of the debt it piled up buying its media assets, the company pivoted away from the strategy entirely, selling Time Warner a year later.

In an unlikely epilogue, Microsoft acquired Xandr (the former AppNexus) in 2021 for a substantially lower sum than AT&T had paid.[13] The company continues to be an important player in the digital advertising space but nowhere near as influential as it was at its peak, when it was widely considered a counterweight to Google's dominance. Now it is more or less the house band for Microsoft's various advertising sideshows.

Even some of the largest companies in the world, with tens or hundreds of millions of paying customers, could not build a counterweight to Google in the advertising space. Politics, mismanagement, and culture generally played a huge role in the failure of telecoms to make a dent, while the opposite values continued to make Google thrive.

CHAPTER 18

IRRATIONALLY HIGH RENTS

We need to up our game and focus on winning this game vs. continuing to extract irrationally high rent from the AdX.[1]

—Pappu Aparna

W hile Google exploited the advantages present when operating on both sides of the advertising market, there was not always consensus inside the company about these activities. Competing factions of product managers, engineers, and executives did not always see eye to eye on which "side" of the business should benefit and which should sacrifice for the greater good. The most contentious issue was the exclusive tie between the demand from the ad network and the supply within AdX. This tie was at the heart of the Three Pillars strategy, a big part of the original rationale for the $3.1 billion purchase of DoubleClick, and the key way publishers were locked in.

From the perspective of the ad network team, they were being rooked. The advertising customers of Google Ads (the ad network) do not necessarily care whether they buy ads on AdX, on the ad serving publishers, or somewhere else. They just want performance, wherever it can be found.

When you log in to Google Ads as an advertiser, you see options for optimizing your campaign to outcomes like clicks, conversions, phone calls, or store visits. The advertisers pay on these outcomes, not on the bulk volume of ads shown to consumers. Suppose an advertiser sells clothing online and they know they can afford to pay $1 per click for every visitor to their site, based on the historical average of how visitors turn into customers. The advertiser can set a target price of $1 per click in Google Ads. The ad network then has to do some very complex calculations on each ad impression to figure out the expected value—and therefore the bid price—that would make Ads its desired 14% margin, while also averaging a click price under $1. To use a simple example, if Ads predicts a single ad impression ad will have a 1% click rate, then it will be willing to bid $0.0086 on the impression ($1.00 per click * 0.01 click rate * 0.86 take rate).

In this way, the performance risk is shifted from the advertisers to Google, which then must pay publishers whether the ads performed or not. This trade-off of risk away from both publishers and advertisers and toward Google is what makes the ad network model work and justifies its margins. As long as the data, algorithms, creatives, and other ingredients to the ad network stew create great flavor, everyone wins.

The ad network team wanted to bid on other exchanges, and they had evidence that doing so would increase their profit and advertiser results. As early as 2012, an internal strategy memo bemoaned the network "is competitively disadvantaged against buy-side competition."[2] This memo explained the situation plainly (GDN refers to the ad network): "In the auction ecosystem, we appear to be running a buyside-subsidizes-sellside model: we are artificially handicapping our buyside (GDN) to boost the attractiveness of our sellside (AdX). Specifically, we have chosen to limit GDN to buying only on AdX, an exclusivity that makes AdX more attractive to sellers."[3]

The network further subsidized AdX with the double bidding, which raised clearing prices, and by letting AdX take a generous 20% of the bid as a fee. If the network were to bid on other exchanges, they would get more inventory, be able to clear it at lower prices, and potentially enjoy higher take rates.

The awkwardly named AWBid was the project to allow AdWords (AW) to bid on other exchanges. While it was clear from the get-go that this project was for the benefit of advertisers and the ad network, even the earliest discussions of the project tellingly focused on the impact to the sell-side business. AdX was growing quickly, but its position in the market remained unstable. In the fierce competitive period before the AdMeld acquisition, the ad network demand was one of the only unique selling propositions for AdX. Even much later, the analysis by News Corp, Gannett, and DMG would show a huge dependence on ad network demand to prop up the exchange. An AWBid memo paints a worst-case scenario: "Given the current market position of AdX versus other Yield Managers, if publishers can get the same AdWords RTB demand from any yield management/exchange partner, we expect many publishers would terminate their AdX relationship in favor of their preferred alternate vendor."[4]

The ad network was critical to maintaining the leadership and profitability of AdX, regardless of whether it benefited the advertiser customers of that product. In a 2014 study, Google estimated that AdX would lose 70% of its revenue if the ad network stopped bidding.[5]

A big part of the conversation around AWBid was the amount charged by AdX when the ad network bid into the exchange. AdX had maintained a strict 20% rate on its exchange and charged the ad network the same amount. In fact, the ad network subsidized AdX by agreeing to this 20% fee, which was much higher than the one when buying on AdSense. Inside Google there were many discussions acknowledging that the 20% AdX take rate was too high and unjustified.

One big hurdle to AWBid's expansion was the quality of the supply from third-party exchanges. Google's internal quality controls were highly dependent on having its tags on the publisher pages so they could run all kinds of forensics to determine whether the user was likely a human versus a bot, and whether the ads in question were actually visible to the consumer. AWBid had a much more limited view into the ads being purchased since it was operating through a third-party exchange and early testing was plagued with quality problems like fake clicks and non-human visitors.

AWBid took years to launch and finally went online in 2015. It was restricted to only a couple of third-party exchanges, who were bound by strict nondisclosure agreements lest they use this as a talking point against AdX. The bidder would be restricted to only bid on campaigns aimed at retargeting, which was significantly less than 10% of the ad network's overall business. AWBid would take the full 32% share before bidding on third-party exchanges, versus the roughly 14% it took when bidding on AdX.* This meant AWBid submitted much lower bids to the external exchanges than on AdX, further depressing results and advantaging its own exchange.

AWBid never expanded beyond retargeting and very limited volume, yet there does not appear to be any email or meeting where this was firmly decided. Rather, inertia at the company and an unwillingness among executives to solve festering political issues seem to have been enough to prevent expansion. Years after the program first launched, in 2019, the question was asked in an internal presentation "Why remarketing only?" and the answer was that the approach "greatly reduces concerns about impact to publisher business."[6] The whole multiyear episode around AWBid shows how conflicted and non-customer-centric the Google decision process had become.

One might stop and wonder whether all the effort to create and build AdX was really necessary for Google's greater goals. So much of AdX's reason for being was to allow the ad network to get access to inventory,

---

* The take rate of around 14% for the ad network and 20% for AdX are applied sequentially, not additively, netting 32%, not 34%. A bid of $1.00 less 14% is $0.86; the $0.86 bid is reduced by AdX's 20% to get to $0.69. The total take rate would average between 31% and 32% total.

but then the ad network ended up captive to the self-perpetuating rationale of maintaining and bolstering the exchange.

———————————

There was a growing school of thought within Google that AdX's
20% take rate was high and that it might not be justified outside of the
tie to the ad network. Chris LaSala was on the commercial side in the
publisher group, working on issues like new product releases and pricing.
He wrote, "The AdX sell-side fee of 20% holds today not because there
is 20% of value in comparing 2 bids to one another, but because it comes
with unique demand via AdWords that is not available any other way."[7]
He continued, "I think we are all in agreement that 'exchange functionality' is not worth 20% and value comes from sourcing demand."[8]

Chris wrote that AWBid "puts pressure on this narrative" but is not
as much of a concern because Google keeps a high margin of 32% even
when bidding on other exchanges. Jonathan Bellack agreed. In a chat to
LaSala, he stated, "I think you are right that AdX buyers at 20% is not
long term defensible."[9] Engineering Manager Pappu Aparna also chimed
in within the same chat, saying, "We need to up our game and focus on
winning this game, vs. continuing to extract irrationally high rent from
the adX [sic]."[10] In another discussion LaSala put a number on it, saying,
"My summary POV is that a sell-side rev share should probably top out
at 10%."[11]

Despite the internal thoughts and feelings that the AdX 20% fee
was too high, the commercial team in charge of discounting, which also
reported up to LaSala, held the line and rarely offered any reductions
to publishers. In 2017, across all 3,815 publishers on AdX, only 13 had
contracts for less than the standard 20% take rate and the weighted
average take rate was 19.8%, only 0.2 off the baseline.[12] How can we
reconcile the belief they were overcharging and the reality that they
enjoyed pricing power?

At this time, header bidding was gaining wide adoption and Google had not yet fully responded to the threat with Open Bidding. The result was that non-AdX exchanges were growing because they had access to premium inventory for the first time. This premium tier of inventory would eventually cause some degree of pricing pressure, as rates for private deals would not remain at 20% and negotiation was possible. On the open exchange, however, AdX's demand came from the ad network, and because that demand was unique, it did not really matter what take rate was applied, so long as publishers made more money. For the competitive demand from DSPs, Poirot had rerouted so much of the market to AdX that, again, there would be little impact from the take rate.

Because of Bernanke and DRS, the effective take rate on *competitive* auctions, where more than one bidder participated, was actually much less than 20%. The systems would make back the margin on noncompetitive auctions, keeping the average at 20%. Finally, the team seemed to miss the underlying point that DRS had proven, that many publishers were not actually very sensitive to take rates, they only cared about yield—they wanted to make more total money. Remember, AppNexus offered much lower rates than AdX to News Corp and others and yet was unable to capture volume in the face of the unique demand.

This is complex and confusing, but the net result is that the team focused on publishers knew their 20% take rate was not justified but were not fully putting together the complete picture, that through auction manipulation, Poirot, the stunting of AWBid, and the exclusive demand from the ad network, they were able to maintain that rate anyway. During the later antitrust trials, Google brought in an expert witness who calculated that the proper rate for AdX in a free market should have been closer to 16%. If that fee were in place, it would result in hundreds of millions of dollars going to media companies and journalism every year.

Reading the internal documents from Google, one gets the sense the culture in the advertising group changed in the mid-2010s. Susan Wojcicki, the longtime head of advertising and a key advocate of the display business, moved to a new role as the CEO of YouTube during this time.[13] Susan was replaced by Sridhar Ramaswamy, an engineer who had worked his way up the ranks at Google from the company's early days and was deeply steeped in the search business. Sridhar gave off a strong whiff of distaste for the display advertising business[14] and eventually the search ads business as well. When he left the company in 2020, he started an ad-free search business called Neeva and told the *New York Times*, "I needed to do something different with my life . . . I came to realize that an ad-supported model had limitations."[15]

Neal Mohan had toyed with leaving the company in 2013, when he was close to joining Twitter only to be retained with a whopping $100 million pay package.[16] In 2015 he was reported by Recode's Kara Swisher to be taking the CEO job at cloud storage company Dropbox, only for those rumors to quiet abruptly.[17] The details of how Google retained Neal this second time are not known, but it likely resulted in his internal transfer to become the chief product officer of YouTube under Susan later that year.[18] With his move, the two most senior executives looking after the display business were gone.

Neal was replaced by Paul Muret, a soft-spoken engineer who was the inventor and founder of Urchin, the precursor to Google Analytics.[19] Paul was a fairly effective executive but was not someone who cared much about publishers, journalism, or web advertising.

The directors and VPs, like Brad Bender, Scott Spencer, and Jonathan Bellack, remained in place for a couple more years, but the senior leadership was now dominated by Mountain View–based search executives with little direct experience of the display ads business and a decidedly "Googley" worldview. Some of the more aggressive missteps the company would make in the second half of the decade could be traced back to the loss of senior executives who really cared about the business they were running.

CHAPTER 19

CREEPY ADS

*To me, it's creepy when I look at something and all of a sudden
it's chasing me all the way across the web.*[1]

—Tim Cook

Apple senior executive Craig Federighi is in charge of software engineering at the company and often gives the second presentation at the company's Worldwide Developer Conference. His presentations are eagerly anticipated by the legions of app and software developers that spend their days building against Apple's specifications and environments. Midway through the keynote in 2017, Craig introduced a new concept within the Safari browser called ITP, or Intelligent Tracking Prevention. ITP would move beyond blocking third-party cookies by default and instead would actively seek out so-called "trackers" on the browser and delete them proactively. Craig proudly announced that "it's not about blocking ads; the web behaves as it always did, but your privacy is protected."[2] That statement is true, if you define "the web" as not including ads, which inconveniently had been a big part of it since 1994.

From the earliest days of web advertising, there was both a dependency on browser cookies and an understanding they were not an ideal tool for the job. Cookies were intended to help collect data in a privacy-friendly way to keep users logged into websites or to remember their preferences. The alternative would be to store or transmit actual personal data, like a username or email, on every page the browser opened.

The problems with cookies became clear in the first wave of commercialization of the web, when third parties who did not have a relationship with the end consumer began widely using them to track consumers' behavior. On a website like nytimes.com, it makes sense and comports with consumer expectations that the *Times* can track what you read and do on the site. When the paper works with another party, called a third party in this case, to serve or sell the ads, cookies like ads.doubleclick.net or ads.yahoo.com can be set and profiles can be collected, thus raising privacy concerns. What obligations do the third parties have to the end consumer, and how might they use the data on their own behalf or on the behalf of other companies the consumer might never have dealt with? These concerns are real, if a little bit theoretical. There is little evidence that the data from the cookies has caused real-world harm, other than a general sense that they violate privacy or facilitate "surveillance capitalism," as some more radical advocates have dubbed it.

Regardless of the harm, the continued support of cookies has been the subject of a push and pull between governments, technology companies, advocates, and the advertising community for decades. The fundamental problem has always been that less consumer data corresponds to lower prices for publishers and worse results for advertisers. Privacy advocates, both in and out of the technology sector, believe data should be minimized. Business interests, like publishers and advertisers, are more focused on the economic costs.

The first major dustup in the privacy arena was DoubleClick's disastrous acquisition of Abacus Direct. The second clash was around a technology called Do Not Track that, depending on whose version of events you listen to, was either an easy way for consumers to control the information in their browser or a back channel for Microsoft to destroy the entire advertising ecosystem. Do Not Track was a technical proposal to allow web browsers to send a signal indicating that the user did not want to be tracked. This would work across browsers and websites and serve as a universal opt-out from tracking. The short version of the story is that in 2012 Microsoft decided to make the signal active by default in the new version of its ubiquitous web browser, Internet Explorer. This meant that all users of the browser would be opted out of tracking, taking a big slice of the entire web advertising world with it. Since compliance with the signal was voluntary and there had been no legislation mandating its use, the coalition supporting the signal fell apart and neither advertising companies nor other competitive web browsers moved forward.[3]

Two lessons were learned from the Do Not Track fiasco: the companies that control browsers have enormous power, and many of them would choose privacy over advertising given the choice.

Apple was the next technology company to make a run at privacy. The Safari browser from Apple has never broken 10% market share on desktop computers. On mobile devices, however, the growth of the iPhone with the default installation of Safari brought the company enormous power. Safari always blocked third-party cookies by default, but as Apple increasingly saw ad-supported Google as their primary competitor, the company started turning the screws on the advertising community. Once Craig launched ITP at the developer conference, Safari was fully blinded for most advertising use cases and loopholes companies were using to track results were closed.[*]

In 2021 Apple went after privacy in ad-supported apps with App Tracking Transparency, or ATT. Under this set of requirements, apps on Apple devices had to explicitly ask consumers for permission to track them. App developers were highly restricted in how they could incentivize opt-ins and were unable to customize the prompt to consumers, which featured quite negative and alarming language designed to get users to

---

[*] The most common scenario that had previously worked but was blocked by ITP was when a cookie was set when a user clicked on an ad or website. Prior to ITP the cookie could track whether the user purchased something on the destination page.

opt out. Apple, meanwhile, tracks users for its own advertising purposes, using a different mechanism without any specific notice.[4]

Throughout Apple's efforts to reduce data availability, they used their typical marketing savvy to appeal to consumers. CEO Tim Cook constantly complained to the press about "creepy ads" that follow you around the web[5] instead of using industry jargon like "cookies" or "retargeting." Apple senior executive Craig Federighi said at the company's Worldwide Developer Conference, "It's not about blocking ads; the web behaves as it always did, but your privacy is protected."[6] If you define "the web" as not including ads, then his statement is true.

The net result of Apple's aggressive push for privacy was undoubtedly bad for advertising. Publisher webpages monetize on the Safari browser at 40% the pricing of the more privacy-agnostic Chrome browser.[7] The ATT rollout at one point cost Facebook $10 billion in lost annual advertising revenue.[8] The impact of these changes across all ad supported companies was profound. They also raised the priority of privacy issues at Google. The Chrome team felt like they had to respond to remain competitive, even if it could potentially damage their own advertising business.

In January 2020 Google's Chrome team announced their long-anticipated plan to do something about third-party cookies. Chrome was the largest browser by market share and Android was a powerhouse in the smartphone market, but both had done little to visibly protect consumer privacy. Apple, meanwhile, was hammering the privacy message home with billboards and TV ads claiming, "What happens on your iPhone, stays on your iPhone."[9] Google was severely conflicted on this issue. While the vast majority of Google's revenue came from advertising, the lion's share was from search, where cookies did not play as much of a role. The large and growing display ad business, though, was highly dependent on cookies and mobile identifiers. The ad-serving technologies that supported most of the world's large publishers and advertisers, as well as AdX and the ad network, could not operate at all without third-party cookies.

The Google Chrome team ended up trying to split the difference. First, they announced that third-party cookies would be eliminated "within two years," which is quite a long time frame and was clearly designed to soften the blow to the advertising businesses. This is probably the only time Google had announced anything at all with a timeline longer than a couple of months. The replacement for cookies, Google indicated, would be a set of privacy-enabling technologies, which collectively became known as the Chrome Sandbox, or Privacy Sandbox. These technologies were barely even proposals at this stage and nowhere near ready for testing. There were many of them, and each had a "cute" bird name, like FLoC or TURTLEDOVE, that was also a tortured acronym: "Two Uncorrelated Requests, Then Locally Executed Decision on Victory" does not exactly roll off the tongue.

Google's announcement tells you everything you ever need to know about the company two decades aged from Susan Wojcicki's garage. Instead of boldly disrupting the status quo like Gmail had with virtually unlimited storage or search had with its simple design and fast response, they tried to split the difference and build an inherently compromised product. The Chrome engineers wanted to do what they perceived as the "right" thing to do about privacy, which was to get rid of third-party cookies. They could not do what Apple did and just remove them because it would hurt their advertising business. Instead, they decided to *engineer* their way out of the problem, with complex proposals designed on blank whiteboards, without much of any regard for the ways the current advertising world operated. They then unveiled the proposals to the world, thinking they would be hailed as saviors. In fact, they were highly conflicted and naive, especially in the assumption of how long it would take to gain adoption of these nascent technologies.

Over the coming years, Google would refine their Sandbox proposals with industry input and attempt to get them codified within the W3C, an international organization that codifies standards for the web. The W3C instead came out numerous times against the proposals. In 2021 a working group called the whole initiative "harmful to the web in its current form,"[10] and in 2023 it rejected the Topics initiative (the renamed FLoC).[11] There was also talk from the Sandbox team about getting Apple to cooperate on some initiatives, but there was no evidence of any actual openness to cooperation.

The difficult position Google found itself in can be clearly outlined in Topics. The idea for Topics was for the browser to anonymously profile users and give advertisers and publishers signals they could use for targeting ads. This was meant to replace one of the key use cases of third-party cookies, where user profiles could be created and shared for better ad relevance. If a consumer spent time on a lot of sports content, Chrome might put that user in a cohort relating to sports, then make that information available to a publisher as the webpage loaded. The engineering on this project did everything possible to make it privacy safe: "Noise" was added to both the creation of the cohorts and the reading of them by the browser. The actual cohorts did not have names like "sports lovers"; they were just a string of letters and numbers you could feed into your algorithm, and so on. All of this missed the point, that the browser should not be collecting and sharing this data in the first place, especially if the goal is privacy! In a sense, Topics makes the browser feel *less* private, even if an expert privacy engineer steeped in the technology might not agree. This is the opposite of Apple's approach. You might even call it "creepy." The W3C's rejection of Topics stated it well: "The user has no fine-grained control over what is revealed, and in what context, or to which parties. It also seems likely that a user would struggle to understand what is even happening; data is gathered and sent behind the scenes, quite opaquely."[12]

Although Topics was rejected by the W3C, it was pushed live by Google in 2023 in the US and, tellingly, only by explicit opt-in within Europe,[13] where privacy enforcement is much stricter.

Aside from Topics, the other Sandbox initiative that received the most attention and testing was the successor of TURTLEDOVE, now called the Protected Audience API. This is probably the most ambitious and complex of the proposals and seeks to replace targeting of audiences based on cookies with a process that takes place entirely in the web browser. This proposal is the closest thing that advertising companies like Criteo might have to replace cookies when retargeting users. A number of tests have been done to determine how much revenue might be lost by publishers if cookies were removed and replaced with this API, with estimates ranging from 30% to 60%.[14]

Changing the entire inner workings of the advertising industry proved more difficult than the Chrome team anticipated. In June 2021 the cookie deprecation date was pushed back from the original "two years" to mid-to-late 2023. The blog post read, "It's become clear that more time is needed across the ecosystem to get this right."[15] In July 2022 they extended the timeline again, this time to the second half of 2024.[16] In early 2024 they pushed it further back to sometime in 2025, five years past the initial announcement.

The timeline pushbacks were not just due to testing issues or code readiness; Google was also under regulatory scrutiny. The UK's Competition and Markets Authority (CMA) opened an investigation in 2021 regarding the potential anticompetitive effects of the cookie deprecation and Sandbox plans.[17] There was an obvious concern over Google potentially preferencing itself, as well as the general sense that the move would hurt publishers and media companies with reduced ad revenue. Google acquiesced to the authority and signed a set of binding commitments that essentially put the whole initiative under the CMA's jurisdiction.[18]

By mid-2024 the deadline was approaching for the final removal of cookies, and the CMA remained dissatisfied with the resolution of key issues. For example, governance remained an issue—who would determine the future direction of the Sandbox once it was released from CMA scrutiny? After many rounds of testing, public comments, and objections from industry bodies, Google threw up its hands and declared they would not be deprecating cookies after all.[19] Instead, they would, in some undefined way, let users choose how much data they would allow to be collected by the browser. While details remain vague and Google controls the narrative, most observers expect this will mean that Chrome users will be given a prompt of some kind that does not exactly remove all cookies but convinces a majority to hobble cookie usage in some way.[20]

Google's arrogance and control over essentially the entire web were on full display throughout the Sandbox debacle. While they constantly emphasized their collaboration and testing with partners, it was always their ball, and they could choose to take it and go home.

While publishers might have been given a brief reprieve from the so-called "cookiepocalypse" promised back in 2020, the clear expectation remains that cookies will decline in importance in some way in 2025 and beyond. The continued uncertainty is also not helpful, leading to a frozen market where privacy-safe solutions remain perpetually out of reach. Meanwhile Apple, Mozilla, and other technology companies that are less invested in the advertising business have made their environments decidedly hostile to media business models. Apple continues to tweak privacy settings in ways that are impediments to advertising businesses, such as allowing users to submit fake, one-time emails when signing up for apps or reducing the ability to determine users' location. Mozilla, the not-for-profit maker of the Firefox browser, rolled out its version, ominously titled the Total Cookie Protection, in 2022.[21] Microsoft announced they will be following Google's direction and replacing cookies with an API modeled after the Sandbox.[22]

Apple's hostility to advertising and Google's bungling of the Sandbox notwithstanding, the long-term trends are undeniable. The web is becoming an increasingly difficult place for publishers to survive. The privacy movement is just another headwind for publishers, one dominated by the largest technology companies in the world and one in which they have little influence.

CHAPTER 20

A JEDI MIND TRICK

Google employees discussed playing a trick—
a "Jedi mind trick"—on the industry.[1]

—State antitrust complaint

A s early as 2010, some people inside Google were worrying that Facebook might be the biggest threat to the company.[2]

By the mid-2010s Facebook was more than an idle threat to Google. The company had gone public in 2012 and was quickly building an ad business that would become second only to Google's. Facebook's ads had started similarly to Google's search ads, with an emphasis on text, but the company had shifted and was now primarily focused on images and video. Unlike Google, which was dependent on placing ads through the exchange on other publishers' websites, these formats fit naturally in properties like the Instagram and Facebook apps and produced great results for advertisers.

Neal Mohan opened a 2013 strategy memo about Facebook with the words "Q2 mobile earnings were startling," and added the prophetic statement "There is a risk that FB becomes the 'starting point' of the internet."[3]

Facebook had made several attempts to run the same Three Pillars strategy that Neal had established at Google, but at critical junctures they pulled back. Despite multiple acquisitions they failed to build a *platform* business. The company had acquired LiveRail, a video ad serving platform and exchange, for a reported $400 million to $500 million[4] only to shutter it two years later due to concerns about fraud.[5] In 2013 the Atlas ad serving technology was bought from Microsoft's aQuantive for just $60 million of the $6.1 billion the software giant had paid,[6] only to be killed by Facebook a couple of years later.[7]

Gokul Rajaram had left Google to do a search start-up, Chai Labs, only for Facebook to acquire the company and put him into roughly the same position he had held when building AdSense.[8] Along with the brilliant and brash former Goldman Sachs trader Antonio Garcia-Martinez, he decided to accelerate Facebook's ad business by capturing the advertising demand present in the growing exchange ecosystem. Antonio built Facebook's homegrown ad exchange, FBX, which launched in 2012.[9] FBX would auction ads on facebook.com to bidders, typically DSPs, and those ads would compete with the ads booked directly by advertisers in the Facebook system. This was analogous to Google's setup with the ad network bidding into AdX and competing with other bidders. FBX was a boon to external bidders like AppNexus and Turn, who could bid on an enormous volume of cheap ad inventory using cookies.

Inside the company it was considered a small business, peaking in revenue at $800 million. More importantly, Facebook executives realized that since they had such rich profiles of their users, including email addresses, location, and sometimes billing information, they would have a much better ability to value their ads than third parties who were dependent on much less rich cookie data.[10] A decision was made by COO and former Googler Sheryl Sandberg to concentrate the company on a "closed" ad strategy rather than an "open" one. Gokul and Antonio both left the company shortly thereafter, the latter memorializing the experience in the memoir *Chaos Monkeys*.[11] After being ignored for years and not expanded to mobile inventory, FBX officially was shuttered in June 2016.[12]

The shutdown of FBX and the adoption of a closed model is an interesting contrast to Google. Despite its enormous presence in the ecosystem, Google had very little of its own ad inventory for display since Google Search, Gmail, and Google Maps only run text ads. While Google has deep user profiles, potentially including search histories, it had thorny issues around using that data in the display ad business and on websites it did not own. Whenever a product team at Google came up with a new way to use search data, there was always the question of whether it might negatively affect that business. The ethos within the company was to never hurt the golden goose, no matter what the opportunity. Facebook essentially had so much inventory and so much data that it did not need to run the Three Pillars strategy; it could just match its own demand to its own supply and become the second-largest advertising company in the world.

In 2014 Facebook did add a pillar, an ad network. The social networking company announced the Facebook Audience Network, or FAN. It would bring Facebook ad demand to apps and websites that the company did not directly own. For the first time, Facebook would not just be a rival of Google but a direct competitor in the ad market. Facebook realized that, like most other ad networks, one of FAN's key challenges was getting access to inventory. Internal documents from the company bemoan the fact that they would always have the challenge of being intermediated: "Google sits between us and the impressions we want to buy."[13]

Product teams within Facebook had been testing the results of buying ads for FAN in mobile and web auctions and found they were being beaten by Google for the best inventory. They knew something was up. "It was like Google was a lion eating the best of the kill, and we were hyenas getting what was left," said a former Facebook executive.[14] As they learned more about how Google controlled the auctions, they realized they would be limited in what they could achieve if they were always in the second-class seats.

Facebook was facing essentially the same problem that the yield managers faced in 2008 and that the exchanges faced in the early 2010s. They turned to the same solution, header bidding. In 2017 Facebook announced it would partner with six different providers, including AppNexus, to access inventory more directly through header bidding.[15] This fueled Google's fears since the only thing that could break Google's sway on publishers was replacing their ad network demand, and Facebook was the only company that could match or exceed that demand.

Header bidding was predominantly a factor for web ads, but Facebook's business was increasingly in mobile apps. Just as the Google ad server was dominant on the web, Google's acquisition of AdMob gave it a strong position for ads serving in mobile apps. Google had purchased AdMob for $750 million in 2009,[16] and the product allowed app publishers to both auction ads in an exchange and do a form of yield management common in the mobile world called "mediation," basically a form of mobile waterfall. The app marketplace had evolved very separately from the web, with different publishers, advertisers, and technologies. It also moved a lot more slowly, since new technology adoption was dependent on publishers installing new code (called SDKs) into their apps, a tedious and time-consuming process. As a result, whereas header bidding had taken the web publishing world by storm, app publishers still were using mediation. Facebook, along with others, wanted to unify the auction to eliminate mediation while also removing any Google advantages in the exchange.

Facebook ended up building its own solution to the mediation problem, called the "bidding kit."[17] This technology would allow app publishers to compare multiple sources of demand from Facebook and others in a single auction, integrated with non-Google exchanges including MoPub, Fyber, and a small start-up that had pioneered in-app header bidding called MAX.[18] Three months later, AppLovin, a leading mobile exchange, acquired MAX, giving further momentum to the move to bring header-like bidding to in-app advertising.[19]

Publishers were very excited about getting Facebook demand. Facebook claimed to increase overall revenue by 10% to 30% when implemented into the header—not a small amount! In the early phases of the rollout of FAN, Facebook even allowed publishers to use the social network's goldmine of consumer data to make their inventory more valuable.[20] These developments did not go unnoticed in Mountain View. Not only was Facebook growing its network business at Google's expense, but also through header bidding, it was routing around the exchange. Chris LaSala at Google wrote that his number-one personal priority in 2017 was to "fight off the existential threat posed by Header Bidding and FAN."[21] Google estimated that Facebook's share of the overall display advertising market that year (including social) was 35% to Google's 19%; it was "the dominant player," and "the gap [was] expected to widen."[22]

About eighteen months after Facebook first entered the fray with header bidding, the industry was somewhat shocked to hear that FAN would bid directly into Google's new header bidding alternative, Open Bidding.[23] This deal was unusual because FAN was a demand source and Google had specifically laid out that only exchanges or other intermediaries would be allowed to bid into Open Bidding. It was also simply shocking that these two Silicon Valley rivals were able to come to an agreement on just about anything.

Behind the scenes, the announcement was the end result of a secret project called Jedi Blue that involved grueling negotiations between the parties to protect against data loss, competitive positioning, and possible government scrutiny. The whole thing was done with complete secrecy. The negotiations would often rely on paper notes and documents and avoid electronics for fear of creating evidence that could later be subpoenaed. The deal was approved by the highest-level executives of both companies, with Sheryl Sandberg, Mark Zuckerberg, and Google CEO Sundar Pichai all directly signing off. Sandberg noted this was "a big deal strategically."[24] The project was the first one managed entirely by

Facebook's London office, and the Google team involved commuted from New York almost every month to get the program operational.

In response to concerns about Last Look and other manipulations, the final agreement between the two companies specified that Google would "not advantage itself or any other third-party demand" in the auction.[25] Facebook was using its power to assure they would not be played by Google like everyone else. The overall agreement read like a tentative truce between two deeply distrustful enemies. Every provision had caveats and carve outs, and the procedures for dispute resolution were detailed to the letter. What was left unsaid in the agreement was whether Jedi Blue represented a de facto truce: Would Facebook get access to publisher inventory at scale and in return stop investing in a header bidding alternative?

"Jedi Blue: A Scandal That Highlights, Yet Again, the Need to Regulate Big Tech"[26] was a pretty typical headline when the details of the agreement were first found out by the public in 2021. The attention was natural, as the press found out about a so-called "secret" pact between two of the leading technology companies of the era, and the allegations included price-fixing and preferential treatment.

There was certainly no direct evidence that Facebook had squashed its header bidding efforts because of this pact. In fact, the evidence pointed to the opposite. In the in-app community, Facebook was quite successful at getting exchanges to adopt unified auctions, and Jedi Blue essentially forced Google's AdMob to follow suit in exchange for the firehose of Facebook demand. Open web advertising was a bit of a moot point, as FAN stopped bidding entirely on this inventory in April 2020 for business reasons unrelated to Google.[27] The risk of fraud and other complexities of the open web were too much to stomach in the aftermath of the Cambridge Analytica scandal.[28]

It is difficult to argue that Jedi Blue hurt advertisers or publishers. Facebook advertisers got more reach for their campaigns. Publishers got more revenue, though with an additional 5% tax going to Google through Open Bidding. The real issue is whether in an alternative world Facebook might have developed its own header solution or even a complete ad platform, increasing overall competition. Facebook's track record of pullbacks from investment in this area suggests that was not likely to happen, and the internal documents leading up to the deal do not indicate much stomach to compete with Google in the platform business.

From the perspective of the competition, the deal was problematic. Other demand sources, like Criteo or the AppNexus DSP,* were only allowed to bid into AdX and incur a 20% fee, whereas Facebook, through Open Bidding, was charged a lower 5% fee. The agreement also set minimum performance standards for the auction traffic, such as a guarantee that 80% of all auctions would have enough data to allow Facebook to identify the users for bidding. Other partners would get no such guarantee. Unlike other partners in Open Bidding, Facebook was also allowed to keep their billing relationships with publishers, a major peeve among competitors.[29] Google made the case that these parameters were effectively volume discounts for a very large customer. Indeed, the dollar amounts involved were substantial—ramping up to a committed $500 million per year in spend from Facebook once the program was fully operational.[30] Google discussed making the same deal available to others and seems to have at least broached the idea with Amazon, Criteo, and maybe The Trade Desk. There were no takers at this huge level of financial commitment.[31] A cynical take is that the lawyers designed the deal explicitly to be *plausibly* available to other competitors but at such a high price that it was unlikely to get any further adoption.

---

* Brian O'Kelley loudly complained that AppNexus was not allowed to bid into Google's Open Bidding when it launched, but sources inside Google claim that only the DSP part of the company was barred, and they were willing to allow the publisher-facing exchange to participate.

Another wrinkle is the difference between web and app. Web advertising was of declining importance to Facebook, and that portion of FAN was shut down soon after Jedi Blue went live. Several former executives from both sides who were involved in crafting Jedi Blue would speculate that Facebook was not really interested in web in the first place but included it in the deal to play on Google's paranoia about header bidding competition.[32] "They wanted AdMob access; the rest was a foil," said one person knowledgeable about the deal. Further, the discounted 5% fee needs to be seen in the context of in-app auctions, where there were no free header bidding options, and having AdMob open for ad network bidding was a very big deal at the time.[33]

In any event, Facebook was not going to be the knight in shining armor to disrupt the advertising market. The social media company seemed content to sell enormous amounts of advertising for high prices to willing advertisers while letting Google continue to get bogged down in the politics, fraud, and overall complexity of the open web and the pesky publishers that make it up.

CHAPTER 21

GOOD NEWS, BAD NEWS

Doing this by itself . . . it looks extremely self-serving.[1]
—Sagnik Nandy

Project Poirot stands out among Google's various auction manipulations as possibly the most reasonable. While the imperative for Poirot was formed in reaction to header bidding, the actual problem it meant to solve was real. The evidence clearly suggests that ad exchanges were running "dirty auctions," where the second-price auction mechanism was being manipulated to raise prices for advertisers. Google's internal data showed that reducing bids on those exchanges produced better results for advertisers with the same level of quality.

There were other ways for ad exchanges to try to juice their results. An exchange might duplicate its bids to the same buyer just to see if the buyer's algorithms might have some throttling or inefficiency to exploit. Some exchanges would send multiple sequential auctions but with slightly lower floor prices each time to try to "fish" for the highest possible bid from the buyer.

Even without cheating, there was enormous inefficiency in the ad exchange world that had developed by the late 2010s. A typical setup for a publisher might include two header bidding wrappers (one from Amazon, one from prebid), plus Open Bidding through the ad server, resulting in three calls to each exchange for each impression. Each exchange would then, in turn, make ad requests to all the DSPs they had connected to, resulting in potentially hundreds of requests to each DSP for each single impression. On top of this spider's web, you have aggressive yield management techniques being implemented by the publishers themselves, trying to eke out additional pennies wherever possible, causing prices on the same inventory to vary enormously depending on the buying path.

All of this is to say there can be culpability for Google for their actions, but we must consider the challenges of operating within this fog of war—programmatic advertising had evolved into a complex and challenging environment without ground rules or regulations and with active and innovative adversaries.

Google is ultimately an engineering company. The driving ethos of the people who work there is to solve problems. They could only continue for so long acting as a leader in advertising while inefficiencies, workarounds, and complexity proliferated. By 2019 the advertising market was certainly filled with all those problems, and the AdX and Open Bidding teams were going to try to solve them all in one swoop.

Following the announcement of Open Bidding as Google's answer to header bidding, the product and engineering teams wanted to clean up various problems that were creeping up and threatening to get worse as the overall environment's complexity increased. For example, because bids could now come in from some exchanges in the header and other exchanges in Open Bidding, each with different auction mechanics and pricing, it was very possible that the highest bid would not actually win every auction.

Since header bidding gained widespread adoption, the argument for second-price auctions became questionable and almost all the non-Google exchanges were switching to first-price auctions, where the highest bid won. AdX, meanwhile, was still on a second-price auction, which was causing all kinds of weird situations. It was possible for a bid to come in from a header as a first-price bid, while the same advertiser's bid would come in through AdX as a second-price bid, and the two would compete with each other.

Header bidding had finally eroded, but not fully killed, Google's unique advantage, Dynamic Allocation. To roll out Open Bidding, Google had made the concession to remove Last Look from competing with those bids since otherwise they would likely have gotten little participation. If they were going to now take the position that they were cleaning up all the mess in the auction, it was hard to maintain their Last Look advantage against header bids.

Finally, Google was aware that many publishers actively manipulated floor prices for better yield. In particular, they set their price floors higher for AdX than for other exchanges. This was rational since AdX's 20% fee was higher than competitors', so making it bid higher would ultimately give publishers more of every dollar spent.

Google wanted to solve all these problems at once. They would follow up on the launch of Open Bidding with several changes. They would move AdX to a first-price auction, get rid of Last Look entirely, and stop customers from pricing AdX higher than other exchanges. They called this whole package of changes the Unified Auction, since in theory it would force all demand (header, AdX, Open, and direct) to compete on a fair basis all at once. There was just one problem: while publishers were happy about the first two changes, the last one, the removal of flexible pricing floors, was about to set off a riot.

A pricing floor is a key tool for publishers to manage their yield through ad exchanges. In the simplest terms, it is the minimum price at which they are willing to sell their inventory. Floors can be set in multiple systems with different effects. A publisher could log in to an ad exchange's user interface and set a floor for just the demand coming through that exchange. They could set a floor in their header bidding setup. Using Google tools, they could set a floor in AdX to apply to its bids or in the ad server to apply to all sources of demand. A lot of this flexibility came from AdMeld, a company that prided itself on understanding publishers' yield management and customizing according to their needs.

The price floors in the ad server were particularly important because they worked across ad exchanges and could also be used for more dynamic purposes, like setting a lower price for a single advertiser who might have a long-term business relationship or setting a higher floor for certain types of ads that might annoy users. They were flexible and ubiquitous.

Publishers were learning, though, that you could make more yield by pushing floors higher on AdX in particular. This was advertising jiujitsu, using your opponent's strength against them. In other ad exchanges, the bid was made with limited information, so the incentive was to bid the least amount needed to win. Publishers would adjust floors based on the bidding history, and an equilibrium between buyer and seller might be reached. AdX was different in two important ways. First, AdX had enormous unique demand from the ad network and was often the only bidder on each auction. We also know that with Dynamic Revenue Share and the habit of sending two bids on each auction, there was a lot of flexibility in what AdX was willing to pay for a given auction. AdX was already manipulating the auction actively with Bernanke, where the algorithm was allowed to raise prices on competitive auctions to win. With Last Look, AdX would pay one cent more than the highest price or floor price in order to win.

All these factors meant that smart ad operations people could make more money by raising AdX floors above those of other exchanges. They did not, at the time, know exactly why this worked, but it did so consistently.

Matthew Wheatland of DMG noticed that AdX reacted differently to floors than other demand sources. He ran a test where he divided all cookied users into twenty buckets and set price floors for each bucket in ten-cent increments from zero to $0.10, $0.20, etc., to create an experimental yield curve of AdX demand. The expected results were that demand should decline as prices rose, but while other exchanges followed this pattern, the demand from AdX showed much less elasticity. He learned he could "push the floors harder and get more revenue than other exchanges."[2]

The team at Google noticed they were losing revenue from higher floors. After Poirot launched, the majority of buying from their DSP was going to AdX, but they still saw that 78% of the spend on other exchanges was on sites that were also available on their exchange.[3] The team suspected this was caused by higher floors, but only once Open Bidding had launched did they have the data to prove it since they could see the full range of prices coming in from other exchanges.[4] One of the key criticisms of Open Bidding was that Google would now see all the bids from all the competitive exchanges, and in fact here was a clear example where the data was being turned around to make major competitive decisions that would benefit the company.

The data showed that in 42% of impressions won by other exchanges, the winning bid's price was lower than AdX's floor on that same impression, meaning there was a range where AdX could have won the auction but was not eligible to bid because the floor was too high. Of those auctions, where floors had made AdX ineligible, AdX was willing to beat the winning price 40% of the time. From the Google team's perspective, this meant they were entitled to win another 16% of auctions,[*] if not for publisher's settings.[5]

---

[*] Forty-two percent of auctions where they were not eligible multiplied by 40% of bids that would be higher.

A lot of ideas were thrown around to solve the problem of AdX floors. They could unify the floors between the ad server and AdX so that the same floors would work for all demand. They could ignore the floor and just let AdX win if the winning bid was lower. They could rebuild the flooring system from scratch.

In internal emails the Google team vacillate between acknowledging this change is for their own benefit and engaging in complex and technical arguments that the very idea of differential flooring would be moot in a first-price auction. They were telling themselves that the flooring strategies were an artifact of inefficient or corrupt auctions and would be moot as soon as the other auction changes within the Unified Auction solved the problem. They apparently did not have the self-awareness to realize the higher AdX floors were an artifact of their own corrupt auction mechanics or the desire of their customers to gain back some measure of control over their own businesses.

Ultimately the decision was made to unify the floors between the ad server and AdX, essentially disabling the ability to set different floors on AdX than on other sources of demand. Some capabilities would remain, like the ability to floor specific brands or geographies, though not exchanges. This change was branded Unified Pricing Rules, or UPR.

All other exchanges allowed publishers to set floors in their systems separately from the ad server, but the ad server was the final decision layer before an ad was chosen. It thus became possible to have higher floors for external exchanges versus AdX (giving Google an advantage) but not lower ones, which would favor those exchanges. Let's take an example. If you logged in to the user interface of PubMatic, you could set a floor of $1 and that would be the lowest bid they would send in to either header bidding or Open Bidding. If you then set a floor of $1.10 in Google, that would apply to both Google and PubMatic, so any bids in the range between $1.00 and $1.10 from PubMatic would no longer be eligible and both systems would effectively have a $1.10 floor. The opposite was not true, however. If the PubMatic floor was higher than Google, say $1.20, bids between $1.10 and $1.20 would not be sent by PubMatic but would be available from AdX.

With the decision made to unify floors, the focus turned to messaging. Google was fully cognizant that this change would be seen as only for their own benefit. The strategy was to bundle the floor price change UPR with the other Unified Auction changes underway, most notably the move to first-price auctions, which publishers were excited about.

Ali Nasiri Amini, an engineering leader, laid it out plainly in an email to Brad Bender, who at this point oversaw both the buy and sell sides of the display business: "We could keep all the current floor-pricing options and move to first-price auction, and this would have achieved most of what we desperately need to fix our ecosystem. However, AdX team wanted to use this migration as an opportunity to significantly limit the ability of publishers to set floor-prices per buyers (which is a good goal to have)."[6]

Ali had an inkling of how it was going to play out, continuing, "Initially, the feedback from first-price announcement was positive. However, recently as we shared details of removing floor-pricing options the feedback has changed dramatically . . . Publishers backlash looks serious to me."

There was some thought inside the company that UPR was good for the customers, in the sense that it was part of the "cleanup" that everyone knew was so necessary. This line of thinking roughly said that publishers were always optimizing for short-term yield gains through things like floor prices and header bidding but they were in the long term making things worse and creating inefficiencies—the more of this friction could be eliminated, the better it would be for everyone. There was no real evidence that this series of assumptions made sense or was justified by the data, but there was a widespread belief that the market had spiraled out of control in some fundamental way, and this was Google's chance, as omnipresent and benevolent dictator of the display advertising world, to solve all the problems at once.

Again, it must be pointed out that publishers were often manipulating the auctions to overcome Google's behaviors and advantages. Had the ad server or AdX supported a unified fair auction at a low take rate years earlier, header bidding would not have been necessary. Had the ad network not continued to manipulate auctions, higher price floors on AdX would have been less common. Had the AdX take rate been lower, there would have been less incentive to work with competitive exchanges. Much of the complexity of the ad exchange business was directly or indirectly caused by Google's hegemony within it, and now the company was determined to clean up the mess.

CHAPTER 22

EMOTIONAL AND UNPRODUCTIVE

The problem seems to be the control sits on Google's plate rather than . . . within publishers.[1]

—Emry Dowinghall

oogle's New York headquarters at 111 Eighth Avenue is only fifteen stories tall but is one of the most massive office buildings in the city. Formerly a Port Authority warehouse, the imposing edifice, which fills a city block, has been made "Googley" with an aggressive application of primary colors, neon signs, and other symbols of the company's performatively fun culture. But zooming out from the whimsical touches, the physical plant gives the distinct impression of power.

In April 2019 Google summoned some of its more important publisher customers to the headquarters to hear about all the changes that had been brewing. News Corp, *Business Insider*, Hearst, and many other leading media companies sent their revenue and ad operations leaders to hear directly from Google in what had been billed as an important preview of the future. You will remember that Sarah Sluis of *AdExchanger* reported at the time, "It did not go well."[2]

The presentation was run by Google product manager Rahul Srinivasan. He framed the conversation around the release of three features: the move to the first-price auction, the elimination of Last Look, and the Unified Pricing Rules (UPR). First-price auctions were the norm at this point, with only AdX still using second price, so this was welcome and would reduce complexity for buyers. Last Look had previously only been removed from Open Bidding, so Google had retained their advantage when bids came in from header bidding. Removing Last Look from all auctions was also a welcome change.

Rahul then pitched UPR, which lets you "centrally control pricing across all indirect sources of demand in a convenient manner."[3] This is not how publishers saw it. They immediately recognized what was happening. A key tool they used to increase yield was being unceremoniously taken away by the company that would benefit the most from its removal. The meeting got quite heated and emotional. The questions started in objection to the substance of the UPR announcement but quickly moved to the nature of the relationship between mighty Google and its publisher vassals.

Steph Layser was among the first to question the rationale. She challenged Rahul, saying, "The problem seems to be the control sits on Google's plate rather than . . . within publishers."

Rahul's answer was very high level and frankly arrogant; he lectured about how the ads market was like the financial markets and how "you need to get to a world where increased market efficiency is what leads to surplus across the board, and that's what will benefit publishers also in the long run."

"The major difference between the financial market and the programmatic market is that the people that own the financial markets are not also bidding on the same markets," Steph retorted. Steph could not be aware that Jonathan Bellack, the product head for this whole business line, had years earlier written nearly the same thing in an internal email that had not yet become public.

There were substantive complaints beyond the ability to extract more money from Google with higher floors. Publishers used floors as negotiating leverage with other exchanges to build better relationships and reduce fees. Even though ad exchange fees were taken out of bids before the net amount was paid to them, smart publishers still wanted to reward those in the supply chain who took lower take rates. Ultimately that benefited buyers and increased the return on investment for advertisers. This and other use cases were collateral damage to Google's belief they were making the world more efficient. UPR was removing a tool for lowering fees and actually *making* the market more efficient in a meaningful, rather than theoretical, way. A *Star Wars* fan might notice the similarity between the language Google used about ad exchanges and the desire to "bring peace to the galaxy."

Jana Meron was quite critical, at one point calling the company a "monopoly," which drew twitters from the assembled crowd, as if breaking a taboo on saying a dangerous word.

Emry Dowinghall of education publisher Chegg got to the problem of arrogance and control, saying, "I just think the biggest problem . . . is that this product is already built. It's done. You could probably turn it live tomorrow . . . when people here are suggesting feedback . . . and there's really no recourse for us whatsoever to force you to change a product that you've already built."

At a lull in questioning, Jana Meron yelled from the audience, "It seems to me that this was all built for header bidding to not exist." Her chutzpah for saying this aloud, especially following the "monopoly" remark, got some laughs and applause from the audience.

Steph would then stick in the dagger with a semi-rhetorical question to which she already could guess the answer: "So say I'm unhappy with this and I want to switch ad servers. Is there anything on the plan? You know, I don't want to give up AdWords or AdX demand and I want it to compete . . . holistically with all the rest of my partners." Rahul did his best to say he would look into it but that was a problem significantly above his pay grade.

When a questioner suggested his coworkers should buy him a stiff drink, Rahul joked, "I think I need it right now," despite it being 11:00 a.m.

In the weeks following the fateful meeting, Steph pushed her account managers for further discussion of the changes and potential amicable resolution of the issues. She wanted a meeting with the product leaders, especially Bellack, who was conspicuously absent from the in-person meeting. Her Google team suggested they have a prep call in advance of meeting with Bellack, of whom the account managers seemed to be in awe and fear. The call, they explained, would assure his time wasn't wasted and Steph's passion on this subject was kept in check.

Steph jumped on the pre-call with account managers Dorothy and Lauren. They dropped the hammer. They weren't going to let Steph on calls with Bellack or senior Google product people anymore as long as she was going to be "emotional and unproductive." This was quite the moment of female empowerment as her legitimate complaints were being turned against her in a moment of gaslighting.

The official posture of Google, as Steph later described it, was "by any means possible, get this girl to shut up!"[4] She represented a large, paying customer of a software vendor, and they had told her unequivocally that they did not want her feedback and would not make their executives available to hear from her. This was following the general announcement that they would release changes to the product she used against her wishes, with no viable recourse. "I felt like they were holding us hostage."[5]

Even though she represented News Corp, one of the largest and most powerful media companies in the world, she had no choice but to accept whatever Google decided, a pattern that was becoming painfully familiar to everyone in the publishing business.

Corporate gaslighting and bullying seem to have become a part of the standard operating procedure at Google. After speaking at a conference and making unflattering remarks about Google's behavior, Jana Meron got a disturbing call from Google product director Sam Cox. The two of them had a strong relationship and had previously collaborated closely on anti-fraud efforts. Jana was shocked to hear Sam tell her she was risking getting cut off from access to Google events and product resources. She felt betrayed and insulted that she, a loyal customer of the company, would get this treatment.[6] Sam, for his part, felt he was doing her a favor and helping her avoid the "Steph Layser treatment."[7]

The arrogance of the Google account teams seemed to know no bounds. Jeremy Hlavacek recalls that early in his tenure as a Google customer with Weather.com, he was reprimanded by a Google account manager for daring to adjust the priorities of the ad exchange and giving competitors advantages in his setup. The account manager followed up by emailing a screenshot of a particularly egregious portion of the contract between the companies, one that said Google could effectively change whatever settings it wanted in his company's ad server setup and effectively warning him to watch his step.[8]

These were not isolated incidents. If you were a Google publisher customer and said something critical of the company, you might be reprimanded, cut off from access, uninvited from industry events, and otherwise given the distinct impression that you were no longer welcome.

There is no definitive answer to the effect the new UPR pricing rules had on customers. Logically it follows that if publishers were previously adding higher floor prices to AdX and then were not allowed to, AdX would win more and at lower prices. Matthew Wheatland found exactly that. In the weeks following the rollout, the percentage of impressions won by AdX skyrocketed from 20% to 60% while revenue was flat, presumably because of price declines.[9] This may have been an exceptionally dramatic outcome since Wheatland and team were veritable ninjas at extracting revenue using floor pricing, but it seems likely this was the overall outcome. Competitors almost certainly suffered ill effects. Pub-Matic's analysis showed somewhere between 3% and 10% reduction in volume after UPR.[10]

From the publisher point of view, they were paying customers of Google's ad server software and in some cases had been so for over two decades. And the company was quite arrogantly telling their customers that it was deploying a bunch of features they had not asked for and could not turn off, all within the shared context that it was impossible to switch ad servers. "UPR was crossing the Rubicon," said one publisher executive.[11]

More than anything else, this was the point where any remaining trust, any remaining "benefit of the doubt," that publishers might have held in regard to Google instantly evaporated. The ad server could cost millions of dollars in fees each year and was effectively the digital operating system for ad-supported publishers. For the vendor offering this critical software to not add any desired enhancement but instead *remove* critical functionality, and to do it for a reason that was so obviously self-serving to the other parts of their organization, was just absolutely infuriating.

And they could not switch.

PART IV

SPINNING OUT

CHAPTER 23

STRANGE BEDFELLOWS

Google simultaneously acts on behalf of
publishers and advertisers, while also trading for itself.
—US House of Representatives report on "Big Tech"

K en Paxton, attorney general of Texas, stood on the steps of the US
Supreme Court surrounded by chief lawyers from other states. A
total of fifty states and territories had banded together to launch an investigation into Google's ad technology and search engine, YouTube,
Google's privacy practices, and more. The pressure on Google had
entered a new and much more dangerous phase. That pressure would
release explosively over the coming years into two major federal suits, a
state case, at least two civil cases, multiple European investigations, and
proposed bipartisan congressional bills.

———

You cannot draw a straight line from the Unified Pricing Rules fiasco
to the legal troubles, but there are certainly connecting dots. Beginning
in the late 2010s, Google got caught in a maelstrom of political and legal

trouble, pushed along by partisan politics, struggling competitors, and an angry mob of media companies and their lobbyists.

The first case to file was led by the Department of Justice and eleven states and focused on Google's search business. The case alleged, among other things, that Google used its market share in search to lock in browser defaults with Safari to perpetuate its position. The suit claimed that Google's large search share allowed it to pay more money for the default search positions than rivals could bear, then use that default position to collect so much data that competition became impossible.

Coming at the very end of the first Trump administration and following contentious hearings and findings about "Big Tech" from Congress, the search suit had the distinct whiff of partisanship. All 11 state cosponsors were "red" states, and the suit was announced in late October, just 13 days before Election Day 2020. It turns out that fighting Google is a bipartisan cause, as 38 more state attorneys general filed a similar search case after the election, and the suits were combined in early 2021.[1]

Two months after the search case was filed, another group of Republican attorneys general filed the first suit against Google's advertising technology stack. This suit alleged that the monopoly ad server was used to lock publishers in and extract profit at their expense. It stated that the company used anticompetitive tactics to defeat header bidding, that it colluded with Facebook on Jedi Blue, and that it manipulated the auction through programs like Bernanke to profit itself. The case remained sealed at the time, so the details were yet to become public. If you assume that legal writing is boring, reviewing the first page of the state complaint might dissuade you:

> The halcyon days of Google's youth are a distant memory. Over twenty years ago, two college students founded a company that forever changed the way that people search the internet. Since then, Google has expanded its business far beyond search and dropped its famous "don't be evil" motto. Its

business practices reflect that change. As internal Google documents reveal, Google sought to kill competition and has done so through an array of exclusionary tactics, including an unlawful agreement with Facebook, its largest potential competitive threat, to manipulate advertising auctions. The Supreme Court has warned that there are such things as antitrust evils. This litigation will establish that Google is guilty of such antitrust evils, and it seeks to ensure that Google won't be evil anymore.[2]

The state case is wide-ranging and accuses Google of malfeasance relating to the auction mechanics, the Facebook partnership, user privacy violations, the Sandbox, AMP, and the kitchen sink.

Scrutiny of Google was nothing new. Rival companies, led by News Corp and Microsoft, had been funding opposition to the company's actions at every turn since before the DoubleClick acquisition. That deal had seen intense lobbying by Microsoft and its proxies, but ultimately the case was hard to make, given the newness of the exchange market.

The opponents had scored a win several years later, when they convinced the DOJ to prevent a commercial deal that would have shifted Yahoo's search business to being powered by Google. This was a messy situation where Yahoo had rebuffed the offer from Microsoft to buy the company[3] and as a counterreaction just five weeks later had signed a deep tie-up with Google around search results and ads.[4] Under intense pressure and lobbying from Microsoft, the DOJ had threatened to bring a Section 2 Sherman Act antitrust case against Yahoo and Google if they pursued the deal, causing the companies to call off the partnership.[5] In the definitive reporting on this episode, reporters Nicholas Thompson and Fred Vogelstein wrote in *Wired* that Microsoft "initiated a campaign that filled

DOJ mailboxes with letters from politicians and nonprofit groups objecting to the deal." Later in the same article, they detail how industry schmoozer Michael Kassan was enlisted to convince advertisers to object to the deal: he got the "largest advertisers to join together to oppose the company in public."[6]

Microsoft's investment in AppNexus also gave the software giant a front seat to what some saw as anticompetitive behavior in the display ads business. Shortly after that investment was made public, Google, for reasons it never disclosed, abruptly shut off AppNexus's access to their ad exchange in the critical period leading up to the holiday season.[7] Microsoft got deeply involved in this conflict, bringing in heavyweight antitrust law firm Paul Weiss and putting Google clearly on the radar of firm partners Jonathan Kanter and Rick Rule. Kanter would later lead the investigation into Google at Biden's Justice Department.

News Corp, DMG, and Gannett all took active steps to alert anyone who would listen about the monopolistic practices of Google. Steph Layser was paraded around the country (and the world) by News Corp lawyers to any competition authority or attorney general who would give them an audience.

DMG filed a civil antitrust suit against the company in April 2021 alleging both advertising and search malfeasance. The DMG suit claimed, "The lack of competition for publishers' inventory depresses prices and reduces the amount and quality of news available to readers, but Google ends up ahead because it controls a growing share of the ad space that remains."[8]

Gannett filed a similar suit in June 2023 in which Michael Reed, the company's chairman and chief executive officer, said, "Google has monopolized market trading to their advantage and at the expense of publishers, readers, and everyone else. Digital advertising is the lifeblood of the online economy. Without free and fair competition for digital ad space, publishers cannot invest in their newsrooms."[9]

At the time they occurred, the most controversial activities of Google, such as projects Bernanke and Poirot, were not known publicly. This changed when New York judge Kevin Castel unsealed the allegations in the state attorneys general suit, showing the world all the messy details about the company's allegedly anticompetitive behaviors.[10] Reactions among publishers ranged from "I knew it!" to "Duh."[11]

The auction manipulations did solve a lot of the gnawing mysteries that had been accruing among smart industry observers. Criteo's tests where they won less with very high bids into the ad exchange could be explained by favoring Google's own demand for valuable auctions. Matthew Wheatland's observation that he could push AdX floors higher and make more money only made sense if there was something funny in the way AdX was bid reducing in a second-price auction. Steph Layser's general inability to get log files that could let her trace backward the chain of payments from Google Ads made a lot more sense if you considered that perhaps Google did not want customers to see their per-advertisement take rate.

Rajiv Goel of PubMatic remarked, "The saddest thing is that people you know at Google would say 'We're here to make the open internet thrive,' then you'd read what they actually had been doing."[12] "It was worse than we thought," Wheatland dryly remarked.[13] Indeed it was.

————————

There was some irony that the embarrassing unsealing of the state complaint happened in a New York court. The suit was brought mostly by red state attorneys general and was originally filed in Texas. Google had maneuvered first to get it moved to their home state of California, then later to what they thought would be a more friendly jurisdiction in New York.[14] The New York court unsealed the complaint revealing the juicy details but would not hold on to the case much longer.

In a sign of how unpopular the big tech companies had become in Washington, the US Congress uncharacteristically passed actual legislation relevant to the case. On December 29, 2022, as part of the omnibus spending bill, Congress passed the State Antitrust Enforcement Venue Act, which made antitrust actions of state attorneys general exempt from the standard venue consolidation process that other suits are subject to.[15] In effect, this gave control back to Ken Paxton, who promptly returned the case to his home state.[16] The state case is expected to go to trial in summer 2025.

European regulators have a reputation as antagonists of American technology companies, and they scored the first wins against Google as related to the abuses within the advertising business. France's Autorité de la Concurrence (ADLC) first launched its investigation in 2019 from complaints by News Corp, *Le Figaro*, and Rossel, a Belgian media group.[17] In June 2021 they came to a settlement, and Google was forced to pay a €220 million fine and agree to end some of their behaviors in Europe. Notably, they agreed to not use data from other exchanges for their own benefit and to share data back with all bidders about the results of auctions. These were small concessions, but it was the first time a government entity had made any alterations to Google's advertising stack.[18]

A much bigger European case was coming. In June 2021 the EU opened an investigation of violations of Article 102 of the Treaty on the Functioning of the European Union, which prohibits the abuse of a dominant market position. Two years later, in 2013, a Statement of Objections was issued, which is essentially a preliminary finding of abuse. The statement recommended a breakup of the company:

> In this particular case, a behavioural remedy is likely to be ineffective to prevent the risk that Google continues such self-preferencing conducts or engages in new ones. Google is

active on both sides of the market with its publisher ad server and with its ad buying tools and holds a dominant position on both ends. Furthermore, it operates the largest ad exchange. This leads to a situation of inherent conflicts of interest for Google. The Commission's preliminary view is therefore that only the mandatory divestment by Google of part of its services would address its competition concerns.[19]

The EU press release included a cute little graphic that showed cartoon scissors cutting along a dotted line that would separate the ad server and AdX from the network and the DSP. The final ruling in the EU case is expected in 2025.

The state case discovery resulted in the uncovering of many of the alleged misbehaviors of Google over the years, increasing the public scrutiny and giving ammunition to the aggressive Biden antitrust teams under Jonathan Kanter. In the face of damning evidence of malfeasance, two years after the state case was filed, the DOJ filed suit with an advertising case alleging much of the same behavior. The DOJ, along with eight "blue" state attorneys general, asked the court to find Google to be a monopoly in display advertising and to force a breakup, specifically of the publisher ad server and the exchange AdX.[20] The government sought in 2024 to crumble the pillars built in 2008.

The DOJ complaint is much more even-tempered than the fire and brimstone coming from the Texas attorney general. It is still just as damning, though: "One industry behemoth, Google, has corrupted legitimate competition in the ad tech industry by engaging in a systematic campaign to seize control of the wide swath of high-tech tools used by publishers, advertisers, and brokers to facilitate digital advertising. Having inserted itself into all aspects of the digital advertising marketplace, Google has used anticompetitive, exclusionary, and unlawful means to eliminate or severely diminish any threat to its dominance over digital advertising technologies."[21]

Not to be left behind, Canada's Competition Bureau filed suit in late 2024 with allegations similar to the US DOJ's. Like the US, Canada also demanded the spinout of the ad server and the ad exchange.[22] The Canadian team had been present in the US courthouse for the DOJ trial, likely taking notes for how the various arguments would play out.

Even Rumble took a shot. Rumble is an erstwhile YouTube competitor with a decidedly rightward political bent. The site grew in popularity during the COVID lockdowns, when politicians like Devin Nunes complained about YouTube censorship and influencers like Dan Bongino joined the community.[23]

Rumble had already filed an antitrust lawsuit against Google alleging that it preferenced YouTube videos over other sources of content. In May 2024 it doubled down on its legal bet and filed antitrust lawsuits against the company focused on the advertising business.[24]

While there is nothing in the Rumble suit that is not already in any of the myriad other legal actions against Google, the filing highlights the somewhat problematic pattern in much of the media business's fight against the search giant. Namely, the companies, law firms, and politicians out in front of this fight often have conflicted motives. It is hard to separate the accusations that Google is a liberal company that censors conservative views from the fact that the State of Texas and News Corp (owner of Fox News, among other right-wing outlets) are two of its primary antagonists. On the other hand, the federal antitrust suit was started under the first Trump administration, avidly pursued by the Biden team, and now will be concluded during the second Trump term. Truly, criticism of Google is a bipartisan issue.

CHAPTER 24

VIRGINIA COURTHOUSE

*The defendant's anti-competitive schemes are as old
as any monopolist's behavior.*

—Julia Tarver Wood

While the state antitrust case against Google meandered between jurisdictions, the case brought by the DOJ moved extremely rapidly. Filed in the Eastern District of Virginia, known as the Rocket Docket, the case went from filing in January 2023 to trial in September 2024. The courthouse's front fresco even includes a metaphorical sculpture, *Justice Delayed, Justice Denied*, featuring a blindfolded justice flanked by a tortoise-and-hare motif.[1] While scheduled for up to six weeks of testimony, the trial concluded ahead of schedule, in just three weeks—a breakneck speed that astounded many observers and participants.

The trial judge, Leonie Brinkema, was appointed in 1993 by President Bill Clinton. Eighty years old at the time of trial,[2] she seemed to struggle at times with the stairs leading up to her bench but had absolutely no problem keeping the contending lawyers in line, parsing the complex evidence, and getting it into the record. More than once during the trial, she ended testimony early with the admonition that the evidence was duplicative or not helpful. There was a reason the trial ended in half the allotted time.

Even before the trial, the deft legal maneuvers raised the drama level. On May 16, months before jury selection would start, Google couriered a Wells Fargo cashier's check for $2,289,751 to the DOJ.[3] The DOJ was suing Google on five counts of violating the Sherman Act, but only one of those counts required a jury trial, so Google simply paid off the full amount, including interest, for that count. Judge Brinkema had no choice but to close the one count in the suit asking for damages. The remaining four counts were seeking injunctive relief rather than damages—under civil law, such charges do not provide for a right to a jury trial.[4] As a result, Google forced the proceedings to become a bench trial, avoiding the uncertainty of a jury.

The DOJ case had based its damages claims on the activities of various federal agencies, like the US Coast Guard and the US Navy, which had utilized Google for advertising services. With their damages dismissed, the scope of evidence and testimony was also shrunk, and the trial would be forced to focus more on technical complexities than on any specific advertiser that might have been hurt by Google's actions.

While Google got rid of the jury, they may have had second thoughts as their interactions with Judge Brinkema progressed. A month before the trial was to begin, the DOJ asked Brinkema for a finding of Adverse Inference based on what they described as "Google's intentional deletion of chat evidence" in the case.[5] An Adverse Inference essentially gives the jury (or the judge, in this case) the assumption that the evidence is against the party even when that evidence is absent. While you can "plead the

Fifth" in a criminal trial, if you stay silent in a civil trial, it can be used against you.

The deletion of chats was a running theme in the DOJ's case against Google. Google employees extensively use a proprietary chat program built into Gmail to have conversations, both substantive and otherwise. Many witnesses ended up being aggressively questioned on the stand about their chat use and whether they had turned the "history" feature on to keep records of important discussions. In a memo sent in November 2020—over a year after the company was made aware it was under DOJ investigation—the message retention team explained that all chat messages would be deleted within twenty-four hours under the *default setting* of "history off." Only if an employee actively and voluntarily switched to "history on" would the messages be kept.[6] This policy was in place until February 2023, well after most of the antitrust litigation was underway.[7]

The default chat setting could be traced back to 2008, when Google's chief legal officer, Kent Walker, wrote a memo focused on document discovery. This memo announced the change in default chat retention, designed to "help avoid inadvertent retention," and kicked off various activities to reduce discoverability in the face of legal scrutiny.[8] This memo had been cited in the company's suit with Epic Games as well, where it was described as a manifestation of "ingrained systemic culture of suppression of relevant evidence within Google."[9] Several advocacy groups recently asked the California Bar to investigate Walker for the memo, writing in a letter, "The behavior is plainly unethical and violates both California State Law and Walker's ethical obligations as a member of the California State Bar."[10]

The DOJ claimed that the destruction of evidence went beyond the default setting but that eight document owners and five trial witnesses had intentionally turned off chat history to avoid discovery. During the trial, witness Chris LaSala admitted as much, saying he asked colleagues to switch to a "history off" chat before continuing a sensitive discussion around pricing.[11]

Another area of concern was the company's internal compliance training program, "Communicate with Care." Also springing from the Walker memo, this program instructed employees to discuss sensitive topics via "off the record" chats rather than emails and to expansively mark communications and documents as "Attorney Client Privilege" where there might not necessarily be a proper legal basis to do so. The DOJ claimed that a whopping forty thousand documents originally claimed by Google to be privileged were later determined to not be eligible for that classification.[12]

At an August 27 hearing, the judge ruled against Google on the Adverse Inference motion, saying, "I'm comfortable saying this is not the way a respected corporate entity should function. A clear abuse of privilege." She also commented it was a "foolish decision not to change defaults on" for those under litigation hold.[13] For the rest of the trial, the judge would assume the worst when the evidence was missing or unclear.

On the first day of the trial, the line to observe snaked around the eighth floor of the court building, with an overflow room set up with video and audio for those who couldn't fit. A reporter for a trade publication had a seizure while in line and medics had to be sent in, adding to the pretrial drama (he was OK). Over the coming three weeks—other than opening arguments—there was very little mainstream press coverage, which was ironic, given the importance of the outcome to newsrooms. The press that did attend bonded over the strict no electronics or food policy, morosely joking about impending writer's cramp from the need to transcribe weeks of testimony longhand.

Julia Tarver Wood, senior litigation counsel for the DOJ, led the case. Mrs. Wood had spent much of her career at the firm Paul, Weiss, Rifkind, Wharton & Garrison LLP, a one-thousand-attorney firm focused on corporate law and litigation and one that was representing Google in this very case! Karen Dunn, the lead litigator for Google, had overlapped with Julia at the firm for at least three years. While the parties were fighting tooth and nail for advantage, the all-female trio of Judge Brinkema plus lead counsels was exceptionally cordial and professional throughout.

Mrs. Wood, in her opening remarks, stated plainly, "The defendant's anticompetitive schemes are as old as any monopolist's behavior."[14] The DOJ's case alleged four anticompetitive behaviors: a monopoly in ad serving, a monopoly in ad exchanges, a monopoly in the advertiser ad network market, and illegal tying of the ad server to the ad exchange. She punctuated her opening with damaging quotes from Google executives: David Rosenblatt saying, "We'll do to the display market what Google did to search"[15] and Scott Spencer saying, "All or nothing, use AdX or no demand." The most evocative quote, one that would be present in all the legal filings and press coverage, was from Jonathan Bellack, who wrote: "Is there a deeper issue with us owning a platform, the exchange, and a huge network? The analogy would be if Goldman or Citibank owned the NYSE."[16]

Google's opening statement, like most of the arguments they would present, was more legalistic. Mrs. Dunn started by touting how the invention of RTB was a game changer and how Google invested billions of dollars to innovate in this market. The core of her argument, though, was not to defend Google's actions but to defend against the case being made by the DOJ. The DOJ's definitions of the different markets (ad serving, ad exchange) were flawed according to the defense, as they all connected in singular transactions. The market definition of "open web display advertising" was not a real market since it did not include Facebook, Amazon, and others.

Finally, a key part of the defense was asserting Google had no "duty to deal" with competitors, as established by a prior US Supreme Court precedent.[17] This last one is interesting and can be parsed many ways. Consider the fact that AdX only integrates in real time with Google's publisher ad server. The DOJ argued this is illegal tying—if you want

AdX, you must also buy the ad server. Google argued that to get real-time bids from AdX into another ad server, you would be requiring Google to do *work*—to create the integrations, sign business contracts, deal with payments, and the like with another party.

The meaty portion of the DOJ's case was a parade of witnesses from publishers and competitors giving evidence of the ad server monopoly and its deep ties with the ad exchange and ad network. Tim Wolfe, the SVP of revenue operations for Gannett (owner of *USA Today* and many local newspapers) testified that he could not leave the Google ad server without sacrificing 50% to 60% of his revenue, which came from AdX. Steph Layser took the stand and reported how Project Cinderella at News Corp had determined the impossibility of switching. Matthew Wheatland from DMG essentially testified the same, that you could not switch without losing significant revenue.

Competitive ad servers also had a say. James Avery, the CEO of Durham, North Carolina, based ad serving company Kevel, testified about how he used to try to compete with Google but gave up and instead now specialized in niche markets. Tim Cadogan, formerly the CEO of OpenX, discussed how they shut down their competitive ad server in the face of impossible competitive constraints against Google.

The third day of the trial was held on September 11. Judge Brinkema made sure to somberly mark the anniversary and pointedly reminded the court that we were in the very courthouse where Zacarias Moussaoui, the only person ever convicted in relation to the tragic events, was tried.[18] On that day they brought Brad Bender to the stand, and so started the pattern where the first witness called each day was a current or former Google employee. The Google witnesses were not there to give unique testimony but were treated as foils for introducing damaging emails and presentations as evidence. Rarely did these witnesses testify to anything interesting, and the repeated use of phrases like "I do not recall" or "I wouldn't characterize it that way" prompted a court observer to hand out printed bingo cards to those following along.[19]

Brad, along with former VP of engineering Eisar Lipkovitz and engineering lead Nirmal Jayaram, were brought to the stand to paint the picture that the ad exchange's business growth came at the expense of investment in the AWBid project, which would have hurt the exchange business by spreading dollars to other exchanges.

To make the tying case between the ad exchange and the ad network, numerous witnesses and documents were presented showing pricing and integration discussions. Pricing for AdX was extremely stable over time, staying at 20% even in the face of competitive pressure. Damning emails were shown, like the email from Chris LaSala stating, "I think we are all in agreement that the 'exchange functionality' is not worth 20%"[20] or another gem where it was stated in a chat that "we extract irrationally high rent from the AdX."[21] Apparently people did not read Kent Walker's memo.

In a long half day of testimony, former product manager Rahul Srinivasan was forced to relive the awful day when Unified Pricing Rules were rolled out. In a shocking moment (at least as far as antitrust trials go), the DOJ convinced the judge to allow the actual audio recording of the meeting to be played.[22] The courtroom heard Steph Layser, Jana Maron, and others react in shock and dismay to the product announcement, as Rahul did his best to get through his slides.

The most anticipated Google witness was Neal Mohan. His career had skyrocketed at Google, and he was now the CEO of YouTube, arguably one of the most important jobs in all media. David Rosenblatt's hunch must have been right. Even the *New York Times* reporters came back to the courthouse to hear him testify, having only previously been present for opening arguments.[23] Neal testified about the core strategy for the display group at Google and how they sought to compete with yield managers. His comment that they wanted to buy a yield manager and "park it" was left dangling for the judge to consider. Unlike many of the other Google witnesses, he did not seem evasive and proudly defended much of the accomplishments of the display group under his management. He pointed out Google's investment in many of the tools in question, such as the years of work needed to rewrite DoubleClick's aging ad server into its modern incarnation.

In one of the most interesting exchanges of the trial, Neal defended Dynamic Allocation as a positive force for publishers, raising their revenue from unsold inventory by 136%. Judge Brinkema broke in to confirm, "That's compared to not having Dynamic Allocation, not compared to if other folks had access?" to which Neal conceded.

———————

In antitrust disputes, often the outcome depends on the market definition. The plaintiffs want the market to be defined as narrowly as possible, while the defendants want it to be as broad as possible. Substitute products must also be considered: Are gas stoves and microwave ovens in the same market or different ones? McDonald's restaurants are certainly competitors to Burger King, but are they also a competitor to Taco Bell?

Was Google really a monopoly? The way Google saw it, the ad network was competitive with all kinds of advertising options that even small advertisers could work with. Internal Google documents from as far back as 2018 showed Facebook with a larger share of the market than the ad network (which was $9.5 billion in 2017) and stated the expectation that Facebook's share would grow to 56% share by 2020.[24]

In this case the DOJ defined the relevant market as "open web display advertising," and if you spent time in the courthouse, you likely could hear these words while sleeping, so often were they repeated.

The "open" in the definition was meant to exclude ads purchased on social networks like Facebook. Since the only way to buy ads on Facebook, TikTok, or other social sites is to use those companies' tools, algorithms, and measurement, they are generally thought of as "closed" systems, sometimes called "walled gardens." Google internal documents and expert witnesses would show their ads business with a small and declining market share in display advertising, but only when the denominator of that share included social media competition.

The "web" in the definition was meant to exclude ads that appear in apps on mobile devices or on connected televisions. Google actively participates in the advertising bought and sold in these sectors but is not nearly as dominant. For in-app, Google had acquired AdMob to try to replicate the network-exchange-serving strategy that had worked so well on the web, but the market was fundamentally different. Ad serving was not considered very important by the biggest gaming apps, and network competitors like AppLovin and Ironsource were able to capture and maintain a significant share. In the video market, FreeWheel remains a strong competitor for ad serving and is owned by Comcast.

The ads in question are graphical, not text. Thus the "display" part of the market definition. There are other types of ads, like so-called "native" ads, that are on the open web and are on the same publisher sites as the ones within the overall ecosystem but are not display ads; they are more similar to search ads. The DOJ definition excluded those types of ads.

The nature of "open web display advertising" became a core part of both sides' case. The DOJ asked most of their non-Google witnesses if they knew what it meant, and while they all agreed with the definition, there was a little squishiness in some of the answers. One witness also included app ads, and another witness complicated his answer with some assumptions about how the ads were bought.

Google went straight to the heart of the matter. They asked Google witnesses whether Amazon and Facebook were competitors and showed internal documents saying as much. Non-Google witnesses were asked pointed questions like whether "native" or video ads are part of the market definition. Media buying witnesses were asked whether they would move clients' budget between social and web, as proof that the two were substitutes. There were some funny exchanges as well. Jay Friedman, from ad agency Goodway Group, was shown an image of facebook.com on a web browser on a laptop and asked, "Why aren't static squares on Facebook the same as display advertising?" His answer: "The Ritz-Carlton and Ramada Inn are both on squares of land."[25]

The market definition would be a key question for Judge Brinkema to answer. More than once the Google attorneys would argue that courts had set a minimum market share of 70% as a guideline for enforcing antitrust laws. Even if the market was tightly defined the way the DOJ suggested, AdX barely had more than 50% share of the ad exchange market after giving up some of its advantages to header bidding and the removal of Last Look. If you broadened the definition any bit, then Google suddenly appeared to be a minor player compared to mighty Facebook. Of course, the perspective changes if search ads are being considered; Google as a whole sells more ads than anyone else.

The DOJ brought forth Professor Gabriel Weintraub as an expert witness to testify about the scope and scale of Google's business. Dr. Weintraub testified about the enormous advantage Google held due to their scale. Even though AdX's market share hovered around 50%—relatively modest compared to the ad server's 90% share—it was about ten times larger than the next leading competitor. When AdX runs an A/B test on a new feature, it can get statistically significant results in one day, whereas other exchanges would take up to thirty days.[26] In this way Google's scale advantage fed a beneficial feedback loop to make its exchange even more dominant.

Weintraub analyzed Google's various conduct and ran simulations on raw data provided by the parties. He found that programs like First Look (really Dynamic Allocation) and Last Look had significantly buoyed Google's share of the market and number of winning auctions.

He highlighted Google's own internal experiments showing that UPR would increase spend on Google by an estimated $220 million and that Poirot increased by almost $270 million. However, the evidence also showed that there were customer benefits. Poirot, for example, was estimated to give advertisers a benefit of 11.5% by bidding on "clean" exchanges.

Dr. Robin Lee of Harvard testified about market definition and power. He showed data indicating that between 2018 and 2022, of the top one hundred Google ad serving customers, only one left for another option, an incredible 99% retention rate. The ad server's share was estimated to be 86.5% in the US and 91% worldwide. Professor Lee showed how dependent publishers were on AdX by calculating how much revenue would be lost by dropping the exchange. Publishers removing AdX would see a 27.9% decrease in revenue, whereas dropping any other competitive exchange would result in a 0.5% decrease, at worst.[27]

———

The DOJ's case took two weeks to present, while Google's defense only lasted four days. Google had intended to bring a parade of advertiser witnesses to the stand to presumably sing the company's praises and explain how important tools like Google Ads were to their business. One such shining example, Courtney Caldwell of ShearShare (a.k.a. Hair BnB), testified about her usage of Google Ads to promote her business across media channels and emphasized that she did not make any distinction between banner ads, video, and social ads.

Google's witness list got severely curtailed, however, when Judge Brinkema declared the expected testimony to be repetitive and not adding any incremental value. If this had been a jury trial, she emphasized, then the additional perspectives might be allowed, but with a bench trial, it was just not a good use of time. Since the government agency plaintiffs' claims had been dismissed, their testimony was also rendered moot. This was another instance in which Google's gambit with the cashier's check may have backfired.

On the first day of Google's case, they brought to the stand Scott Sheffer, the VP of publisher partnerships. It was unclear to observers what his testimony was supposed to illustrate. Sheffer was asked by counsel to diagram how complex all the Google products are and to draw lines showing how they interacted with one another, generating a giant mess of an oval on the courtroom screens. If this diagram was supposed to show that Google was *not* in control of every aspect of publisher businesses, it did the opposite. Perhaps the message was intended to show that there was so much complexity that it defies even the intervention of the US government; we will never know. We do know that the demonstration quickly turned to farce. The DOJ's lawyer for cross-examination took the stand and dryly asked the court AV guy to put the "spaghetti football" on the screen. Certainly the funniest moment of the trial and the origin of quite a few social media memes among court observers.

For the next week Google did very little to dispel or counterargue the alleged monopoly in ad serving or the ad exchange. The argument against these monopolies was focused on market definition. Their second line of defense focused on the investment and innovation that the company made in this business. Jessica Mok, a finance director who oversaw the display business at Google, testified that the whole business was not even profitable until 2018, a full decade after the Google acquisition. Professor Paul Milgrom from Stanford, an actual Nobel Laureate,[28] was brought in to defend AdX's auction dynamics, like Dynamic Allocation, First Look, and UBR. Even with a gold medal from Oslo, he could not defend Last Look as good for anyone but Google.

Google's final witness, and the person they would hang their market definition argument on, was Dr. Mark Israel, a frequent expert witness for corporations facing antitrust scrutiny. Dr. Israel's thesis was that subdividing the overall advertising market into product areas like ad serving or an ad exchange was wrong and that really there was a single all-encompassing market for digital advertising. "If you're not happy with Google's ad tech, you switch to another ad tech," he stated confidently from the stand. "If the ad server isn't good, maybe advertisers will not want to work with you and go to Facebook instead," he offered as a hypothetical.

Israel made similar statements about other aspects of publisher businesses, claiming that there were choices available to them that would obviate the monopolistic grasp that Google supposedly had. If you are unhappy with selling ads on the web, why don't you just move all your consumers to your mobile app? If you are unhappy selling ads through an exchange, why not just sell more ads directly?

On cross-examination, the DOJ attorney asked Israel a hypothetical: Could the *New York Times* use Facebook to sell an impression? Israel said the question did not matter given his market definition. This line of argument defied any kind of logic. There were real companies using real products, and the expert witness refused to validate that the use cases even existed.

The next day, Friday, was likely going to be the final day of testimony. After Google rested, the DOJ had the option to bring one or more rebuttal witnesses, and depending on the number and the extent of their testimony, that could mean we would spill into the following week. Judge Brinkema started the day with a love-in of a sort, offering attorneys from both sides praise for their professional conduct and demeanor during the rapid trial. That praise may have been a bit premature as the last witness turned out to be the most contentious of the whole trial.

The DOJ asked for a single rebuttal witness, Matthew Wheatland from DMG. As soon as his name was announced, the courtroom broke into objections, while observers and the press connected the dots on what seemed to be a stroke of genius. Wheatland had testified a week earlier from the publisher's perspective as a DOJ witness and had been among those to give evidence of the difficulty of switching ad servers.

He was not being called back to the stand to give more evidence about Google's products; he was being called back to give a real-world rebuttal to the leaps of logic and reason from Dr. Israel. The Google expert witness from the day before had given testimony with no basis in reality. It was the theoretical musings of a paid academic hack. Instead of countering his arguments with a different expert witness, the DOJ brought back a day-to-day practitioner. It was obvious this strategy would be devastating to Dr. Israel's credibility.

Google objected on the grounds that they should not be rebutting an expert with a "fact" witness and that Wheatland had already provided the needed facts. This went on for a while, and almost every question to Wheatland brought forth objections and discussion. In the end, Wheatland was allowed to testify and provided the publisher point of view, destroying Israel's credibility. The testimony went, more or less, as follows:

> **Question:** If advertisers can move ad spend, how does that help you negotiate for better rates with Google?
> **Answer:** No, that doesn't help.

> **Question:** If users move to viewing your content on apps, how does that help you negotiate for better rates with Google?
> **Answer:** No, that doesn't help.

> **Question:** Why can't you just move more of your users to use your apps?
> **Answer:** It is extremely hard. We only have 2% of usage on apps after a lot of effort.

> **Question:** Is there a cost with building and maintaining apps (Dr. Israel had said it was easy to do so)?
> **Answer:** Yes, we have ten full-time engineers on our Apple and Android apps and our website also monetizes better, so moving to the app would lose us money.

Question: Could you disable Last Look when it existed?
Answer: No.

Question: Did most publishers grow to like UPR after launch?
Answer: No.

Question: Do you have alternatives to using UPR?
Answer: No.

Question: Is AdX cheaper than alternatives?
Answer: No. AdX is twice the price of other exchanges.[29]

The Monday of Thanksgiving week, the court was back in session for closing arguments. Mrs. Tarver Wood would describe the discussion as "A Tale of Two Cities" given the divergent points of view on display between the plaintiffs and the defense. As expected, much of it came down to market definition.

The DOJ's arguments remained solidly based on facts and witness testimony. They preemptively made the point that market definition should be a "pragmatic tool" that helps identify submarkets that are the basis of competition for real participants, not just a theoretical exercise. Thus the testimony of real practitioners within the advertising business indicating they could not switch ad servers and were dependent on AdX for irreplaceable revenue.

Google's attorney Karen Dunn spent her closing focused mostly on the legal issues. She boldly made the claim to the judge that finding for the DOJ would require overturning two different Supreme Court precedents and then laid out in detail her arguments for each of the two cases.*

---

* The two cases are *Verizon Communications, Inc. v. Law Offices of Curtis V. Trinko* and *Ohio v. American Express Co.*

Using Google's very broad market definition, she was able to make assertions that minimized the company's apparent dominance and power. For example, she argued that most publishers do not pay for Google's ad server or use AdX—this is a strange framing since Google offers the ad server for free to very small publishers (of whom there are many) and shunts those customers to AdSense instead of the exchange.

There was also some sleight of hand with regard to Google's DSP. Dunn argued that since the DSP did bid outside of AdX, publishers were not dependent on AdX for unique demand. Unless this was a mistake, this argument had to be seen as an intentional falsehood. She was trying to confuse the demand from the DSP (which is available) with the demand from the ad network (which is not). A tale of two cities, indeed.

Dunn's conclusion was severely curtailed due to time constraints. The Rocket Docket had taken another victim.

Judge Brinkema ended the closing arguments by confidently asserting she wanted the case wrapped up by the end of the year. The holiday season came and went, with court observers frantically refreshing the court-filings websites looking for a ruling. Months passed, and the mystery of the case's outcome grew. One lawyer went so far as to pop by the judge's chambers unannounced to do a wellness check and make sure she was feeling OK. Rumors spread that there was a grand bargain underway or that Trump was going to swoop in and save Google at the last minute. One hundred days past her self-imposed deadline, Judge Brinkema dropped a 115-page ruling that definitively and clearly ruled against Google and declared its behavior anticompetitive and monopolistic. The ad server is a monopoly. The ad exchange is a monopoly. The tie between the two products is an unlawful one. Publishers were harmed by the monopoly and deserve justice. Google's market definition arguments were nonsense. Google's legal arguments were invalid.

The ruling was a clear victory for the DOJ and created a roadmap for breaking Google's iron grip on the advertising market. The judge's conclusion speaks for itself:

> Plaintiffs have proven that Google has willfully engaged in a series of anticompetitive acts to acquire and maintain monopoly power in the publisher ad server and ad exchange markets for open-web display advertising. For over a decade, Google has tied its publisher ad server and ad exchange together through contractual policies and technological integration, which enabled the company to establish and protect its monopoly power in these two markets. Google further entrenched its monopoly power by imposing anticompetitive policies on its customers and eliminating desirable product features. In addition to depriving rivals of the ability to compete, this exclusionary conduct substantially harmed Google's publisher customers, the competitive process, and, ultimately, consumers of information on the open web. Accordingly, Google is liable under Sections 1 and 2 of the Sherman Act.[30]

It was not a clean sweep, as some aspects of the ruling fell short for the DOJ. The ruling found that both the original DoubleClick acquisition and the contentious AdMeld buy were not anticompetitive, since at the time of those acquisitions, Google did not have monopolistic power in these areas. The ruling also dismissed allegations that Google Ads (the ad network) was a monopoly, which was not unexpected since the DOJ seemed to put very little effort into making that part of the case. These points, as well as the judge's reasoning around the case law, are potential avenues for an appeal.

In the final paragraphs of the ruling, Judge Brinkema asks the parties to regroup to consider remedies. What should be done, exactly, about this monopoly? The answer will determine much of the future of publishing and media.

CHAPTER 25

BREAKING UP IS HARD TO DO

If we think about remedies, wouldn't breaking the parts up reduce scale and hurt advertisers?[1]

—Hon. Leonie Brinkema

The conventional wisdom around antitrust cases in the US is that they tend to create change just as the abuses in question become less relevant. Put another way, they attack yesterday's problems.

Certainly, there's a sense of that in the Google case. Most of the alleged abuses happened in the past and many no longer even apply. When Google gave up Last Look and moved to a first-price auction, many of the opportunities to manipulate the auction, like Bernanke, went away. UPR remains, but at this point is baked in to the marketplace.

Google used to have perfect information about every auction in real time and use that data to change its bids and floor prices. In the modern day, they still have the information, but much of it is also shared with the competition. Technology has also evolved enough that instead of using perfect insights in real time, Google (and competitors) can use AI and machine learning to predict bids and prices with almost as much accuracy. They do not need to maintain an unfair platform advantage in ad serving to use their scale advantage in data and intelligence.

Open Bidding turned out to be a bust. The Trade Desk, the largest independent DSP, bans any purchasing through this channel.[2] The Jedi Blue deal with Facebook lost a lot of relevance once they shuttered their web ads business. While it remains in the app advertising market, that business is quite competitive, and Google is not necessarily the leader.

These changes in the market have hurt Google's business, which remains large but is no longer growing. In Google's financial reporting, they divide out the "Network" business to include AdMob, AdX, AdSense, the DSP, the ad network, and the ad servers. Since there is a hodgepodge of different businesses here that have different dynamics, it can be hard to figure out exactly where the growth is coming from. Overall, the segment roughly tripled in size in a decade, from $10.3 billion in 2011 to $31.7 billion in 2021. This last figure was bolstered by increased online activity during the COVID lockdowns, especially for the mobile AdMob business. Even without the exceptional 2021, though, the business had almost doubled, reflecting Google's execution of Neal Mohan's donut strategy and the growth of the DSP, the ad network, and AdX from virtually nothing to industry leaders.

Since 2021, though, growth has gone negative and the business remains at around $31 billion several years later.[3] If you reasonably assume mobile AdMob business outpaces the web businesses, it appears the businesses that are subject to the antitrust scrutiny are shrinking, perhaps quite rapidly. In terms of market share within the display market, various exhibits were shown in court that indicated a flattening or slight decline in Google's share in the period leading up to 2020 (the most recent period for which private data was shared under court order).

Within the larger context, the clear consumer trend has been toward consuming content on mobile devices and within social apps, marginalizing the exact types of publishers and media companies that have been fighting against Google's grip. The time consumers spent on mobile exceeded desktop sometime in 2018 or 2019,[4] and recent estimates show time spent on social media exceeds two hours per day.[5] Some mainstream publishers, like Weather.com and the *New York Times*, have thrived in the mobile-app-driven media ecosystem, but most have struggled. Use of websites for news dropped ten percentage points from 2018 through 2023, with all the gains going to social media, and these trends are present globally. The gap by age groups is also striking, with only 24% of young people using the web for news.[6]

Despite the whiff of "yesterday's problems" in the antitrust cases, for the media companies trapped in this maelstrom, they remain quite real. Their actual day-to-day businesses run on the Google ad serving "stack," and that is not going to change overnight. There are three questions that need to be answered: What should be done to stop future abuses? How much did Google siphon out of the market because of its monopoly? And how much of Google's market share and control was bolstered by ties between products?

What once seemed unthinkable is now a regular part of conversation in the courts and the advertising world. What if mighty Google was forcibly broken up?

The DOJ, the EU, and the Canadian government have all asked their courts to force Google to separate its sell-side advertising business, which includes the ad server and AdX. Google offered to just spin out AdX to satisfy EU regulators, but publishers rejected this as insufficient because the ad server would stick with the company.[7] A full breakup would sever the tie between the ad network's demand and the exchange and the ad server, thereby allowing other exchanges and ad servers to compete. But would this be good for publishers?

Publishers are apprehensive about the prospect of a spinout of Google's advertising assets. Like it or not, they are still highly dependent on the publisher ad server, and the prospect of it having uncertain ownership entails significant risk to their business's operations. While the ad server is a meaningfully sized software business on its own and likely could be made break-even or profitable on a standalone basis, in its current state, it is heavily subsidized by margin from AdX. If AdX had never existed, it is unlikely Google would have spent all the time and money modernizing the software, let alone acquiring it in the first place!

If the ad server was spun without AdX, that subsidy would disappear, resulting in fewer resources to maintain and improve the technology, and perhaps higher prices to publishers. Even if AdX and the ad server were spun together, the exclusive relationship with the ad network would disappear or be reduced. The unique demand from the ad network would be spread more evenly across exchanges, and as a result, revenue and resources for the spun-out entity would decline.

The fire hose of demand from the ad network could also be subject to uncertainty in a spinout. It may seem logical that absent the self-dealing, Google would naturally spread its demand across many exchanges, thus giving publishers more control over their monetization. In this line of thought, the remedy would free AWBid from the artificial constraints it has been under for years. That is an optimistic scenario, though. Currently the ad network generously splits its margin with either AdSense or AdX, depending on the path. When it bids on AdX, it only takes a 14% margin, so AdX can keep 20%. Freed of constraints and treating AdX at arm's length, the ad network would follow a profit-maximizing strategy and would seek to increase margin across all supply paths. You could imagine the ad network keeping 20% or 30% on every bid, thus reducing the amount paid to publishers. Further, we know that for years the ad network propped up AdX priced with double bids; while the move to first-price auctions made this unnecessary, it is certainly possible that there remain some forms of bid inflation between buy and sell sides, which would disappear when separated.

The bidding from Google's DSP could also be affected. Since the rollout of Poirot in 2017, more than half of the bids have gone to AdX. An independent AdX might not enjoy that privilege, and you would expect the bidding to be more even across exchanges. Once again, while a simple economic analysis might say that this should pressure exchanges to lower take rates, it could also cause less predictable outcomes, like a push from Google for lower publisher floors and prices when bidding.

There's also the issue of systematic efficiencies in Google's stack that come from being all in the same company. On the stand in the trial, one of the company's expert witnesses made this point. Google's expert witness, Dr. Israel, showed evidence that regardless of the (high) 20% fee from AdX, when you looked at paths between buyers and sellers, and added up the total fees, it was the intra-Google paths that were among the most efficient (cheapest).[8] For example, a buyer using the Google DSP and buying on AdX would have a lower total fee than a buyer using Criteo to buy ads on PubMatic. Some of these pricing efficiencies are born of explicit subsidies within the company and noneconomic decision-making. Testimony at the trial indicated that the whole display group ran unprofitably for many years and that only when AdMob and mobile took off did they become profitable. Former Google executives have indicated that the DSP is quite unprofitable to this day. It is very unclear what happens when all these subsidies disappear and the senior executives at Google take a fresh look at the remaining parts.

Data is also part of the equation. The sharing of cookies between all the parts of the stack gave advantages to buyers and sellers when targeting user behavior and reporting on advertising outcomes. Even with cookies becoming less relevant, the sharing of data remains a key advantage of Google's scale and scope of offerings. "If scale is critical and Google is blown apart, would that make it more difficult to buyers?" Judge Brinkema asked John Dederick, the chief revenue officer of The Trade Desk, while he was on the stand.[9] This is a very complex topic, and much of how Google uses data between products is not known, but it is a reasonable assumption that the broken-off parts of Google would lose much of the benefits they currently enjoy from Google's data.

One publisher executive made a stark historical analogy: "Like it or not, Google is a stable empire. Bring down the empire, and you might have the Dark Ages with no indoor plumbing. It could get worse before it gets better." They also pointed out that there could be economic considerations, saying, "If a private equity firm were to buy the ad server business and suddenly hike up prices, it could put some marginal publishers out of business." Finally, and most concerningly, they asked, "If Google no longer has a stake in the open web, why do they have an incentive to send anyone to the open web?"[10] This last point is crucial. Optimistic views of a breakup or spinout assume that the remaining Google business continues as usual and that the outcome is mostly a change in economics. This view discounts Google's increasing emphasis on YouTube and declining dependence on the Network business. What if Google simply picked up their toys and went home?

Estimating the damage done to publishers from Google's activities is difficult. If you look at some of the very specific actions that Google undertook, in many cases they could prove that they *increased* publisher revenue. Bernanke improved publisher payouts by 8% as some auctions that would not otherwise have cleared did so at manipulated prices.[11] This came at the expense of competitive exchanges, who might have otherwise helped publishers in other ways, but that's hard to quantify since it did not, after all, happen.

The simplest way to get a handle on the damage done to publishers is to assume that AdX has retained more than its deserved share of the exchange market and then to try to estimate how much more they extracted from publishers due to this share than they reasonably should have. This argument was made in the DOJ trial by their expert witness Dr. Timothy Simcoe of Boston University. While AdX's take rate was a consistent 20%, competitors experienced a gradual decline in take rates into the mid-teens percentage range. Simcoe asserted that the overall rates in this business were artificially bolstered by AdX's 20%, like cyclists following the leader of a peloton. If the market were truly competitive and absent monopolistic behavior, the take rates for all players would have declined across the board.

Ultimately, Simcoe derived 16% as AdX's proper take rate if not for the monopoly ties with the ad network and the ad server. According to other evidence in the trial, total AdX revenue peaked at around $10 billion per year, which would put the damages to publishers at $400 million per year (4% over charge * $10 billion). This analysis does not consider the lack of innovation in the ad server market or the inability of publishers to properly negotiate for lower rates from AdX and other partners. It also does not consider the cross-subsidies with other Google products.

One of the flaws of the Google antitrust trials is the exclusion of YouTube from consideration. YouTube has been absent from government enforcement action around the world because as a matter of market definition, it exists within the video market, which includes giants like Netflix, Comcast, TikTok, and many others. While YouTube is a huge cultural and commercial force in the market, it cannot be said to have monopoly market share. This is one reason the DOJ's market definition specified "display ads."

Yet YouTube is part of the story. In 2014 Google changed its policies to only allow its own DSP to buy ads on YouTube. This was a kidney punch to independent DSPs who lost access to the largest source of video supply on the internet. Brian O'Kelley testified before Congress on this point, saying, "This was a devastating move for AppNexus and other independent ad technology companies. YouTube was (and is) the largest ad-supported video publisher, with more than 50% market share in most major markets."[12] Joe Zawadski estimated it was 15% of his revenue at MediaMath before getting cut off.[13]

In 2021 Google announced the general availability of a new optimization capability within Google Ads, called PMax. This new capability optimizes against advertiser goals with limited input for the user. It is the "set it and forget it" tool. According to some estimates, more than half of campaigns in Google Ads now use this technology. PMax is the ultimate expression of the sentiment that performance is all that matters to advertisers.

PMax is tied to YouTube and has access to the enormous number of ad impressions on that platform, along with all the data about how those ads perform. No other ad system has that level of data access. Not surprisingly, large amounts of PMax-controlled budgets are spent on YouTube. Very likely these budgets are shifting to YouTube at the expense of the ad inventory that is sold by AdX, which is more competitive and has higher floor prices, and is a business where Google must share more revenue with publishers. While we do not have any information about how individual budgets are shifting to YouTube, we know that on a macro basis, Google's financial statements have shown a notable shift in revenue from Network business to YouTube, with the former shrinking and the latter growing consistently. YouTube ad revenue became larger than the Network as of the third quarter of 2023 and shows no signs of slowing down.* [14]

While it is not part of a court case, the YouTube exclusive tie with the DSP and the shifting of budgets from PMax likely also cost publishers significant revenues. Even for publishers that partner with YouTube, their yield from ads is far less than when consumers visit their sites or apps directly to watch video. Integrating with other DSPs would likely increase

---

* Call it the "Neal Mohan effect": the network grows from nothing to $30 billion under his watch, then as soon as he joins YouTube, that business takes all the growth.

YouTube revenues, but they refuse on policy grounds.* CPMs on YouTube remain stubbornly lower than on other video platforms, and that comes before the revenue share to Google. Google also pushes consumers to YouTube in search over other video content, an accusation Rumble detailed in their lawsuit against the company.

Google's strategic disadvantage against Facebook was always the lack of O & O, or Owned and Operated properties. Facebook has so much consumer attention on its apps that it never had to run the Three Pillars strategy or convince publishers to use its technology to show more ads. YouTube is belatedly solving this problem, with enormous consumer growth across all devices and great opportunities for monetization. It is no surprise Google as a whole is slowly moving to the same "closed" ad strategy on YouTube that Sheryl Sandberg and Mark Zuckerberg endorsed on Facebook a decade earlier. The difference is Google *also has* an open ecosystem in their DSP to use for cross-subsidization.

One of the stranger themes of the Google antitrust case was the suggestion, from a number of witnesses, that perhaps the ad server should become a common good, as a form of advertising socialism. Self-described libertarian and former VP of engineering at Google Eisar Lipkovitz suggested on the stand, "I'd rather DFP be a public good."[15] Steph Layser wrote an op-ed that the Google legal team showed her during cross-examination where she had opined, "Community assets should not be owned by private companies,"[16] which she later mocked on LinkedIn with the hashtag #adtechsocialist.[17] Tom Kershaw, one of the founders of prebid.org and the former CTO of Rubicon, also advocated on the stand for a socialized ad server of some kind.

---

* Google claims that they saw little revenue decline when first removing YouTube access, but this was before widespread buying of online video ads.

Some outside of the trial took these suggestions seriously. Richard Kramer, an equity analyst who often criticizes Google, wrote that the network business should be spun out into a B Corp—designating a for-profit entity that also considers social goals—existing to help journalism and publishing rather than any specific profit motive.[18]

Brian O'Kelley, with an equal amount of humor and malice, suggested that Google be forced to operate the ad server indefinitely at zero profit.[19] That is one way to pay penance for your sins. "What's missing from the equation is a competitive landscape," said another publisher executive.[20]

Aside from the feasibility of these suggestions, it is important to consider that a spinout of the Google assets could also be dangerously abused if not also regulated. After the AT&T breakup of the 1980s, the Baby Bells largely recreated the monopoly through acquisitions. An independent ad serving company would still have near monopoly power over publishers, opening the opportunity for abuse. The spun-out company could raise prices, manipulate the auction for its own benefit, acquire related companies, or do any kind of thing that might not be in the interests of its customers. Does anyone think that the ad server would be less abusive if owned by Microsoft, Meta, or Oracle?

———————————

In a separate DOJ antitrust trial that concluded spring 2024, Judge Amit Mehta found Google to be operating a monopoly in both search and the text ads relating to search. The company was found to be maintaining its monopoly by plowing the money it made from its dominant search business into distribution deals that reinforced the monopoly in Apple products, as well as its own Chrome browser and Android operating system. While the Network business is in decline and Google might be willing to spin it out, search is the company's cash cow and flagship product, and the government is likely to face stubborn resistance pursuing any remedy.

The departing DOJ team in the Biden administration asked the court for a radical remedy in the case: the end of the Apple payments and the divestment of the Chrome browser. The remedies trial commenced in the spring of 2025 and is expected to conclude in the summer.

The range of potential remedies in the search trial are problematic and unsatisfying. Would a Chrome spinout help consumers? The browser business is largely subsidized by payments from Google, so without that flow of funds, there would be far less resourcing to an independent Chrome. Removing the Apple payment would save Google over $20 billion per year, as consumers likely will choose that search engine as their default anyway.

To critics of the case, the DOJ is also litigating the last battle, as Google search comes under pressure from a new wave of AI-based search engines like Perplexity and OpenAI and the paradigm of the "blue links" erodes. The two trials can also be seen as linked and all part of the overwhelming data advantage Google holds over all the markets in which it operates. The Google ad team is near obsessed with keeping their tag on publisher pages, not just because it helps get more yield on ads but also because it collects data about the page, the user, and the environment more readily. Ownership of the Chrome browser also puts Google in the driver's seat with regard to privacy and policy issues that ultimately protect their advertising interests as seen from their actions on cookies and the Sandbox.

Politics plays a role in thinking about outcomes. With both the search and the advertising remedies on the agenda at the time the new, ostensibly "anti-tech" Trump administration comes to power, perhaps these two cases can be seen as pieces on the board for trading. The Microsoft antitrust case, for example, evaporated with a change in the executive branch in Washington, with the new George W. Bush administration uninterested in pursuing remedies after a guilty verdict. It is possible that the new administration will seek a "grand bargain" of some kind that perhaps gives concessions in the search case while forcing an advertising spinout.

CHAPTER 26

WINNING THE PEACE

What we're looking for is sustainability for journalism.[1]
—Richard Caccappolo

C ould Google have been just as successful but done things differently? Hindsight is twenty-twenty, but there are a couple of junctures where the company's dysfunction seems to have blinded it to the flaws in its approach.

The ad exchange, AdX, was never as important to the strategy as it seemed. The exchange was incubated as Project Wolf within DoubleClick, which made sense because that company did not have a media arm or an ad network to sell ads. If you cannot sell ads, then being a middleman for their sale to others makes sense and is a great business opportunity. Once part of Google, though, Neal Mohan's Three Pillars strategy could have collapsed to just two, the ad server and the ad network. Google's ad network wanted access to the ad server's inventory and could have built that as a feature into the ad server rather than spin up a whole second-price mechanism with all the complexity and politics that went with it. Call it "Dynamic Allocation for AdSense" and be done with it. Publishers and other ad exchanges would still have an issue with Google giving itself preferences, but optically there would no longer be any assumption that it was running a fair exchange or had any obligation to other parties. AdX was also a highly subsidized business. More than half of its revenue came from the ad network, and the prices the network paid were for many years highly inflated by the double bidding.

Consider a thought experiment: What would the Google strategy have been if header bidding already existed at the time of the DoubleClick acquisition? The Google ad network might have just bid into the header instead of pursuing the acquisition in the first place. Even with the acquisition, it would have been far simpler to enable direct ad network bidding instead of trying to manage and grow a middleman business in the exchange.

The obvious area where Google crossed a line was just that—when they crossed between the interests of their advertisers and their publishers. In the first iteration of AdX, the exchange through Dynamic Allocation could win an auction for one cent more than the highest order in the ad server. While this damaged competitors, it was still mostly to the benefit of the publisher because it made them more money. The ethics of that same mechanism changes, though, when the buy-side ad network is given the pricing data and can manipulate its bid to come in just high enough to win. That still makes publishers money but eliminates the opportunity to make more money from bids without the information advantage.

When Jonathan Bellack was confronted by his customer Joey Trotz about why he should support header bidding, it was a wake-up call. Emails show that inside Google people knew what customers really wanted—a free and fair unified auction—but internal politics killed it. Instead, the Open Bidding solution charged too high of a fee to be viable and did not have enough flexibility to get wide-scale adoption. Open Bidding failed at its goal of being better than header bidding. A version of Open Bidding that was cheap (or just charged ad serving fees), where the participants could choose to contract directly, and where there was an on-ramp for DSPs and buy-side bidders to participate at lower than the 20% fee of AdX would have had the potential to solve many of the industry's problems.

As for the worst sins of the era, Global Bernanke and Unified Pricing Rules, all one can say is there was a failure of leadership. At some point the people inside the company who cared about publishers and their business model were either too powerless or uninterested to make a difference and stand up to do the right thing.

———————

It is worth spending a bit of time thinking about what went wrong with web advertising as a whole. The web as we know it has been commercially available for three decades, since about 1994, when the first banner ad for AT&T ran on hotwired.com. Consumers have benefited enormously from content on the web: just looking at Wikipedia sometimes feels like a miracle. For anyone old enough to remember, there is still a sense of awe when you can access the hundred-year archive of the *New York Times*, post your own blog, or research vacations in seconds. All that needs to be paid for.

Web advertising works but in many ways was never a great business. One just has to remember how fast Google Search or Facebook advertising grew from nothing to be the two largest advertising businesses in the world. Traditional web display had all the advantages on paper but never experienced that kind of sustained growth. The web was backed by hundred-year-old media companies, with all the best advertiser relationships, with great brands, editorial capabilities, and sales relationships, yet the business is much smaller and less attractive than what was built by the technology-first West Coast companies.

There are a bunch of flaws to the web advertising business model, but most of them come down to fragmentation. There are hundreds of publishers and thousands of sites that make up the premium portion of the advertising-supported web. Despite many efforts to set standards, these sites are all laid out differently, with different ad opportunities. Cookies were always a brittle and unreliable way to track consumers. Compare this to the always logged-in users on Instagram and the standard square ad units in the feed, and you start to see the flaws of the web model.

Consumers also voted with their feet (really their eyeballs). Social apps have directly siphoned away time and attention from news and journalism websites because consumers simply use those apps more. The transition of time from the web to apps has also hurt traditional publishers, as consumers do not generally download news or magazine apps, other than a select few.

Google is being accused of doing too much to manipulate and capture the web advertising market, but an argument can be made that they did too little to really fix the problems. Consider the Privacy Sandbox. The Chrome team attempted to replace cookies with less effective but privacy-friendly alternatives. Never was there a discussion about giving consumers value for their data consent, like allowing Google single-sign-on to be used for advertising purposes, or other approaches that might help, rather than hinder, the advertising community.

As video and app consumption grew to surpass the web, the actions of Google, Facebook, and the other big tech companies did nothing to sustain an "open" environment for journalism or publishing. YouTube restricted both supply and demand to throttle efforts of traditional media companies to thrive on the platform. Google News, Apple News, and Facebook Instant Articles have all been half-hearted attempts, without meaningful positive impacts. To be clear, the big tech companies are not charities, but still their attitude toward traditional media can be characterized as flippant at best.

The years 2023 and 2024 may have seen the greatest vibe shift among media companies, as they realized the old paradigm of traffic acquisition and monetization was breaking down. Google postponed the "cookiep-ocalypse" but Chrome intends to do *something* about them, even if we do not know exactly what. Facebook traffic to news sites is down 50%. Tech giants like Amazon are winning sports rights away from traditional broadcasters. The hottest "media" companies are Uber, DoorDash, and Walmart. And of course, there is the specter of AI.

It is hard to predict how AI is going to play out in the media world, but it is already having dramatic effects. In May 2024, before the Virginia antitrust trial started but after Google Search had been declared a monopoly by Judge Mehta, the company announced the expansion of its AI-driven powered search results, dubbed AI Overviews. The implications for publishers that rely on traffic from Google were clear and unsurprising. When consumers get the entire answer they need from the search results on Google, clicking out to media company websites becomes moot.

A flurry of AI licensing deals has been struck, such as Reddit's $30 million annual license to OpenAI[2] or, in contrast, the *New York Times'* lawsuit against OpenAI and Microsoft for *not* licensing their data.[3] These new revenues will have to make up for the drop in traffic, as referrals from Google and social networks are way down and show no sign of returning. Elon Musk's X platform has systematically reduced the reach of any post that includes a URL, thus neutering the news traffic it gives off.[4]

It is fair to say that no one knows how the media business is going to look in even five years. Journalism and media are already at the intersection of trends in AI, with questions of authenticity and generated content at the forefront. The problem of ever-growing advertising-supported content is even more critical in an era where the machines can create the content themselves.

AI is also accelerating the growth of the big platforms over the independent internet. Only companies as large as Google, Meta, and Amazon have enough data to make the transition to AI-driven advertising. Google's PMax now competes with Meta's Advantage+ and Amazon's

Performance Plus in the drive to automate as much of advertising as possible.

On the agency and advertiser side, the uncertainty is acute. Sam Altman, the CEO of OpenAI, recently said, "Ninety-five percent of what marketers use agencies, strategists, and creative professionals for will easily, nearly instantly, and at almost no cost be handled by the AI."[5] In a sense this is a modest prediction because it assumes that the tasks those people do will be the same tasks delegated to the machines, which seems increasingly like a leap of faith in normalcy. Consider a world where the consumer does not even visit a website to get information about a product but instead an autonomous agent collects and collates the information to make a purchase decision—what is the role of media, agencies, or advertising in that transaction?

AI is set to radically transform the relationship between media, technology, and consumers, and no one knows how it will play out.

Richard Caccappolo is CEO of DMG and a leader in the media insurrection against Google. Along with Gannett, DMG is one of the plaintiffs in a civil antitrust suit against Google that has yet to come to trial as of this writing. I met with him in his office off Saint Mark's Place in the East Village and asked what he really wanted the result of all this to be: Is it just a money grab, or is it about justice or something else?

His answer really surprised me. He said he wants to focus on "winning the peace." He sees the antitrust and legislative checks on Google's power as part of a rebalancing of the tone and relationship between technology and Google. "Google is going to innovate, and we want to be there with them," he said.

There's no going back to the good old days of sustainable ad supported journalism. The traditional media companies are in a critical state and are fighting for their future. Kicking Google—one of the world's most powerful companies—out of the game doesn't assure victory. The framing of media versus tech is at fault. It's not a contest, it's a partnership.

WHERE ARE THEY NOW?

M any of the people involved in these events have gone on to become powerful CEOs outside of advertising. Below are some highlights as of early 2025, with names listed alphabetically.

Tim Armstrong: CEO, Flowcode, a private QR-code start-up

Ben Barokas: CEO, SourcePoint, privacy tech for publishers

Michael Barrett: CEO, Magnite, a publicly traded company

Jonathan Bellack: Director of the Applied Social Media Lab at Harvard

Brad Bender: After a stint as head of Google News, he left the company and is now investing and participating in boards

Richard Caccappolo: CEO, DMG Media (owner of the *Daily Mail*)

Tim Cadogan: CEO, GoFundMe

Rajiv Goel: CEO, PubMatic, a publicly traded company

Chris LaSala: Professor, Columbia Business School

Steph Layser: Worldwide head, Publisher Ad Tech Solutions, Amazon

Brian Lesser: CEO, GroupM

Marissa Mayer: CEO, Sunshine, a private consumer app company

Jana Meron: Vice president of revenue operations and data, the Washington Post Company

Wenda Harris Millard: Sitting on many board seats

Neal Mohan: CEO, YouTube

Brian O'Kelley: CEO, Scope3, carbon measurement start-up

David Rosenblatt: CEO, 1stDibs, publicly traded marketplace for design and furniture

Michael Rubenstein: CEO, FirstHand.ai, an AI start-up founded with FreeWheel alumnus Jon Heller

Payam Shodjai: Senior director, Meta

Scott Spencer: CEO, Rewarded Interest, privacy start-up

Nat Turner: Cofounder with Zach Weinberg of Tribeca Health, sold to Roche for over $3 billion, now CEO of Collectors, a start-up focused on sports memorabilia

Michael Walrath: CEO, Yext, publicly traded SMB marketing company

Zach Weinberg: Cofounder with Nat Turner of Tribeca Health, sold to Roche for over $3 billion, now CEO of Curie.bio, a biotech start-up

Susan Wojcicki: Susan left YouTube to focus on her health and tragically passed away from lung cancer in 2024

ACKNOWLEDGMENTS

A big thanks to the beat reporters and editors at *AdExchanger, Adweek, Digiday*, and *Business Insider*. Lara O'Reilly, Zach Rodgers, Allison Schiff, Ronan Shields, Sarah Sluis, and many others spent a decade documenting the ins and outs of this confusing and colorful industry. If we are keeping score, Sarah absolutely dominates the leaderboard for endnotes in this book.

I also relied on the work of Arielle Garcia of Checkmyads for much of the Google material disclosed. Arielle took the effort to organize and index so many of the exhibits from the DOJ antitrust trial, making it easier for journalists and interested parties to get access to that material.

And a special thanks to all the sixty or so people who shared their insights with me. The world of advertising can be dull, but it shines when we hear the stories of those who were in the trenches.

NOTES

Chapter 1: Welcome to Silicon Alley

1   Author conversation with Wenda Harris Millard

2   "Interview with Kevin Ryan," *TechCrunch*, May 22, 2011, https://techcrunch.com/2011/05/22/founder-stories-doubleclick-kevin-ryan/

3   "77% of Advertising on the Web Is Bought by 'Dot-Com' Firms," *Los Angeles Times*, September 6, 2000, https://www.latimes.com/archives/la-xpm-2000-sep-06-fi-16112-story.html

4   "DoubleClick Sells Its Media Sales Business to L90," *New York Times*, July 1, 2002, https://www.nytimes.com/2002/07/01/business/doubleclick-sells-its-media-sales-business-to-l90.html

5   DoubleClick's FY 2002 10K shows the TechSolutions business with $187 million in revenue against $303 million in total revenue, including Abacus and other businesses

6   "2003 Full-Year IAB Internet Advertising Revenue Report," April 1, 2004, https://www.iab.com/insights/2003-full-year-iab-internet-advertising-revenue-report/

7   "DoubleClick Retains Banking Firm to Explore 'Strategic Options,'" *Ad Age*, November 1, 2004, https://adage.com/article/digital/doubleclick-retains-banking-firm-explore-strategic-options/41439

8   "Buyout Firm to Acquire DoubleClick for $1 Billion," *New York Times*, April 26, 2005, https://www.nytimes.com/2005/04/26/technology/buyout-firm-to-acquire-doubleclick-for-1-billion.html

9   DoubleClick, Inc. 10K dated December 31, 2004 shows $126 million in cash on hand, https://www.sec.gov/Archives/edgar/data/1049480/000095012305003222/y06461e10vk.htm#302

10   Ibid.

11   Nasdaq, https://www.nasdaq.com/market-activity/ipos/overview?dealId=7108-5111

12   "DoubleClick Buys NetGravity," *New York Times*, July 14, 1999, https://archive. nytimes.com/www.nytimes.com/library/tech/99/07/cyber/articles/14advertising.html

13   Neal Mohan, March 23, 2009, "Re. sale reductions," email filed in *US et al v Google LLC*

14   "DoubleClick Sells E-Mail Unit for $90M," *Digital Marketing News*, February 15, 2006, https://www.dmnews.com/doubleclick-sells-email-unit-for-90m/

15   "Doubleclick Sells Abacus to Epsilon-for-435m," *MediaPost*, December 29, 2006, https://www.mediapost.com/publications/article/53117/doubleclick-sells-abacus-to-epsilon-for-435m.html

16   "DoubleClick Acquires Klipmart," *Ad Age*, June 29, 2006, https://adage.com/article/digital/doubleclick-acquires-klipmart/110264

17   Author interview with David Rosenblatt, November 2024

Chapter 2: A Stupid Feature

1   "40. Brian O'Kelley (Part 2)—The Right Media Experience," *Paleo Ad Tech* podcast, December 10, 2023, https://paleoadtech.com/2023/12/10/40-brian-okelley-part-2-the-right-media-experience/

2   Author interview with Michael Walrath, December 2024

3   Author interview with Bill Wise, December 2024

4   Author interview with Joe Zawadski; note this version of events slightly contradicts some of Brian O'Kelley's in minor ways

5   Author interview with Brian O'Kelley, November 2024

6   "40. Brian O'Kelley (Part 2)—The Right Media Experience," *Paleo Ad Tech* podcast, December 10 2023, https://paleoadtech.com/2023/12/10/40-brian-okelley-part-2-the-right-media-experience/

7   "RMX Direct: Alternative Ad Networks Battle for Your Blog," *TechCrunch*, August 12, 2006, https://techcrunch.com/2006/08/12/rmx-direct-alternative-ad-networks-battle-for-your-blog/

8   Author interview with Brian O'Kelley, November 2024

9   "RMX Direct: Alternative Ad Networks Battle for Your Blog," *TechCrunch*, August 12, 2006, https://techcrunch.com/2006/08/12/rmx-direct-alternative-ad-networks-battle-for-your-blog/

Chapter 3: Supply and Demand

1   Author interview with Gokul Rajaram, December 2024

2   "The House that Helped Build Google," *USA Today*, September 26, 2019, https://usatoday30.usatoday.com/tech/techinvestor/corporatenews/2007-07-04-google-wojcicki_N.htm

3   Author interview with Gokul Rajaram, December 2024

4   Ibid.

5   "Introducing Google Ad Planner," *Inside AdWords* company blog, June 24, 2008, https://adwords.googleblog.com/2008/06/introducing-google-ad-planner.html

Chapter 4: Project Wolf

1   Author interview with a former DoubleClick and Google employee who remains anonymous and is not authorized to speak on these issues

2   Ibid.

3   Clayton M. Christensen, *The Innovator's Dilemma: When New Technologies Cause Great Firms to Fail* (Boston: Harvard Business Review Press, 1997)

4   Ibid.

5   "Project Centillion," undated, slide deck from DoubleClick, provided by a former employee

6   Ibid.

7   "DoubleClick to Buy Falk," *AdWeek*, March 20, 2006, https://www.adweek.com/brand-marketing/doubleclick-buy-falk-84567/

8   Author interview with Joe Zawadski, December 2024

9   Interview with Michael Rubenstein, November 2024

10   Ibid.

11   Interviews with former DoubleClick employees, left anonymous to not be mean spirited

12   "Dynamic content selection and delivery," US Patent US8306857B2

13   To see how this concept has evolved over time, see the current era Google help article "Line item types and priorities," https://support.google.com/admanager/answer/177279?hl=en

14   "The DoubleClick Marketplace (a.k.a. Project Wolf) Presentation to DoubleClick Board," June 21, 2006, provided by former DoubleClick employee

15   Ibid.

16   "IAB Internet Advertising Revenue Report," May 2007, https://www.iab.com/wp-content/uploads/2015/05/resources_adrevenue_pdf_IAB_PwC_2006_Final.pdf

17   "DoubleClick to Set Up an Exchange for Buying and Selling Digital Ads," *New York Times*, April 4, 2007, https://www.nytimes.com/2007/04/04/business/media/04adco.html

Chapter 5: YMAG

1   David Rosenblatt, February 11, 2009, transcript of talk given to Google sales team as captured by Clay Bavor, filed in *US et al v Google LLC*

2   Author interview with David Rosenblatt, November 2024

3   David Rosenblatt, February 11, 2009, transcript of talk given to Google sales team as captured by Clay Bavor, filed in *US et al v Google LLC*

4   Ibid.

5   Unnamed Google employee, likely Jason Harinstein, May 19, 2007, "Project Liberty Revisited: EMG Deal Review," presentation filed in *US et al v Google LLC*

6   Ken Auletta, *Googled: The End of the World as We Know It* (New York: Penguin Press, 2009)

7   Interview with David Rosenblatt, November 2024

8   "Scoop: We Found the Deck DoubleClick Used to Sell Itself to Google," *The Monopoly Report*, September 4, 2024, https://monopoly.marketecture.tv/p/the-deck-doubleclick-used-to-sell-to-google

9   Ibid.

10   "DoubleClick Explores a Sale," *Wall Street Journal*, March 28, 2007, https://www.wsj.com/articles/SB117505407416851554

11   David Rosenblatt, February 11, 2009, transcript of talk given to Google sales team as captured by Clay Bavor, filed in *US et al v Google LLC*

12   David Drummond, March 23, 2007, "Project Liberty—CONFIDENTIAL," email filed in *US et al v Google LLC*

13   Ibid.

14   "Satya Nadella Tells a Court that Bing Is Worse than Google—and Apple Could Fix It,"
       The Verge, October 2, 2023, https://www.theverge.com/2023/10/2/23900233/microsoft-
       ceo-satya-nadella-us-google-antitrust-trial-testimony

15   "Google Buys DoubleClick for $3.1 Billion," *New York Times*, April 14, 2007, https://
       www.nytimes.com/2007/04/14/technology/14DoubleClick.html

16   "Brits Buy Up the Ad Business," *New York Times Magazine*, July 2, 1989, https://www.
       nytimes.com/1989/07/02/magazine/brits-buy-up-the-ad-business.html. Note: The byline
       on this article is Randall Rothenberg, who would later run the IAB, the main trade orga-
       nization in digital advertising

17   Author interview with Rob Norman, November 2024

18   Author interview with Michael Walrath, December 2024

19   "Yahoo to Buy Rest of Right Media for $680 Mln," Reuters, August 9, 2007, https://
       www.reuters.com/article/us-rightmedia-yahoo-idUSN3037037520070430/

20   Author interview with Michael Walrath

21   "Dot-Com Fever Stirs Sense of Déjà Vu," *New York Times*, October 16, 2007, https://
       www.nytimes.com/2007/10/16/business/worldbusiness/16iht-bubble.4.7915048.html

22   Author interview with Brian O'Kelley, November 2024

23   "Microsoft to Acquire aQuantive, Inc.," Microsoft press release, May 18, 2007, https://
       news.microsoft.com/2007/05/18/microsoft-to-acquire-aquantive-inc/

24   Interview with former Google executive who spoke off the record to not seem like a
       jackass

25   "Ad Exchange AdECN Acquired By Microsoft," *AdExchanger*, July 27, 2007, https://
       www.adexchanger.com/investment/ad-exchange-adecn-acquired-by-microsoft/

26   "Microsoft to Acquire AdECN, Inc.," Microsoft press release, July 26, 2007, https://
       news.microsoft.com/2007/07/26/microsoft-to-acquire-adecn-inc/

27   "AOL Buys an Online Ad Company," *New York Times*, July 25, 2007, https://www.
       nytimes.com/2007/07/25/technology/25aol.html

28   "AOL Buys German Online Ad Company Adtech," Reuters, https://www.reuters.com/
       article/lifestyle/aol-buys-german-online-ad-company-adtech-idUSN16474846/

29   "WPP to buy 24/7 Real Media for $649 million," Reuters, August 9, 2007, https://www.
       reuters.com/article/business/media-telecom/wpp-to-buy-247-real-media-for-649-mil-
       lion-idUSN17274450/

Chapter 6: Bring in the Snacks

1   "Statement of Federal Trade Commission Concerning Google/DoubleClick," December
       20, 2007

2   "Trump's 'War on 'Losers': The Early Years," *Vanity Fair*, August 12, 2015, https://
       www.vanityfair.com/news/2015/08/spy-vs-trump

3   "Google Buys Deja Archive," *Wired*, Feb 12, 2001, https://www.wired.com/2001/02/
       google-buys-deja-archive/

4   "Google Offering Print Ads to More Advertisers & Papers," Search Engine Land, July 18,
       2007, https://searchengineland.com/
       google-offering-print-ads-to-more-advertisers-papers-11723

5   Author interview with Tom Phillips, November 2024

6   "Google Enters TV Ad Sales Market with EchoStar," NBC News, April 3, 2007, https://
       www.cnbc.com/2007/04/03/google-enters-tv-ad-sales-market-with-echostar.html

7   Interview with Tom Phillips, November 2024

8   "Google/DoubleClick Inside Story: 'FTC Will Approve,'" *Business Insider*, September
       27, 2007, https://www.businessinsider.com/2007/9/googledoublec-1

9   "Google Deal Said to Bring U.S. Scrutiny," *New York Times*, May 29, 2007, https://
      www.nytimes.com/2007/05/29/technology/29antitrust.html
10   Ibid.
11   "DoubleClick, Abacus Tie," *CNN Money*, June 14, 1999, https://money.cnn.
      com/1999/06/14/technology/doubleclick/
12   "Privacy Advocates Rally against DoubleClick-Abacus Merger," *CNET*, Jan. 2, 2002,
      https://www.cnet.com/tech/services-and-software/privacy-advocates-rally-against-
      doubleclick-abacus-merger/; editorial note—the date on the article appears wrong, since
      the deal closed in 2000
13   "DoubleClick Buys Abacus (A)," *Harvard Business School*, April 2000 (Revised June
      2001), https://www.hbs.edu/faculty/Pages/item.aspx?num=27164. This case study makes
      the claim it was the *USA Today* article, cited as "Cookies: How sites know what they
      know," *USA Today*, January 25, 2000
14   "Critics Aim at DoubleClick," *CNN Money*, March 6, 2000, https://money.cnn.
      com/2000/03/06/technology/privacy_doubleclick/
15   "DoubleClick in New Suit," *CNN Money*, February 17, 2000, https://money.cnn.
      com/2000/02/17/technology/doubleclick/
16   "DoubleClick Buys Abacus (A)," *Harvard Business School*
17   "Ad Big Rips Google Deal," *New York Post*, April 23, 2007, https://nypost.
      com/2007/04/23/ad-big-rips-google-deal/
18   Auletta, *Googled*; author cites an anonymous source
19   "An Examination of the Google-DoubleClick Merger and the Online Advertising Indus-
      try: What Are the Risks for Competition and Privacy? Hearing Before the Subcommittee
      on Antitrust, Competition Policy and Consumer Rights," September 27, 2007
20   Ibid.
21   Ibid.
22   Ibid.
23   "Google Vows to Double Protect Consumer Privacy," *Wired*, Apr 17, 2007, https://www.
      wired.com/2007/04/google-vows-to-doubleprotect-consumer-privacy/
24   "Rivals Get Business Over 'Google Click' Threat," *New York Post*, May 9, 2007, https://
      nypost.com/2007/05/09/rivals-get-business-over-google-click-threat/
25   "Statement of Federal Trade Commission Concerning Google/DoubleClick," December
      20, 2007
26   Ibid.
27   Ibid.
28   Ibid.
29   Ibid.
30   "Google to Sell off DoubleClick's Performics Unit," *Computerworld*, April 03, 2008,
      https://www.computerworld.com/article/1574655/google-to-sell-off-doubleclick-s-
      performics-unit.html
31   "Google HR Boss Explains Why GPA and Most Interviews Are Useless," *Business
      Insider*, June 19, 2013, https://www.businessinsider.com/
      how-google-hires-people-2013-6
32   Author interview with Tom Phillips, November 2024
33   Author interview with David Rosenblatt, November 2024
34   "Google to Lay Off About 300 at DoubleClick," *New York Times*, April 2, 2008, https://
      www.nytimes.com/2008/04/02/technology/02cnd-google.html
35   Nikesh Arora, March 22, 2009. "Sale reductions," email filed in *US et al v Google LLC*
36   "Google Is Wrecking DoubleClick, Says Unhappy Client," *Business Insider*, February 1,
      2010, https://www.businessinsider.com/unhappy-client-says-google-is-killing-doubleclick-
      2010-2

37   "Google's Trojan Horse: Let the Free Ad Serving Begin," *New York Times*, March 13, 2008, https://archive.nytimes.com/bits.blogs.nytimes.com/2008/03/13/googles-trojan-horse-let-the-free-ad-serving-begin/

38   Author interviews with various Google employees

39   "Control Your Own Advertising Empire With Google Ad Manager," *Wired*, March 13, 2008, https://www.wired.com/2008/03/control-your-own-advertising-empire-with-google-ad-manager/

40   Neal Mohan, September 2, 2008, "Display Strategy Status and Next Steps," email filed in *US et al v Google LLC*

41   Author interview with Brad Bender, December 2024

42   David Rosenblatt, February 11, 2009, transcript of talk given to Google sales team as captured by Clay Bavor and filed in *US et al v Google LLC*

43   Mohan, "Display Strategy Status and Next Steps"

44   Scott Spencer, May 16, 2008, "Google Ad Exchange. GPS Review Meeting," slide deck filed in *US et al v Google LLC*

45   "Google Tops Global Brand League," BBC, April 3, 2007, http://news.bbc.co.uk/2/hi/business/6581653.stm

46   "A Guide to Google's New Privacy Controls," *New York Times*, March 12, 2009, https://archive.nytimes.com/bits.blogs.nytimes.com/2009/03/12/a-guide-to-googles-new-privacy-controls/

47   Author interview of Jonathan Bellack

48   Ibid.

49   Neal Mohan, testimony in *US et al v Google LLC* as transcribed by the author

50   Scott Spencer, May 16, 2008, "Google Ad Exchange. GPS Review Meeting," slide deck filed in *US et al v Google LLC*

51   Unknown author, unknown title, Google Excel spreadsheet filed in *US et al v Google LLC* with case filename PTX1097._Native.xls indicated AdX $9.4 billion in revenue in 2020, so a reasonable assumption is it crossed $10 billion around 2021

52   Scott Spencer et al., April 2009, "L&S Review," slide deck filed in *US et al v Google LLC*

Chapter 7: You Can't Get Faster Than Real Time

1   Scott Spencer, January 30, 2013, "Re: TMG, AdX, AFC and . . . Rubicon," email filed in *US et al v Google LLC*

2   "TechCrunch40 Session 6: Revenue Models & Analytics," *TechCrunch*, September 18, 2007, https://techcrunch.com/2007/09/18/techcrunch40-session-6-revenue-models-analytics/

3   "Chipshot.com Bogeys into Bankruptcy," *CNET*, January 2, 2002, https://www.cnet.com/tech/tech-industry/chipshot-com-bogeys-into-bankruptcy/

4   Amar Goel, January 31, 2009, "Re: doubleclick API/integration question," email filed in *US et al v Google LLC*

5   Neal Mohan, January 31, 2009, "Re: doubleclick API/integration question," email filed in *US et al v Google LLC*

6   Neal Mohan, June 25, 2009, "Re; Fwd: PubMatic Transforms Online Publisher Ad Sales with Ad Price Prediction," email filed in *US et al v Google LLC*

7   Scott Spencer, January 30, 2013, "Re: TMG, AdX, AFC and . . . Rubicon," email filed in *US et al v Google LLC*

8   Author interview with Ben Barokas, October 2024

9   Author interview with Michael Barrett, November 2024

10 "Ad Exchange and Network Optimizer, AdMeld, Hires Barrett, Former Fox Exec," *AdExchanger*, November 10, 2008, https://www.adexchanger.com/online-advertising/ad-exchange-and-network-optimizer-admeld-hires-barrett-former-fox-exec/

11 Interview with Brian O'Kelley, November 2024

12 Author interview with Rajeev Goel, November 2024

13 "AdMeld CEO Barrett on New Funds and Next Steps," *AdExchanger*, August 2, 2010, https://www.adexchanger.com/yield-management-tools/admeld-ceo-barrett-on-new-funds-and-next-steps/

14 "AdMeld to Host Industry-Leading Conference on Real Time Bidding (RTB)," *Ad Tech Daily*, January 21, 2010, https://adtechdaily.com/2010/01/21/admeld-to-host-industry-leading-conference-on-real-time-bidding-rtb/

15 Interview with Michael Barrett, November 2024

16 "Back from the AdMeld Partner Forum," *Rob's Musings*, February 8, 2010, http://www.robdeichert.com/2010/02/back-from-admeld-partner-forum.html

17 "What was the world's first DSP?," Quora answer by Brian O'Kelley

Chapter 8: Pork Bellies and Digging for Gold

1 "BITS; If Ads Were Traded Like Pork Bellies," *New York Times*, March 3, 2008, https://archive.nytimes.com/query.nytimes.com/gst/fullpage-9C04EEDF1E3EF930A35750C0A96E9C8B63.html

2 "AOL to Buy Advertising.com," NBC News, June 24, 2004, https://www.nbcnews.com/id/wbna5282082

3 "Yahoo Buys Ad Network," *New York Times*, September 5, 2007, https://www.nytimes.com/2007/09/05/technology/05yahoo.html

4 Author interview with Joe Zawadski, December 2024

5 Ibid.

6 Author interview with Brian Lesser, December 2024

7 "GroupM Launches Xaxis—Ad Industry's Most Comprehensive Audience Buying Solution," GroupM press release, June 27, 2011, https://www.businesswire.com/news/home/20110627005401/en/GroupM-Launches-Xaxis-%E2%80%93-Ad-Industry%E2%80%99s-Most-Comprehensive-Audience-Buying-Solution

8 "Publicis Groupe Launches VivaKi a New Growth Engine for the New Media and Digital Environment," Publicis press release, June 25, 2008, https://www.publicisgroupe.com/sites/default/files/press-release/20080625_VivaKi_EN_Final.pdf

9 "Adnetik Growing a Trading and Targeting Firm Says CEO Montes," *AdExchanger*, October 12, 2010, https://www.adexchanger.com/platforms/adnetik/

10 "Turner Digital Does About Face on Programmatic, Rolls Out Private Marketplace," *AdExchanger*, October 24, 2013, https://www.adexchanger.com/publishers/turner-digital-does-an-about-face-on-programmatic-rolls-out-private-marketplace/

11 "For Turner Digital, Audience Buying Risk Outweighs Reward," *AdExchanger*, October 9, 2012, https://www.adexchanger.com/online-advertising/for-turner-digital-audience-buying-risk-outweighs-reward/

12 "Turner Digital Does About Face On Programmatic, Rolls Out Private Marketplace," *AdExchanger*, October 24, 2013, https://www.adexchanger.com/publishers/turner-digital-does-an-about-face-on-programmatic-rolls-out-private-marketplace/

13 Author's personal recollection

14 Author interview with Zach Weinberg, December 2024

15 Ibid.

16 Author interview with Sam Bloom, December 2024

17 Author interview with Zach Weinberg, December 2024

18   Jason would later leave Google to work for Nat and Zach at their next start-up, Flatiron Health

19   Author's personal recollection, as an attendee of this meeting

20   According to the most recent data disclosed in the DOJ trial AdX's spend was $9.3 billion in 2020 and the DSP's spend was $6.1 billion; source: PTX1097, unknown title and author, slide presentation filed in *US et al v Google LLC*

21   "Google Confirms Invite Media Acquisition, Brings Bidding to Display Ads," *Tech-Crunch*, June 3, 2010, https://techcrunch.com/2010/06/03/google-confirms-invite-media/

22   Author interviews with various former Google employees who wished to remain anonymous

23   "Google to Limit the Number of Ways Brands Can Buy YouTube Ads," *Wall Street Journal*, August 6, 2015, https://www.wsj.com/articles/BL-269B-4211

Chapter 9: Parking It Somewhere

1   Neal Mohan, October 20, 2010, "Re: how are we doing building out our YM services capability?," email filed in *US et al v Google LLC*

2   Scott Spencer, et al., April 2009, "L&S Review," slide deck filed in *US et al v Google LLC*

3   Neal Mohan, October 18, 2010, "Re: Yield Management," email filed in *US et al v Google LLC*

4   Lexi Reese, Undated, likely 2010, "Non-Premium Display Competitive Deep Dive," slide deck filed in *US et al v Google LLC*

5   Jonathan Bellack, et al., date unclear, likely late 2010, "Yield Management Product Plan," slide deck filed in *US et al v Google LLC*

6   Ibid.

7   Ibid.

8   Ibid.

9   "Google Tried to Buy Ad Startup Admeld, but Talks Broke Down over Price," *Business Insider*, February 11, 2011, https://www.businessinsider.com/google-admeld-2011-2

10   "Leaders of Digital Advertising and Marketing Converge as IAB Annual Leadership Meeting Convenes," IAB press release, Feb. 27, 2011, https://www.iab.com/news/leaders-digital-advertising-marketing-converge-iab-annual-leadership-meeting-convenes/

11   Dave Sobota, March 17, 2011, "Project 17 (Admeld and Pubmatic)," slide deck filed in *US et al v Google LLC*

12   Ibid.

13   "Google Acquires AdMeld For $400 Million," *TechCrunch*, June 9, 2011, https://tech-crunch.com/2011/06/09/google-acquires-admeld-for-400-million/

14   Author interview with Ben Barokas, November 2024

15   Author interview with Brian Kane, November 2024

16   Author interview with Brian Kane, November 2024

17   "Google Integrates Admeld Into DoubleClick AdX, Preps 'Unified' Publisher Solution," *AdExchanger*, March 22, 2012, https://www.adexchanger.com/ad-exchange-news/google-integrates-admeld-into-doubleclick-adx-preps-unified-publisher-solution/

18   David Hertog, September 20, 2012, "AdX and AdMeld, A Brief Preview of the Combined Platform," presentation filed in *US et al v Google LLC*

19   Joe Pedro, March 27, 2013, "Re: AdMeld Migration Update," email filed in *US et al v Google LLC*

20   Louis Goldenbroit, April 10, 2013, "Re: AdMeld Migration Update," email filed in *US et al v Google LLC*

21   Neal Mohan testimony in *US et al v Google LLC* as transcribed by the author

Chapter 10: YAM, MAY, AMY

1 David Rosenblatt, February 11, 2009, transcript of talk given to Google sales team as captured by Clay Bavor and filed in *US et al v Google LLC*

2 Author interview with various former Right Media executives

3 Earliest mention of the consortium that remains online is this article, which indicated the launch was in the previous November (2006): "Yahoo Expands Its Newspaper Consortium," *Danbury News-Times*, April 20, 2007, https://www.newstimes.com/news/article/yahoo-expands-its-newspaper-consortium-233230.php

4 "Why We Sold TechCrunch to AOL, and Where We Go from Here," *TechCrunch*, September 28, 2010, https://techcrunch.com/2010/09/28/why-we-sold-techcrunch-to-aol-and-where-we-go-from-here/

5 "AOL Agrees to Acquire The Huffington Post," *The Huffington Post*, February 7, 2011, https://www.huffpost.com/entry/aol-huffington-post_n_819375

6 Author interviews with various former DoubleClick employees; Tim Armstrong did not respond to requests for an interview

7 Author interview with Dave Jacobs, December 2024

8 "AOL Is Acquiring Video Ad Platform Adap.tv For $405M," *TechCrunch*, August 7, 2013, https://techcrunch.com/2013/08/07/aol-is-acquiring-video-ad-platform-adap-tv-for-405m/

9 "The AppNexus Reveal: We're a Demand-Side Platform Says Pres Rubenstein," *AdExchanger*, November 12, 2009, https://www.adexchanger.com/ad-exchange-news/the-appnexus-reveal-were-a-demand-side-platform-says-pres-rubenstein/

10 "AppNexus Raises a Meaty $50 Million Series C For Realtime Ad Bidding Platform," *TechCrunch*, October 5, 2010, https://techcrunch.com/2010/10/05/appnexus-raises-a-whopping-50-million-series-c-for-realtime-ad-bidding-network/

11 "Microsoft, AOL, and Yahoo Form Alliance as the Display Market Shifts Again," *Campaign Asia*, November 10, 2011, https://www.campaignasia.com/article/microsoft-aol-and-yahoo-form-alliance-as-the-display-market-shifts-again/279679

12 "Yahoo Gives Up, Turns Search Over to Bing," *Wired*, July 29, 2009, https://www.wired.com/2009/07/yahoo-gives-up/

13 Author interview with David Jacobs, December 2024

14 "Super Panel—AppNexus Summit NYC 2011," December 6, 2011, YouTube, https://www.youtube.com/watch?v=iz2DNhmd98k

15 "Google Executive Marissa Mayer Named Yahoo's New Chief Executive," *Los Angeles Times*, July 16, 2012, https://www.latimes.com/business/technology/la-fi-tn-yahoo-ceo-marissa-mayer-20120716-story.html

16 Author interview with Brian O'Kelley and confirmed in interview with Andrew Kraft

17 "Marissa Meyer [sic]: Just Don't Call Her 'Googirl,'" *Guardian*, February 29, 2008, https://www.theguardian.com/media/pda/2008/feb/29/marissameyerjustdontcallh

18 "Why AOL Came Back While Yahoo Came Up Short," *AdExchanger*, July 27, 2016, https://www.adexchanger.com/online-advertising/aol-came-back-yahoo-came-short/

19 "Yahoo Finally Pulls the Plug on Right Media Exchange," *AdExchanger*, January 9, 2015, https://www.adexchanger.com/platforms/yahoo-finally-pulls-the-plug-on-right-media-exchange/

20 "How French Publishers Are Winning Together," *ExchangeWire*, March 31 2015, https://www.exchangewire.com/blog/2015/03/31/how-french-publishers-are-winning-together/

21 Author interview with Brian O'Kelley, December 2024

22 "Microsoft Shuts Down Its Ad-Exchange Acquisition," ZDNet, February 1, 2011, https://www.zdnet.com/finance/microsoft-shuts-down-its-ad-exchange-acquisition/

23   "AOL in Deal With Microsoft to Take Over Display Ad Business," *New York Times*, June 29, 2015, https://www.nytimes.com/2015/06/30/business/aol-in-deal-with-microsoft-to-take-over-display-ad-business.html

Chapter 11: The Platform, the Exchange, and a Huge Network

1   Jonathan Bellack, September 2, 2016, "Re: Header bidding wrapper," email filed in *US et al v Google LLC*

2   Unknown author, October 2013, "Display Ads Deep Dive: Buyside October 2013," slide presentation as filed in *US et al v Google LLC*

3   Jonathan Bellack, "Re: Header bidding wrapper"

4   Kai Hansen, January 2008, "Ads Quality from A–Z in 16 Chapters," slide deck filed in US v Google LLC (search case), https://www.justice.gov/d9/2023-10/417378.pdf

5   "The AdSense revenue share," *Inside Adsense* Google blog, May 24, 2010, https://adsense.googleblog.com/2010/05/adsense-revenue-share.html

6   Giles, Jim (April 2016), "Overall Pub Yield with DRS (v2)," slides filed in *US et al v Google LLC*

7   David Pal, May 9, 2014, "Dynamic Sell-side Revshare on AdX," memo filed in *US et al v Google LLC*

8   *State of Texas et al v Google, LLC* in the United States District Court Southern District of New York

9   Unknown author, May 10, 2016, "AdX Auction Optimizations," slide presentation as filed in *US et al v Google LLC*

10   Max Loubser, May 13, 2016, "Dynamic Revenue Share," document filed in *US et al v Google LLC*

11   "Google Sweetens Deal for Publishers with Dynamic Price Floors," *Digiday*, March 5, 2015, https://digiday.com/media/google-sweetends-deal-publishers-dynamic-price-floors/

12   Unknown author, "AdX Auction Optimizations"

13   "DSPs To SSPs: 'Clean Up Or We Cut You Off,'" *AdExchanger*, May 11, 2017, https://www.adexchanger.com/platforms/dsps-ssps-clean-cut-off/

14   Unknown author, July 2018, "Ecosystem—margins, auction dynamics, supply path opt," slide presentation filed in *US et al v Google LLC*

15   Alok Aggarwal, October 2014, "AdX + gTrade Overview," slide presentation filed in *US et al v Google LLC*

16   Ibid.

17   Unknown author, October 21, 2013, "Project Bernanke. Launch Presentation," slide deck filed in *US et al v Google LLC*

18   "Google's Project Bernanke Explained," *Ad Tech Explained*, January 24, 2022, https://www.adtechexplained.com/p/google-project-bernanke-explained

19   Ibid.

20   Ibid.

21   *State of Texas et al v Google, LLC* in the United States District Court Southern District of New York

22   Unknown author, November 2014, "First call signal, and GDN bidding," presentation filed in *US et al v Google LLC*

23   Unknown author, unknown date (likely 2016), "Exchange Buying Dynamics. 2017 Quality & Formats Summit," filed in *US et al v Google LLC*

24   Ibid.

25   *State of Texas et al v Google, LLC* in the United States District Court Southern District of New York

26   "Leaving the Trading Desk Model Behind, Holding Companies Embed Specialists At Agencies," *AdExchanger*, September 6, 2017, https://www.adexchanger.com/agencies/abandoning-trading-desk-model-holding-companies-embed-specialists-agencies/

27   "Rubicon Project Eliminates Buy-Side Fees," *AdExchanger*, November 2, 2017, https://www.adexchanger.com/platforms/rubicon-project-eliminates-buy-side-fees/

28   "Index Exchange Called Out for Tweaking Its Auction," *AdExchanger*, August 16th, 2018, https://www.adexchanger.com/platforms/index-exchange-called-out-for-tweaking-its-auction/

29   "Ritson: P&G's Marc Pritchard Has Made the Biggest Marketing Speech for 20 Years," *MarketingWeek*, January 31 2017, https://www.marketingweek.com/mark-ritson-marc-pritchard-viewability-fraud-speech/

30   "ANA Study Finds 25% of Programmatic Ad Dollars Are Wasted," *MarTech*, December 5, 2023, https://martech.org/ana-study-finds-25-of-programmatic-ad-dollars-are-wasted/

31   Criteo 10K for the Fiscal Year Ended December 31, 2015

32   Author interview with Aly Nurmohamed, November 2024

33   Email from Stephanie Layser, August 2024

34   "Project Cheat Sheet: A Rundown on All of Google's Secret Internal Projects, as Revealed by the DOJ," *AdExchanger*, September 6, 2024, https://www.adexchanger.com/antitrust/project-cheat-sheet-a-rundown-on-all-of-googles-secret-internal-projects-as-revealed-by-the-doj/

35   Author interview with former Google executive who requires anonymity because they are not authorized to speak on behalf of the company

Chapter 12: Ad Tech Urban Legends

1   "The Rise Of 'Header Bidding' and the End of the Publisher Waterfall," *AdExchanger*, June 18, 2015, https://www.adexchanger.com/publishers/the-rise-of-header-bidding-and-the-end-of-the-publisher-waterfall

2   *State of Texas et al v Google, LLC* in the United States District Court Southern District of New York

3   Ibid.

4   Website is defunct, but can be found on the Internet Archives here: https://web.archive.org/web/20010124044800/http://3bigshows.com/

5   Author interview with Andrew Casale

6   "Casale Media Rebrands as Index Exchange," *Media in Canada*, January 28, 2015, https://mediaincanada.com/2015/01/28/casale-media-rebrands-as-index-exchange/

7   Ibid.

8   Author interview with Matthew Wheatland, November 2024

9   Interview with Jana Meron, November 2024

10   Prebid release notes, GitHub, August 6, 2015, https://github.com/prebid/Prebid.js/releases/tag/0.1.1

11   Author interview with Brian O'Kelley, November 2024

12   Author interview with Matt Goldstein, November 2024

13   Author interview with Andrew Casale, November 2024

14   "Sleeping Ad Giant Amazon Finally Stirs," Reuters, April 24, 2013, https://www.reuters.com/article/business/sleeping-ad-giant-amazon-finally-stirs-idUSBRE93N06E/

15   "Amazon's Header Tag Goes Server-Side and Brings in Outside Demand," *AdExchanger*, December 2, 2016, https://www.adexchanger.com/ad-exchange-news/amazons-header-tag-goes-server-side-brings-outside-demand/

16   "5 Reasons Why Exchanges Are Signing Up for Amazon TAM," *AdExchanger*, June 21, 2017, https://www.adexchanger.com/ad-exchange-news/5-reasons-exchanges-signing-amazon-tam/

17   "Ashton Kutcher Launches New Online Platform Called A+," *Los Angeles Times*, January 23, 2015, https://www.latimes.com/entertainment/envelope/cotown/la-et-ct-aplus-ashton-kutcher-media-platform-20150123-story.html

18   "Inside Ashton Kutcher's Celebrity-Powered Viral Media Empire, Which No One Knows Exists," *Business Insider*, February 19, 2015, https://www.businessinsider.com/ashton-kutcher-startup-aplus-media-viral-plagiarism-celebrities-2015-2

19   "Header-Bidding Wrappers: Another Step Toward the End of the Waterfall," *AdExchanger*, February 2, 2016, https://www.adexchanger.com/ad-exchange-news/header-bidding-wrappers-another-step-toward-the-end-of-the-waterfall/

20   "Chicken Soup for the Soul Acquires a Majority of A Plus, the Positive Journalism Site Founded by Ashton Kutcher," *Business Wire*, September 21, 2016, https://www.businesswire.com/news/home/20160921006334/en/Chicken-Soup-Soul-Acquires-Majority-Positive-Journalism

21   "Wrapper Wars: Exchanges And Publishers Question Fairness Of Index Exchange's Wrapper," *AdExchanger*, October 1, 2018, https://www.adexchanger.com/platforms/wrapper-wars-exchanges-and-publishers-question-fairness-of-index-exchanges-wrapper/

22   Author interview with anonymous witness to the events discussed, who is restricted by their NDA

23   "Announcing the Formation of an Independent Prebid.org," Prebid.org blog post, September 11, 2017. Not available in original form any longer, archived version here: https://web.archive.org/web/20240227012020/https://prebid.org/announcing-prebid-org/

24   "Prebid.org Hits 100+ Members!," Prebid.org blog post, March 29, 2021

25   "The Year Header Bidding Went Mainstream," *AdExchanger*, December 27, 2016, https://www.adexchanger.com/publishers/year-header-bidding-went-mainstream/

26   "Rubicon Loses 35% of Its Value after Terrible Earnings Report, Says It Was 'Slow to React to Header Bidding,'" *AdExchanger*, August 2, 2016, https://www.adexchanger.com/platforms/rubicon-hurt-by-header-bidding/

Chapter 13: Something Slightly Better

1   Payam Shodjai, March 16, 2018, "Re: Header Bidding Observatory/ Edition #3," email filed in *US et al v Google LLC*

2   Aparna Pappu, June 18, 2015, "The Rise Of 'Header Bidding' And The End Of The Publisher Waterfall | AdExchanger," email filed in *US et al v Google LLC*

3   Drew Bradstock, June 18, 2015, "The Rise Of 'Header Bidding' And The End Of The Publisher Waterfall | AdExchanger," email filed in *US et al v Google LLC*

4   Nunzio Thron, June 18, 2015, "The Rise Of 'Header Bidding' And The End Of The Publisher Waterfall | AdExchanger," email filed in *US et al v Google LLC*

5   Michelle Sarlo Dauwalter, June 22, 2015, "The Rise Of 'Header Bidding' And The End Of The Publisher Waterfall | AdExchanger," email filed in *US et al v Google LLC*

6   Ibid.

7   Interview with publisher executive who remains off the record because he was not authorized to speak on behalf of his company, December 2024

8   Author interview with former Google employee who remains off the record because he was not authorized to speak on behalf of his company, December 2024

9   "Jonathan Bellack, Google, Tom Shields, AppNexus Debate Header Bidding 2015 IAB Ad Operations Summit," YouTube, November 2, 2015, https://www.youtube.com/watch?v=suszUQMJz3I

10   Payam Shodjai, Oct 28, 2016, "Re: DVAA Sellside Review: Jedi++ Strategy," email filed in *US et al v Google LLC*

11   "AppNexus Acquires Yieldex, Publisher Forecasting and Pricing Platform," *AdExchanger*, March 18, 2015, https://www.adexchanger.com/publishers/appnexus-buys-yieldex-which-helps-publisher-forecast-and-price-inventory/

12   "Jonathan Bellack, Google, Tom Shields, AppNexus Debate Header Bidding 2015 IAB Ad Operations Summit," YouTube, November 2, 2015, https://www.youtube.com/watch?v=suszUQMJz3I

13   Quote is a paraphrase from memory and may not be entirely accurate. This is from an author interview with former Google executive who is not authorized to speak on behalf of the company, December 2024

14   Lisa Lehman, October 7, 2015, "Re: The REAL Header Bidding Threat . . .," email filed in *US et al v Google LLC*

15   Unknown author, March 1, 2017, "Header and Exchange Bidding Update," presentation filed in *US et al v Google LLC*

16   Jim Giles, December 15, 2016, "Re: Need financial target for EB in 2017," email filed in *US et al v Google LLC*

17   Jonathan Bellack, March 16, 2018, "Fwd: Header Bidding Observatory / Edition #3," email filed in *US et al v Google LLC*

18   Payam Shodjai, March 16, 2018, "Re: Header Bidding Observatory / Edition #3," email filed in *US et al v Google LLC*

19   Jerome Grateau, November 22, 2016, "Re: Rubicon," email filed in *US et al v Google LLC*

20   Jerome Grateau, February 14, 2017, "Re: [FYI] Key Questions for Pricing Discussion," email filed in *US et al v Google LLC*

21   Chris LaSala, June 19, 2018, "Re: EB," email filed in *US et al v Google LLC*

22   Unknown author, March 1, 2017, "Header and Exchange Bidding Update," slide presentation filed in *US et al v Google LLC*

23   Nirmal Jayaran, November 7, 2016, "Re: 0.1% experiment on DBM/Skyray," email filed in *US et al v Google LLC*

24   Adapted from Tim Cadogan's court testimony in *US et al v Google LLC* as transcribed by the author

25   Matthew Brown, August 15, 2019, "Re: Google & Rubicon Weekly Call Agenda—August 15," email filed in *US et al v Google LLC*

26   Tim Cadogan, November 21, 2018, "GCP / DBM problem," email filed in *US et al v Google LLC*

27   "Ad Exchange OpenX Commits to $110 Million Google Cloud Deal," *Reuters*, January 24, 2019, https://www.reuters.com/article/technology/ad-exchange-openx-commits-to-110-million-google-cloud-deal-idUSKCN1PI2M1/

28   "OpenX Lays Off 100 Employees and Pivots to Video," *AdExchanger*, December 18, 2018, https://www.adexchanger.com/platforms/openx-lays-off-100-employees-and-pivots-to-video/

29   Unknown author, July 2018, "Ecosystem—margins, auction dynamics, supply path opt," presentation filed in *US et al v Google LLC*

30   Ibid.

31   Ibid.

32   Author interview with Rajiv Goel, December 2024

33   Chris LaSala, March 11, 2016, "Re: Notes from Today's OPA Sync," email filed in *US et al v Google LLC*

34   Professor Rabii testimony in *US et al v Google LLC* as transcribed by the author

35   "Big Changes Coming to Auctions, as Exchanges Roll the Dice on First-Price," *AdEx-changer*, September 5, 2017, https://www.adexchanger.com/platforms/big-changes-coming-auctions-exchanges-roll-dice-first-price/

36   "Nearly Half of Programmatic Impressions Are Sold through First-Price Auctions," *eMarketer*, May 7, 2018, https://www.emarketer.com/content/nearly-half-of-programmatic-impressions-are-sold-through-first-price-auctions

Chapter 14: Garbage In, Garbage Out

1   Jed Dederick testimony in *US et al v Google LLC* as transcribed by the author

2   Author interview with Susan Parker, December 2024

3   "Our Fight against Fraud," *MediaMath* blog post, September 14, 2015, https://www.mediamath.com/blog/our-fight-against-fraud/

4   "Under Pressure from Buyers, Fraud-Plagued AppNexus Girds for Battle," *AdExchanger*, October 15, 2014, https://www.adexchanger.com/platforms/appnexus-has-a-day-of-reckoning-on-the-ad-fraud-issue/

5   "AppNexus Launches Industry-First Certified Supply Program to Eradicate Fraud," PR Newswire, November 5, 2014, https://www.prnewswire.com/news-releases/appnexus-launches-industry-first-certified-supply-program-to-eradicate-fraud-281620131.html

6   "After Filtering for Fraud, AppNexus Transactions Fell by 65 Percent," *Digiday*, September 15, 2015, https://digiday.com/marketing/appnexus-filters-65-percent-impressions-fraudulent/

7   Luke Fenney tweet: https://x.com/lukefenney/status/643415294476742656

8   Author interviews with Sam Cox and Jonathan Bellack, December 2024

9   Author interview with Sam Cox, December 2024

10   Author interview with Sam Cox, December 2024

11   Interview with Jana Meron, November 2024

12   "IAB Tech Lab Launches Assault on Illicit Advertising Inventory," IAB press release, May 17, 2017, https://iabtechlab.com/press-releases/iab-tech-lab-launches-assault-on-illicit-advertising-inventory

13   "Ads.txt Adoption Continues Its Steady Growth," *eMarketer*, March 6, 2018, https://www.emarketer.com/content/ads-txt-adoption-continues-its-steady-growth

14   Author interview with Rob Norman, November 2024

15   "Pixalate Releases March 2024 Rankings for Open Programmatic Ad Sellers on Made-for-Advertising (MFA) Websites: 18% of Global Ad Spend on MFA Sites Was Sold by Magnite," Yahoo Finance, April 12, 2024, https://finance.yahoo.com/news/pixalate-releases-march-2024-rankings-171000820.html

16   "Adalytics Report Torches Ad Tech for Touting MFA Prevention While Scarfing MFA Supply," *AdExchanger*, March 11, 2024, https://www.adexchanger.com/advertiser/adalytics-report-torches-ad-tech-for-touting-mfa-prevention-while-scarfing-mfa-supply/

17   Author interview with Rob Leathern, December 2024

18   "Cheetah Mobile Statement on Reported Facebook Halt of Chinese Utility App Ads," Reuters, February 14, 2017, https://www.reuters.com/article/legal/government/cheetah-mobile-statement-on-reported-facebook-halt-of-chinese-utility-app-ads-idUSF-WN1FZ1EJ/

19   "Google Has Banned Almost 600 Apps for Pushing 'Disruptive' Ads," *BuzzFeed News*, February 20, 2020, https://www.buzzfeednews.com/article/craigsilverman/google-bans-android-apps-disruptive-ads

20   Author interview with Steph Layser and Matthew Wheatland

21 "Does Forbes Operate 'Made for Advertising' Pages and Transact Mis-Declared Ad Inventory?," *Adalytics* blog, March 2024, *https://adalytics.io/blog/ ads-observed-on-www3-forbes-subdomain*

22 Author interview with Jeremy Hlavacek, formerly of Weather.com, December 2024

23 "Viewability Has Arrived: What You Need to Know to See Through This Sea Change," IAB blog post, Mar. 31, 2014, https://www.iab.com/news/ viewability-has-arrived-what-you-need-to-know-to-see-through-this-sea-change

24 "Google on How It Handles Sites with Too Many Ads," *Search Engine Journal*, December 14, 2020, https://www.searchenginejournal.com/ google-on-how-it-handles-sites-with-too-many-ads/390751/

25 "Media Companies Have Never Had More Readership, but a Group of Adtech Companies Are Making It Tough to Monetize," *Business Insider*, March 30, 2020, https://www.businessinsider.com/integral-ad-science-doubleverify-help-brands-avoid-coronavirus-news-2020-3

26 "Adalytics Report Challenges Verifiers and Pubs That Claim 100% Brand-Safe Media," *AdExchanger*, August 7, 2024, https://www.adexchanger.com/marketers/ adalytics-report-challenges-verifiers-and-pubs-that-claim-100-brand-safe-media/

27 "Why Time's Taylor Swift Feature Was Marked Brand Unsafe," *AdWeek*, April 18, 2024, https://www.adweek.com/media/why-times-taylor-swift-feature-was-marked-brand-unsafe/

Chapter 15: Google's Version of the Web

1 "Facebook's Pivot to Video Didn't Just Burn Publishers. It Didn't Even Work for Facebook," Nieman Lab, September 15, 2021, https://www.niemanlab.org/2021/09/ well-this-puts-a-nail-in-the-news-video-on-facebook-coffin/

2 "Google to Buy YouTube for $1.65 Billion," *CNN Money*, October 9, 2006, archived version: https://web.archive.org/web/20201112015618/https://money.cnn. com/2006/10/09/technology/googleyoutube_deal/index.htm?cnn=yes

3 "NBC Signs Promo Deal with YouTube," *Guardian*, June 27, 2006, https://www.the-guardian.com/media/2006/jun/27/digitalmedia.broadcasting

4 Author's recollection of conversation with Susan Wojcicki

5 "Viacom v. YouTube," Electronic Frontier Foundation, undated, https://www.eff.org/ cases/viacom-v-youtube

6 Complaint in *Viacom v. YouTube*, Court of Appeals, 2nd Circuit 2012, https://scholar. google.com/scholar_case?case=13644579048975596329

7 "Searching for Video? Google Pushes YouTube over Rivals," *Wall Street Journal*, July 14, 2020, https://www.wsj.com/articles/google-steers-users-to-youtube-over-rivals-11594745232

8 "NBC Universal and News Corp. Announce Deal with Internet Leaders AOL, MSN, MySpace and Yahoo! to Create a Premium Online Video Site with Unprecedented Reach," *Business Wire*, March 22, 2007, archived: https://web.archive.org/ web/20110101212907/http://www.businesswire.com/news/home/20070322005690/ en/NBC-Universal-News-Corp.-Announce-Deal-Internet

9 "Joost Reaches Video Deal With Viacom," *New York Times*, February 20, 2007, https:// archive.nytimes.com/dealbook.nytimes.com/2007/02/20/joost-reaches-video-deal-with-viacom/

10 The author was the creator and original product manager for DoubleClick's video ad server, DART Video, which was later rebuilt by Google

11 Author interview with Doug Knopper, December 2024

12   "Google, Viacom Settle Landmark YouTube Lawsuit," Reuters, March 18, 2014, https://www.reuters.com/article/us-google-viacom-lawsuit-idUSBREA2H11220140318/

13   Author interview with Doug Knopper, December 2024

14   "Comcast Buys Advertising Startup Freewheel for $360 Million," Reuters, March 6, 2014, https://www.reuters.com/article/lifestyle/comcast-buys-advertising-startup-freewheel-for-360-million-idUSBREA251SJ/

15   "Exclusive: Comcast Emerges as New Google Antitrust Foe—Sources," Reuters, October 1, 2019, https://www.reuters.com/article/technology/exclusive-comcast-emerges-as-new-google-antitrust-foe-sources-idUSKBN1WG3J7/

16   "Disney Drops FreeWheel in Favor of Google Ad Manager," *AdExchanger*, November 27, 2018, https://www.adexchanger.com/tv-2/disney-drops-freewheel-in-favor-of-google-ad-manager/

17   "Google May Have Pulled off a TV Ad-Tech Coup Just as Comcast and Disney Were Duking It Out over Fox and Sky," *Business Insider*, October 1, 2018, https://www.businessinsider.com/comcast-and-disney-duked-it-out-google-may-have-won-2018-9

18   "FreeWheel to Launch Enhanced YouTube and YouTube TV Integration," FreeWheel press release, April 25, 2022, https://www.freewheel.com/news/freewheel-to-launch-enhanced-youtube-and-youtube-tv-integration

19   "YouTube Accounts for 10.4% of All TV Viewing in July, Surpasses Disney as Top Watched Media Company," *NextTV,* September 3, 2024, https://www.nexttv.com/news/youtube-accounts-for-104-of-all-tv-viewing-in-july-surpasses-disney-as-top-watched-media-company

20   "What the Shift to Video Means for Creators," Facebook blog, January 7, 2015, https://www.facebook.com/formedia/blog/what-the-shift-to-video-means-for-creators

21   "Why Facebook And Mark Zuckerberg Went All In On Live Video," *BuzzFeed News*, April 6, 2016, https://www.buzzfeednews.com/article/mathonan/why-facebook-and-mark-zuckerberg-went-all-in-on-live-video

22   "Mashable Fires News Staff, Replaces Executives as Part of Pivot to Video Infotainment," Vox, April 7, 2016, https://www.vox.com/2016/4/7/11585950/mashable-fires-news-staff-executives

23   "Facebook Overestimated Key Video Metric for Two Years," *Wall Street Journal*, September 22, 2016, https://www.wsj.com/articles/facebook-overestimated-key-video-metric-for-two-years-1474586951

24   "Facebook Will Pay $40 Million to Settle a Lawsuit Claiming that it Misled Advertisers about the Success of Video," Nieman Lab, October 8, 2019, https://www.niemanlab.org/2019/10/facebook-will-pay-40-million-to-settle-a-lawsuit-claiming-that-it-misled-advertisers-about-the-success-of-video/

25   "Introducing Instant Articles," Facebook blog, May 12, 2005, archived article: https://web.archive.org/web/20150514162847/http://media.fb.com/2015/05/12/instantarticles/

26   "Facebook Faces Increased Publisher Resistance to Instant Articles," *Digiday*, April 11, 2017, https://digiday.com/media/facebook-faces-increased-publisher-resistance-instant-articles/

27   "'It Doesn't Negate the Negatives': 'Facebook's Instant Articles Update Ignores Revenue Issues," *Digiday*, May 30, 2017, https://digiday.com/media/doesnt-negate-negatives-facebooks-instant-articles-update-ignores-revenue-issues/

28   "Facebook's Referral Traffic for Publishers Down 50% in 12 Months," *Press Gazette*, May 9, 2024, https://pressgazette.co.uk/media-audience-and-business-data/media_metrics/facebooks-referral-traffic-for-publishers-down-50-in-12-months

29   "As Clicks Dry Up for News Sites, Could Apple's News App Be a Lifeline?," *Semaphor*, May 19, 2024, https://www.semafor.com/article/05/19/2024/as-clicks-dry-up-for-news-sites-could-apples-news-app-be-a-lifeline

30 "Introducing the Accelerated Mobile Pages Project, for a Faster, Open Mobile Web," Google blog, October 07, 2015, https://blog.google/products/search/ introducing-accelerated-mobile-pages/

31 "Google Has Launched a Major Project that Aims to Make the Entire Mobile Web Load a Lot Faster," *Business Insider*, October 7, 2015, https://www.businessinsider.com/ google-launches-accelerated-mobile-pages-2015-10

32 "Chartbeat: Only a Third of Google AMP Publishers See Traffic Boost," *AdExchanger*, August 23, 2018, https://www.adexchanger.com/platforms/chartbeat-only-a-third-of-google-amp-publishers-see-traffic-boost/

33 "Google Throttled Non-AMP Page Speeds, Created Format to Hamper Header Bidding, Antitrust Complaint Claims," *Search Engine Land*, October 24, 2021, https://searchengineland.com/google-throttled-amp-page-speeds-created-format-to-hamper-header-bidding-antitrust-complaint-claims-375466

34 "Google's Mobile Web Dominance Raises Competition Eyebrows," *Politico*, June 1, 2018, https://www.politico.eu/article/google-amp-accelerated-mobile-pages-competition-antitrust-margrethe-vestager-mobile-android/

35 "Google News App Will Display Non-AMP Content and Send Readers to Publisher Pages," *Search Engine Land*, September 8, 2021, https://searchengineland.com/ google-news-app-will-display-non-amp-content-and-send-readers-to-publisher-pages-374291

36 "Finally, The Publisher Pushback On AMP; This Is Why We Can't Have Nice News," *AdExchanger*, February 25, 2022, https://www.adexchanger.com/ad-exchange-news/ finally-the-publisher-pushback-on-amp-this-is-why-we-cant-have-nice-news/

37 "Rupert Murdoch: 'There's No Such Thing as a Free News Story,'" *Guardian*, December 1, 2009, https://www.theguardian.com/media/2009/dec/01/ rupert-murdoch-no-free-news

38 "Jerry Dias: We Need a Canadian Model to Save Canadian Journalism," *National Post*, October 27, 2020, https://nationalpost.com/opinion/jerry-dias-we-need-a-canadian-model-to-save-canadian-journalism

39 "Google Licenses Content from News Publishers under the EU Copyright Directive," Google blog post, June 15, 2023, https://blog.google/around-the-globe/google-europe/ google-licenses-content-from-news-publishers-under-the-eu-copyright-directive/

40 "Australia Passes New Media Law that Will Require Google, Facebook to Pay for News," CNBC, February 24, 2021, https://www.cnbc.com/2021/02/25/australia-passes-its-news-media-bargaining-code.html

41 "Meta Begins the Process of Ending News Links In Canada," *TechDirt*, August 2, 2023, https://www.techdirt.com/2023/08/02/meta-begins-the-process-of-ending-news-links-in-canada/

42 "An Update on Canada's Bill C-18 and Our Search and News Products," Google blog post, November 29, 2023, https://blog.google/intl/en-ca/company-news/ outreach-initiatives/an-update-on-canadas-bill-c-18-and-our-search-and-news-products/

43 Linkedin post by Benedict Evans: https://www.linkedin.com/posts/benedictevans_an-update-on-canadas-bill-c-18-and-our-search-activity-7080332396490842112-aAjy/

Chapter 16: Acts of God

1 "Big Brands Fund Terror through Online Adverts," *The Times*, February 9, 2017, https:// www.thetimes.com/business-money/technology/article/ big-brands-fund-terror-knnxfgb98

2   "News Corp Chairman Rupert Murdoch Takes Swings at Google, Facebook," Reuters, November 17, 2021, https://www.reuters.com/business/media-telecom/news-corp-chairman-rupert-murdoch-takes-swings-google-facebook-2021-11-17/

3   "AppNexus Closes Strategic Investment Round," PR Newswire, Sep 28, 2016, https://www.prnewswire.com/news-releases/appnexus-closes-strategic-investment-round-300335766.html

4   Ibid.

5   "WPP Invests Technology Plus $25 million for a Significant Stake in AppNexus," WPP press release, September 22, 2014, https://www.wpp.com/en/news/2014/09/wpp-invests-technology-plus-25-million-for-a-significant-stake-in-appnexus

6   Author interview with Steph Layser, along with her testimony in *US et al v Google LLC* as transcribed by the author

7   Unknown authors from News Corp, April 2017, "Project Cinderella Analysis—April 2017," document filed in *US et al v Google LLC*

8   Ibid.

9   Matthew Wheatland testimony in *US et al v Google LLC* as transcribed by the author

10   Matthew Wheatland, date unknown (likely July 2019), "Google AdX value," presentation filed in *US et al v Google LLC*

11   Interview with Matthew Wheatland, October 2024

12   Tim Wolfe testimony in *US et al v Google LLC* as transcribed by the author

13   James Avery, April 24, 2019, "Re: Question about your tweet :)," email filed in *US et al v Google LLC*

14   "OpenX Lays Off 100 Employees and Pivots to Video," *AdExchanger*, December 18, 2018, https://www.adexchanger.com/platforms/openx-lays-off-100-employees-and-pivots-to-video/

15   "Verizon Media to Shutter Oath Ad Server," *AdWeek*, March 4, 2019, https://www.adweek.com/programmatic/verizon-media-to-shutter-oath-ad-server/

16   "AppNexus + Axel Springer," 2018, promotional case study published by AppNexus, https://www.appnexus.com/sites/default/files/case-studies/Axel-Springer-Case-Study_0.pdf

17   "Schibsted Media Group and AppNexus Announce Global Partnership," September 15, 2015, Schibsted press release, https://schibsted.com/news/schibsted-media-group-and-appnexus-announce-global-partnership/

18   Interview with Michael Rubenstein, October 2024

Chapter 17: ARPU

1   "Why Can't Telcos Make Their Ad Tech Acquisitions Work?," *Video Ad News*, August 9, 2020, https://videoweek.com/2020/09/08/why-cant-telcos-make-their-ad-tech-acquisitions-work/

2   "Verizon Settles with F.C.C. Over Hidden Tracking via 'Supercookies,'" *New York Times*, March 7, 2016, https://www.nytimes.com/2016/03/08/technology/verizon-settles-with-fcc-over-hidden-tracking.html

3   "Singtel Offloads Amobee to Tremor for $239 Million (Nearly $100 Million Less than It Paid for Amobee in 2012)," *AdExchanger*, July 25, 2022, https://www.adexchanger.com/ad-exchange-news/singtel-offloads-amobee-to-tremor-for-239-million-nearly-100-million-less-than-it-paid-for-amobee-in-2012/

4   "Ericsson Is Shutting Down Its Ad Division, the Latest in a Long Line of Telco-Adtech Divorces," *Business Insider*, June 4, 2024, https://www.businessinsider.com/ericsson-to-shut-emodo-advertising-divison-2024-6

5   "Verizon to Acquire AOL," Verizon press release, May 12, 2015, https://www.prnews-wire.com/news-releases/verizon-to-acquire-aol-300081541.html

6   "Verizon to acquire AOL," Verizon press release, May 12, 2015, https://www.verizon.com/about/news/verizon-acquire-aol

7   "Verizon to Acquire Yahoo's Operating Business," Verizon press release, July 25, 2016, https://www.verizon.com/about/news/verizon-acquire-yahoos-operating-business

8   "Verizon's Internet Boss Tim Armstrong in Talks to Leave," *Wall Street Journal*, September 7, 2018, https://www.wsj.com/articles/verizons-internet-boss-in-talks-to-leave-1536321413

9   "Apollo Completes Its $5B Acquisition of Verizon Media, Now Known as Yahoo," *TechCrunch*, September 1, 2021, https://techcrunch.com/2021/09/01/apollo-completes-its-5b-acquisition-of-verizon-media-now-known-as-yahoo/

10   "Report: Trump Asked Gary Cohn to Block AT&T-Time Warner Merger," CNN, March 4, 2019, https://www.cnn.com/2019/03/04/media/att-time-warner-trump-gary-cohn/index.html

11   "AT&T in Talks to Acquire AppNexus for About $1.6 Billion," *Wall Street Journal*, June 19, 2018, https://www.wsj.com/articles/at-t-in-talks-to-acquire-appnexus-for-about-1-6-billion-1529464400

12   "Brian O'Kelley Steps Down As AppNexus CEO," *AdExchanger*, October 5, 2018, https://www.adexchanger.com/online-advertising/brian-okelley-steps-down-as-appnexus-ceo/

13   "Xandr, Formerly AppNexus, Is Now Formerly AT&T, After Its Acquisition By Microsoft," *AdExchanger*, December 21, 2021, https://www.adexchanger.com/online-advertising/xandr-formerly-appnexus-is-now-formerly-att-after-its-acquisition-by-microsoft/

Chapter 18: Irrationally High Rents

1   Pappu Aparna, June 25, 2018, "Re: PRIVILEGED AND CONFIDENTIAL," chat transcript or other type of meta commentary associated with email of this title filed in *US et al v Google LLC*

2   Woojin Kim et al., August 2012, "Display Strategy Working Document," document filed in *US et al v Google LLC*

3   Ibid.

4   Unknown author, date unknown (but likely 2010–11), "AdWords cross-exchange bidding," memo filed in *US et al v Google LLC*.

5   Nirmal Jayaram, January 2014, "Impact of GDN not participating in AdX auctions," memo filed in *US et al v Google LLC*

6   Unknown author, November 2019, "Awbid," presentation filed in *US et al v Google LLC*

7   Chris LaSala, June 25, 2018, "Re: PRIVILEGED AND CONFIDENTIAL," email filed in *US et al v Google LLC*

8   Ibid.

9   Jonathan Bellack, June 25, 2018, "Re: PRIVILEGED AND CONFIDENTIAL," chat transcript or other type of meta commentary associated with email of this title, filed in *US et al v Google LLC*

10   Pappu Aparna, June 25, 2018, "Re: PRIVILEGED AND CONFIDENTIAL," chat transcript or other type of meta commentary associated with email of this title, filed in *US et al v Google LLC*

11   Chris LaSala, January 4, 2019, "Re: OpenX lays off 100, more pressure on sellside take rates," email filed in *US et al v Google LLC*

12 Unknown author, September 2017, "PBSx Discount Guidance," presentation filed in *US et al v Google LLC*

13 "Google's 16th Employee Susan Wojcicki Is Now YouTube's New CEO," *Business Insider*, February 5, 2014, https://www.businessinsider.com/susan-wojcicki-may-become-youtube-ceo-2014-2

14 Author interview with multiple former Google executives

15 "A Former Google Executive Takes Aim at His Old Company With a Start-Up," *New York Times*, June 19, 2020, https://www.nytimes.com/2020/06/19/technology/google-neeva-executive.html

16 "Google Paid This Man $100 Million: Here's His Story," *Business Insider*, April 6, 2013, https://www.businessinsider.com/neal-mohan-googles-100-million-man-2013-4

17 "It Looks Like Google's '$100 Million Man' Is Leaving for Dropbox," *Business Insider*, June 8, 2015, https://www.businessinsider.com/google-neal-mohan-goes-to-dropbox-2015-6

18 "Google's Neal Mohan Jumps to YouTube, as DoubleClick Gets a Product Chief from the Analytics Side," *AdExchanger*, November 18, 2015, https://www.adexchanger.com/online-advertising/googles-neal-mohan-jumps-to-youtube-as-doubleclick-gets-a-product-chief-from-the-analytics-side/

19 Ibid.

Chapter 19: Creepy Ads

1 "Apple's Cook Says Ads that Follow You Online Are 'Creepy,'" *CNET*, April 6, 2018, https://www.cnet.com/news/politics/apple-tim-cook-says-facebook-ads-that-follow-you-are-creepy-daca-dreamers-privacy-taxes/

2 "Apple—WWDC 2017 Keynote," YouTube, https://www.youtube.com/watch?v=oaqHdULqet0

3 "Here's the Gaping Flaw in Microsoft's 'Do Not Track' System For IE10," *Business Insider*, August 29, 2012, https://www.businessinsider.com/heres-the-gaping-flaw-in-microsofts-do-not-track-system-for-ie10-2012-8

4 "Cheat Sheet: How Apple's ATT Is Giving It More Influence over Ad Dollars," *Digiday*, September 20, 2021, https://digiday.com/marketing/cheat-sheet-how-apples-att-is-giving-it-more-influence-over-ad-dollars/

5 "Apple's Cook Says Ads that Follow You Online Are 'Creepy,'" *CNET*, April 6, 2018, https://www.cnet.com/news/politics/apple-tim-cook-says-facebook-ads-that-follow-you-are-creepy-daca-dreamers-privacy-taxes/

6 "Apple—WWDC 2017 Keynote," YouTube, https://www.youtube.com/watch?v=oaqHdULqet0

7 LinkedIn post by Paul Bannister, January 2024, https://www.linkedin.com/posts/pauljbannister_super-early-chrome-deprecation-data-analysis-activity-7150484855074553856-vvQr/

8 "Facebook Says Apple iOS Privacy Change Will Result in $10 Billion Revenue Hit This Year," CNBC, February 2, 2022, https://www.cnbc.com/2022/02/02/facebook-says-apple-ios-privacy-change-will-cost-10-billion-this-year.html

9 "Apple Has a Message for Amazon and Google and It's Plastered on the Side of a Hotel at the Biggest Tech Conference of the Year," CNBC, January 6, 2019, https://www.cnbc.com/2019/01/06/apple-privacy-ad-ces-2019.html

10 "Influential W3C Working Group Calls Privacy Sandbox Proposal 'Harmful,'" *AdExchanger*, April 14, 2021, https://www.adexchanger.com/privacy/influential-w3c-working-group-calls-privacy-sandbox-proposal-harmful/

11 Post on GitHub rejecting the proposal: https://github.com/w3ctag/design-reviews/issues/7 26#issuecomment-1379908459

12 Ibid.

13 "Episode 58: All About the Privacy Sandbox with Alex Cone from Google," *Marketecture Podcast*, February 9, 2024, https://www.marketecturepod.com/ episode-58-all-about-the-privacy-sandbox-with-alex-cone-from-google/

14 "State of the Sandbox, July 4th edition," *Marketecture Newsletter*, July 1, 2024, https:// news.marketecture.tv/p/state-of-the-sandbox

15 "An Updated Timeline for Privacy Sandbox Milestones," Google blog post, June 24, 2021, https://blog.google/products/chrome/updated-timeline-privacy-sandbox-milestones/

16 "Expanding Testing for the Privacy Sandbox for the Web," Google blog post, July 27, 2022, https://blog.google/products/chrome/update-testing-privacy-sandbox-web/

17 "Investigation into Google's 'Privacy Sandbox' Browser Changes," CMA blog, originally published January 2021, https://www.gov.uk/cma-cases/investigation-into-googles-privacy-sandbox-browser-changes

18 "Our Commitments for the Privacy Sandbox," Google blog, June 11, 2021, https://blog. google/around-the-globe/google-europe/our-commitments-privacy-sandbox/

19 "Google Reneges on Plan to Remove Third-Party Cookies in Chrome," CBS Money-watch, July 22, 2024, https://www.cbsnews.com/news/google-third-party-cookies-chrome/

20 "Google Lets the Users Do the Dirty Work," *Marketecture Newsletter*, July 29, 2024, https://news.marketecture.tv/p/chrome-users-dirty-work

21 "Firefox Gets a Privacy Boost as Total Cookie Protection Becomes the Default for All Users," *TechCrunch*, June 14, 2022, https://techcrunch.com/2022/06/14/ firefox-gets-a-privacy-boost-as-total-cookie-protection-becomes-the-default-for-all-users/

22 "Microsoft Edge is Getting Rid of Third-Party Cookies. What about Their Replace-ment?," *AdGuard Blog*, April 5, 2024, https://adguard.com/en/blog/microsoft-edge-cookies-api-privacy.html

Chapter 20: A Jedi Mind Trick

1 "In Re: Google Digital Advertising Antitrust Litigation," filing in United States District Court Southern District of New York

2 Jag Duggal, April 6, 2010, "OCQ Meeting Notes," email filed in *US et al v Google LLC*

3 Neal Mohan et al., 2013, "FB Compete for Ads Strategy 2014," document filed in *US et al v Google LLC*

4 "Facebook Acquires LiveRail for $400M To $500M to Serve Video Ads Everywhere, Improve Its Own," *TechCrunch*, July 2, 2014, https://techcrunch.com/2014/07/02/ facebook-liverail/

5 "Facebook Is Shutting Down the Video-Ad Company It Bought for about Half a Billion Dollars 2 Years Ago," *Business Insider*, May 26, 2016, https://www.businessinsider.com/ facebook-shutting-down-liverail-2016-5

6 "Facebook Confirms It Will Acquire Atlas Advertiser Suite from Microsoft to Close the Ad Spend Loop," *TechCrunch*, February 28, 2013, https://techcrunch.com/2013/02/28/ facebook-acquires-atlas/

7 "Facebook Shutters Atlas Ad Server, Ending Its Assault on DoubleClick; Atlas to Live On as Measurement Pixel," *AdExchanger*, November 18, 2016, https://www.adexchanger. com/platforms/facebook-shutters-atlas-ad-server-ending-assault-doubleclick-atlas-live-measurement-pixel/

8   "Facebook Buys Semantic Search Firm Chai Labs for More than $10M," *VentureBeat*, August 15, 2010, https://venturebeat.com/entrepreneur/facebook-buys-semantic-search-firm-chai-labs-for-more-than-10m/

9   "Facebook Ad Exchange (FBX) Opens for Business with 16 Partners," *MarTech*, September 13, 2012, https://martech.org/facebook-ad-exchange-fbx-opens-for-business-with-16-partners/

10 "The Billion-Dollar Facebook Business that Never Happened," *Business Insider*, March 6, 2015, https://www.businessinsider.com/the-history-of-facebooks-fbx-ad-exchange-2015-3

11 Antonio García Martínez, *Chaos Monkeys: Obscene Fortune and Random Failure in Silicon Valley*, first edition (New York: Harper, 2016)

12 "Facebook Will Shut Down FBX, Its Desktop Ad Exchange," *TechCrunch*, May 25, 2016, https://techcrunch.com/2016/05/25/facebook-will-shut-down-fbx/

13 Unknown author, July 17, 2017, "Charting a Different Course," internal Facebook memo filed in *US et al v Google LLC*

14 Interview with a former Facebook executive who was only willing to speak on background because they were not authorized to comment

15 "Facebook Made an Unprecedented Move to Partner with Ad Tech Companies—Including Amazon—to Take on Google," *Business Insider*, March 22, 2017, https://www.businessinsider.com/facebook-announces-move-into-header-bidding-to-take-on-google-2017-3

16 "Google Acquires AdMob For $750 Million," *TechCrunch*, November 9, 2009, https://techcrunch.com/2009/11/09/google-acquires-admob/

17 "Facebook F8'19, Fair and Open Ad Bidding Ecosystem," YouTube video by former Facebook product lead Kaushik Subramanian, https://www.youtube.com/watch?v=go2A0jf5Yc4

18 "Introducing Bidding for App Publishers and Developers," Facebook press release, June 5, 2018, https://www.facebook.com/audiencenetwork/resources/blog/introducing-bidding-for-app-publishers-and-developers

19 "AppLovin Acquires MAX in a Bid to Spur In-App Header Bidding Adoption," *AdExchanger*, September 5, 2018, https://www.adexchanger.com/mobile/applovin-acquires-max-in-a-bid-to-spur-in-app-header-bidding-adoption/

20 Justin Pang, August 2017, "Sell-side Competitive Review. Facebook and Amazon," slide deck filed in *US et al v Google LLC*

21 Chris LaSala, December 9, 2016, "GSL Thoughts for Sell-Side Marketing Support," email filed in *US et al v Google LLC*

22 Unknown author, January 2018, "Google Display & Video Ads Market Share," presentation filed in *US et al v Google LLC*

23 "Facebook Audience Network Joined Google's Open Bidding Program," *AdWeek*, December 14, 2018, https://www.adweek.com/programmatic/facebook-audience-network-joined-googles-open-bidding-program/

24 "Zuckerberg and Google CEO Approved Deal to Carve Up Ad Market, States Allege in Court," *Politico*, January 14, 2022, https://www.politico.com/news/2022/01/14/facebook-google-ad-market-lawsuit-527108

25 "Network Bidding Agreement" between Facebook and Google as provided to the author by a source involved in the project

26 "Jedi Blue: A Scandal That Highlights, Yet Again, the Need to Regulate Big Tech," *Forbes*, January 19, 2021, https://www.forbes.com/sites/enriquedans/2021/01/19/jedi-blue-a-scandal-that-highlights-yet-again-the-need-to-regulate-bigtech/

27 "Changes to Web and In-Stream Placements," Facebook support page, https://www.facebook.com/business/help/645132129564436

28   Author interview with former Facebook executive who was not authorized to speak on behalf of the company

29   "Behind a Secret Deal Between Google and Facebook," *New York Times*, April 6, 2021, https://www.nytimes.com/2021/01/17/technology/google-facebook-ad-deal-antitrust.html

30   "Network Bidding Agreement" between Facebook and Google as provided to the author by a source involved in the project

31   Various internal emails and conversations with former Google employees who spoke on background as they were not authorized to speak for the companies

32   Author interviews with both Google and Facebook executives involved in Jedi Blue who were not authorized to discuss these matters

33   "Google's AdMob Bids Adieu to the Waterfall with Its Take on In-App Header Bidding," *AdExchanger*, March 15, 2018, https://www.adexchanger.com/mobile/admob-bids-adieu-to-the-waterfall-with-in-app-header-bidding/

Chapter 21: Good News, Bad News

1   Sagnik Nand, May 9, 2019, "Re: First-price & Removing pricing knobs," email filed in *US et al v Google LLC*

2   Author interview with Matthew Wheatland, November 2024

3   Jonathan Bellack, date unknown, "ATTY CLIENT PRIVILEGED Sell-side pricing 2.0," comments on a Google Doc as filed in *US et al v Google LLC*

4   Jim Giles, July 21, 2017, "Re: Display RevForce," email filed in *US et al v Google LLC*

5   Unknown author, July 9, 2018, "DRX Unified Yield Management Strategy," presentation filed in *US et al v Google LLC*

6   Ali Nasiri Amin, May 9, 2019, "Re: First-price & Removing pricing knobs," email filed in *US et al v Google LLC*

Chapter 22: Emotional and Unproductive

1   This quote and all others in this section that aren't otherwise attributed are from an audio recording and transcription of the April 2019 meeting as filed in US et al v Google LLC

2   "Publishers Lash Out against Google over 'Unified Pricing' Changes," *AdExchanger*, April 18, 2019, https://www.adexchanger.com/online-advertising/publishers-lash-out-against-google-over-unified-pricing-changes/

3   This and all other quotes in this section are from an audio recording and transcription of the April 2019 meeting as filed in *US et al v Google LLC*

4   Author interview with Steph Layser, November 2024

5   Steph testimony in *US et al v Google LLC* as transcribed by the author

6   Author interview with Jana Meron, November 2024

7   Author interview with Sam Cox, December 2024

8   Author interview with Jeremy Hlavacek, December 2024

9   Matthew Wheatland, February 18, 2020, "RE: google question," email filed in *US et al v Google LLC*

10   Ahmed Samsuddin, October 14, 2019, "UPR Impact," email filed in *US et al v Google LLC*

11   Author interview with publisher executive who wished to remain anonymous

Chapter 23: Strange Bedfellows

1   "DOJ, AGs Get Google Cases Combined For Discovery," *Law360*, January 8, 2021, https://www.law360.com/articles/1342942
2   *State of Texas et al. v Google LLC*
3   "Microsoft Drops Bid after Yahoo Rejects Higher Offer," ABC News, May 3, 2008, https://abcnews.go.com/Technology/story?id=4781757
4   "Google and Yahoo Form Search Advertising Partnership," *New York Times*, June 13, 2008, https://www.nytimes.com/2008/06/13/business/worldbusines s/13iht-yahoo.1.13686722.html
5   "The Plot to Kill Google," *Wired*, January 19, 2009, https://www.wired.com/2009/01/ ff-killgoogle/
6   Ibid.
7   "Google (Temporarily) Blocks AppNexus from Its Ad Exchange," *TechCrunch*, November 30, 2010, https://techcrunch.com/2010/11/30/ google-temporarily-blocks-appnexus-from-its-ad-exchange/
8   "Daily Mail Owner Sues Google for Monopoly over Ad Business," Reuters, April 20, 2021, https://www.reuters.com/technology/ daily-mail-files-antitrust-lawsuit-against-google-2021-04-20/
9   "Gannett Files Federal Lawsuit against Google," Gannett press release, June 20, 2023, https://www.gannett.com/pr/gannett-files-federal-lawsuit-against-google/
10   "Dominance and Collusion: Inside the Unredacted Antitrust Lawsuit against Google's Ad Tech Business," *AdExchanger*, October 25, 2021, https://www.adexchanger.com/ platforms/ dominance-and-collusion-inside-the-unredacted-antitrust-lawsuit-against-googles- ad-tech-business/
11   "The Industry Bristles from Latest Unredacted 'Revelations' in Google Antitrust Suit—but Does Anything Change?" *AdExchanger*, January 19, 2022, https://www.adex- changer.com/online-advertising/ the-industry-bristles-from-latest-unredacted-revelations-in-google-antitrust-suit-but- does-anything-change/
12   Interview with Rajiv Goel, December 2024
13   Interview with Matthew Wheatland, November 2024
14   "U.S. Judicial Panel Moves Texas Lawsuit against Google to New York," Reuters, August 10, 2021, https://www.reuters.com/technology/us-judicial-panel-rejects- google-effort-move-texas-antitrust-case-2021-08-10/
15   "New Year, New Venue Law: Newly Passed Law Means State Attorneys General Can Avoid Having Their Antitrust Cases Consolidated in Multidistrict Litigation," White & Case blog, January 17, 2023, https://www.whitecase.com/insight-alert/ new-year-new-venue-law-newly-passed-law-means-state-attorneys-general-can-avoid
16   "Paxton Defeats Google's Efforts to Avoid Transfer of Landmark Antitrust Case Back to Texas," Texas AG press release, October 04, 2023, https://www.texasattorneygeneral. gov/news/releases/ paxton-defeats-googles-efforts-avoid-transfer-landmark-antitrust-case-back-texas
17   ADCL website: https://www.autoritedelaconcurrence.fr/en/decision/ regarding-practices-implemented-online-advertising-sector
18   "Google Commits to a More Level Ad Tech Playing Field in Big Antitrust Settlement with France," *AdExchanger*, June 7, 2021, https://www.adexchanger.com/platforms/ google-commits-to-a-more-level-ad-tech-playing-field-in-big-antitrust-settlement- with-france/

19 "Antitrust: Commission Sends Statement of Objections to Google over Abusive Practices in Online Advertising Technology," EU press release, June 13, 2023, https://ec.europa.eu/commission/presscorner/detail/en/ip_23_3207

20 "Justice Department Sues Google for Monopolizing Digital Advertising Technologies," DOJ press release, January 24, 2023, https://www.justice.gov/opa/pr/justice-department-sues-google-monopolizing-digital-advertising-technologies

21 *US et al v Google LLC* complaint

22 "Competition Bureau Sues Google for Anti-Competitive Conduct in Online Advertising in Canada," Government of Canada press release, November 28, 2024, https://www.canada.ca/en/competition-bureau/news/2024/11/competition-bureau-sues-google-for-anti-competitive-conduct-in-online-advertising-in-canada.html

23 "Meet Rumble, the YouTube Rival That's Popular with Conservatives," *Fortune*, November 30, 2020. https://fortune.com/2020/11/30/rumble-video-service-youtube-rival-popular-among-conservatives/

24 "Rumble Sues Google over Digital Advertising Practices," Reuters, May 13, 2024, https://www.reuters.com/legal/rumble-sues-google-over-digital-advertising-practices-2024-05-13/

Chapter 24: Virginia Courthouse

1   *Justice Delayed, Justice Denied*, sculpture by Raymond Kaskey

2   "The 'Rocket Docket' Judge Who Will Decide the Fate of Google's Ad Technology," *New York Times*, November 25, 2024, https://www.nytimes.com/2024/11/25/technology/google-antitrust-leonie-brinkema.html

3   "Google Dodged a Jury Trial in Its Big Adtech Case with a $2,289,751 Check," *Business Insider*, September 15, 2024, https://www.businessinsider.com/google-dodged-jury-advertising-antitrust-trial-with-check-damages-2024-9

4   "Judge Versus Jury in Focus after Google Writes $2.3 Million Check," Bloomberg, July 8, 2024, https://news.bloomberglaw.com/antitrust/judge-versus-jury-in-focus-after-google-writes-2-3-million-check

5   No. 1:23-cv-00108-LMB-JFA, *United States et al v Google LLC*

6   Unknown author, November 2020, "Google Chat Retention Policy," document filed in *US et al v Google LLC*

7   Document 1116, Memorandum Of Law In Support Of Plaintiffs' Motion For An Adverse Inference, *United States et al v Google LLC*

8   Ibid.

9   Ibid.

10 "Tech Critics Want a Google Exec Punished for Deleted Chats," *The Verge*, October 22, 2024, https://www.theverge.com/2024/10/22/24275745/kent-walker-google-california-bar-evidence-antitrust

11 Chris LaSala testimony in *US et al v Google LLC* as transcribed by the author

12 Ibid.

13 Jason Kint's tweet: https://x.com/jason_kint/status/1828445438376062981

14 Author's transcription from the *US et al v Google LLC*

15 Ibid.

16 Jonathan Bellack, September 2, 2016, "Re: Header bidding wrapper," email filed in *US et al v Google LLC*

17 *Verizon Communications, Inc. v. Law Offices of Curtis V. Trinko, LLP*

18 "EDVA Commemorates the 20th Anniversary of 9/11," press release from US Attorney's Office of the Eastern District of Virginia, September 7, 2021, https://www.justice.gov/usao-edva/pr/edva-commemorates-20th-anniversary-911

19   "Trial Update, September 18: Judge Brinkema Keeps the Case Moving at the Speed of Light, as DOJ Case-in-Chief Nears Its Conclusion," US v Google, September 18, 2024, https://www.usvgoogleads.com/trial-updates/trial-update-september-18-judge-brinkema-keeps-the-case-moving-at-the-speed-of-light-as-doj-case-in-chief-nears-its-conclusion

20   Chris LaSala, June 25, 2018, "Re: PRIVILEGED AND CONFIDENTIAL," email filed in *US et al v Google LLC*

21   Chris LaSala, unknown date, "Re: PRIVILEGED AND CONFIDENTIAL," chat or document comments filed in *US et al v Google LLC*

22   PTX1853, audio-visual file filed in *US v Google*, https://media.justice.gov/vod/atr/PTX1853-Video-Public.mp4

23   "YouTube CEO Says Google Faces Plenty of Ad Tech Competition," *New York Times*, September 16, 2024, https://www.nytimes.com/2024/09/16/technology/google-antitrust-youtube-ceo.html

24   Brad Bender, April 5, 2018, "AdWords Display Overview," presentation filed in *US et al v Google LLC*

25   Jay Friedman testimony in *US et al v Google LLC* as transcribed by the author

26   Professor Gabriel Weintraub testimony in *US et al v Google LLC* as transcribed by the author

27   Professor Robin Lee, exhibit PTX1395 as filed in *US et al v Google LLC*

28   "Stanford Economists Paul Milgrom and Robert Wilson Win the Nobel in Economic Sciences," *Stanford Report*, October 12, 2020, https://news.stanford.edu/stories/2020/10/stanford-economists-paul-milgrom-robert-wilson-win-nobel-economic-sciences

29   Author summary of Matthew Wheatland's testimony in *US et al v Google LLC*

30   Ruling of Judge Brinkema in *US et al v Google LLC*

Chapter 25: Breaking Up Is Hard to Do

1   Author's transcription from US et al v Google LLC

2   "The Trade Desk Turns Off Open Bidding as It Goes after Google Again," *IT News*, February 16, 2022, https://www.itnews.com.au/news/the-trade-desk-turns-off-open-bidding-as-it-goes-after-google-again-576123

3   All figures and commentary from Google, Inc. and Alphabet, Inc. 10(K)s

4   "Distribution of Average Daily Time Spent Online Worldwide from 3rd Quarter 2013 to 2nd quarter 2024, by Device," Statista, November 4, 2024, https://www.statista.com/statistics/1380539/time-spent-online-daily-by-device/

5   "Daily Time Spent on Social Networking by Internet Users Worldwide from 2012 to 2024," Statista, April 10, 2024, https://www.statista.com/statistics/433871/daily-social-media-usage-worldwide/

6   Reuters Institute Digital News Report as reported in *The Conversation*, June 13, 2023, https://theconversation.com/young-people-are-abandoning-news-websites-new-research-reveals-scale-of-challenge-to-media-207659

7   "Exclusive: Google Offered to Sell Part of Ad Tech Business, Not Enough for EU Publishers," Reuters, September 18, 2024, https://www.reuters.com/technology/google-offered-sell-advertising-marketplace-adx-eu-antitrust-probe-sources-say-2024-09-18/

8   Figure 76 of Dr. Israel's report as filed in *US et al v Google LLC*

9   Author reporting on events at the trial

10   Author interview with publishing executive who was not authorized to speak on behalf of his company, December 2024

11   Unknown author, October 21, 2013, "Project Bernanke" slide presentation as filed in *US et al v Google LLC*

12   Testimony of Brian O'Kelley before the U.S. Senate Judiciary Committee Hearing, "Understanding The Digital Advertising Ecosystem And The Impact Of Data Privacy And Competition Policy," May 21, 2019

13   Author interview with Joe Zawadski, December 2024

14   "Alphabet Q2 2024 Earnings: Search Growth Outpaces YouTube, Network Continues to Decline," Mobile Dev Memo, July 24, 2024, https://mobiledevmemo.com/alphabet-q2-2024-earnings-growth-slows-network-continues-to-decline/

15   Author reporting on events at the trial

16   This article cannot be located at this time, but the DOJ and Steph Layser both acknowledge its existence

17   Linkedin post by Steph Layser, November 2024, https://www.linkedin.com/posts/slayser8_usvgoogle-activity-7259606150638137344-DJZc

18   "How to Make Google's Network Business a Force for Good," *AdExchanger*, October 9, 2024, https://www.adexchanger.com/data-driven-thinking/how-to-make-googles-network-business-a-force-for-good/

19   Author interview with Brian O'Kelley, December 2024

20   Author interview with publisher executive who wished to remain anonymous

Chapter 26: Winning the Peace

1   Author interview with Richard Caccappolo

2   "Reddit to Give OpenAI Access to Its Data in Licensing Deal, *Wall Street Journal*, May 16, 2024, https://www.wsj.com/tech/ai/reddit-signs-data-licensing-deal-with-openai-14993757

3   "The Times Sues OpenAI and Microsoft Over A.I. Use of Copyrighted Work," *New York Times*, December 27, 2023, https://www.nytimes.com/2023/12/27/business/media/new-york-times-open-ai-microsoft-lawsuit.html

4   "Elon Musk Acknowledges Something that Was Obvious about the New Twitter: It's No Longer a Good Place for Links," *Business Insider*, November 25, 2024, https://www.businessinsider.com/elon-musk-twitter-x-links-lazy-linking-2024-11

5   "Sam Altman Says AI Will Handle '95%' of Marketing Work Done by Agencies and Creatives," Marketing Artificial Intelligence Institute, March 5, 2024, https://www.marketingaiinstitute.com/blog/sam-altman-ai-agi-marketing

ABOUT THE AUTHOR

Ari **Paparo** was an executive at DoubleClick and Google who was part of the acquisition and witness to many of the events in the early portions of this book.

Ari is a writer, podcaster, and commentator on all things advertising. He is the CEO of Marketecture Media, a network of podcasts, newsletters, and events covering the digital media business that includes publications under the Marketecture brand, as well as AdTechGod, the Advertising Forum, and Ad Tech Explained.

Ari has worked in the advertising industry for two decades, including at many of the companies discussed in this book. He was an executive in charge of the advertiser and agency-facing products at DoubleClick through the company's acquisition by Google. He served as a director of product management at Google for several years before leaving to head Nielsen's digital measurement team. He later served as the head of product management for AppNexus, where he was fired by Brian O'Kelley. Later he founded his own advertising technology company, Beeswax, which was sold to Comcast in 2021.

Ari is the author of the VAST standard, which virtually all digital video advertising runs, as well as the patent holder on Nielsen's Digital Audience Ratings product for measuring online ratings. He has invested in twenty or more advertising start-ups.

Ari lives in the Union Square area of New York with his wife and two kids.

INDEX